The
Star-
Spangled
Screen

The Star-Spangled Screen

The American World War II Film

Bernard F. Dick

Scholarly publisher for the Commonwealth,
serving Bellarmine College, Berea College, Centre
College of Kentucky, Eastern Kentucky University,
The Filson Club, Georgetown College, Kentucky
Historical Society, Kentucky State University,
Morehead State University, Murray State University,
Northern Kentucky University, Transylvania University,
University of Kentucky, University of Louisville,
and Western Kentucky University.

Editorial and Sales Offices: The University Press of Kentucky
663 South Limestone Street, Lexington, Kentucky 40508-4008

00 99 98 97 96   5 4 3 2 1

Library of Congress Cataloging-in-Publication

Dick, Bernard F.
    The star-spangled screen : the American World War II film /
Bernard F. Dick
      p.   cm.
    New ed., with new afterword.
    Includes bibliographical references and indexes.
    ISBN 0-8131-0885-3 (pbk. : alk. paper)
    1. World War, 1939-1945—Motion pictures and the war.   2. Motion
pictures—United States—History.   I. Title.
D743.D44   1996
791.43′658—dc20   96-24072

Manufactured in the United States of America

Contents

For my mother, Anita Platus,
And in memory of my stepfather,
Wallace A. Burns

Preface

Some dates are so emblazoned on the memory that their mere mention makes it possible to relive them or at least remember where one was at the time. 29 October 1929 and 22 November 1963 are such dates. But neither has quite the conjuring power of 7 December 1941, which, unlike the date of a stock market crash or a president's assassination, is able to evoke nostalgia in the true sense of the word—a yearning to go back to that time despite the pain, the *algos*, it has caused, because at least it would be a return to a simpler, perhaps even a better, time.

It is precisely the nostalgic aspect of World War II that has made it difficult to discuss the American World War II film critically. The films are either approached dreamily like old magazines meant for rainy afternoons; or patronizingly like senile relatives that must be coddled. The other alternative is to place them within the context of the World War II film in general where, dwarfed by documentaries and international prize winners, they shrink to the size of the shadow in Robert Louis Stevenson's poem—the shadow that "sometimes gets so little that there's none of him at all."

The Star-Spangled Screen is an attempt to examine the American World War II film from the standpoint of the studio system that created it and the culture that embraced it. To Hollywood, it was not a war that began on 1 September 1939 or even on 7 December 1941; to use the movie cliché, it was many years in the making. The real story of the American World War II film begins with Hollywood's awakening to fascism in the early thirties. But it was a slow awakening; like a sleeper prematurely roused, the industry moved cautiously, veiling fascist aggression in allusion and metaphor until 1939 when history intervened.

Some films make sport of history; others respect it. While it is possible to check the historical accuracy of World War II films, it has not always been possible to study their production history. Now, with the availability of production files and screenplay drafts at such archives as The Wisconsin Center for Film and Theater Research, the UCLA Theater Arts Library, and USC's Archives of Performing Arts, the evolution of many films can be traced from treatment to cutting continuity; and with such studios as Twentieth Century–Fox and MGM/UA opening their files to scholars, the conditions under which the movies were made can be recreated. Thus, wherever possible, I have documented my discussion with archival data.

I have focussed mainly on the 1940s since the most memorable World War II films appeared during that decade. Examples of later films are used primarily to distinguish between the American World War II film and the films about World War II. The difference is that, by the mid 1950s, the war had become a mythico-historical event to be approached in the way a historical novelist might approach the past. A historical novelist, however, uses facts to establish an authentic milieu and then weaves a narrative around it. Most of the post-1940s World War II films either recreate history at the expense of plot (*The Longest Day, Battle of the Bulge*) or sacrifice history for the sake of the plot (*The Sea Chase, Hanover Street*).

The American World War II film, on the other hand, transforms history into plot, inventing boldly, sometimes rashly, but at least inventing. Although that transformation is sometimes naive, it is still a true transformation; there is never that jarring separation of fact and fiction that occurs in *A Bridge Too Far* and *Battle of the Bulge*.

Since no film is without credits, a book on film should not be, either. My credits, however, are in alphabetical order:

Jeanne Aversa, typist; Robert Blees; Robert Buckner; Jack Colldeweih, Chair, Communications Department, Fairleigh Dickinson University (Teaneck-Hackensack Campus); Lee Gerber, Manager, Studio Legal Administration, Twentieth Century–Fox; Samuel A. Gill, Archivist, Margaret Herrick Library; John M. Hall, West Coast Manager, RKO Pictures, Inc.; Stefan Heym; Robert Knutson, Head, Archives of Performing Arts, University of Southern California; Jim Kottman, Head, Story Files, Twentieth Century–Fox; Mrs. Mary McMahon, Periodicals Librarian, Fairleigh Dickinson University (Teaneck-Hackensack Campus); Audrée Malkin, Head, Theater Arts Library, University of California at Los Angeles; Martin Nocente; Attorney Herbert S. Nussbaum, MGM/UA; Arnold Pickelney; my uncle Charles A. Sarambo; Emily Sieger, Reference Librarian, Motion Picture, Broadcasting, and Recorded Sound Division, The Library of Congress; Sister Jeanne Tierney, C.S.J.P. of St. Peter's College at Englewood Cliffs; and Professor Raymond E. White, Ball State University.

Some individuals transcend alphabetization. I am especially grateful to Lou Harris, former Paramount publicist, for locating a copy of Lester Cole's screenplay of *None Shall Escape* that I could read; to Lester Cole, for writing a film with one of the most powerful speeches heard on the screen during the war; and to my wife, Katherine M. Restaino, for choosing to spend her vacation doing research with me instead of reading her beloved mysteries.

Semper fi.

Teaneck, New Jersey
March 9, 1984

1. Prologue to Pearl

Shortly after noon on 17 July 1943, I set out for the West Side Theater; it was a thirty-minute walk from the wrong side of the tracks, where I lived in a Central European enclave in Scranton, Pennsylvania, to the other, not exactly the right but merely the less primitive side. Environment provides the first metaphor, and the railroad tracks were mine; they were the line of demarcation between the valley and the hill, the border beyond which lay civilization.

Beyond the tracks rose a hill, more arduous than steep, occasionally sinking into small depressions where the houses had settled with such finality that they resembled lopsided nests where birds stubbornly brooded. Although the hill was a trial to one who lived in the valley, scaling it was one of youth's few triumphs over nature.

The hill curved at the top, then flattened into sidewalks that dipped periodically, breaking the rhythm that had been generated in the ascent. But what nature withholds, the will provides. I generated my own rhythm, the rhythm of anticipation. The windings and turnings culminated in Main Avenue, which like everything in West Scranton was not straight. It was an arc of contiguous buildings that folded into each other like accordion pleats, forming a natural declension as they sloped away from the top of the street where the West Side Theater stood.

Only the undiscriminating could love the West Side at first sight; for the fastidious, love came with the acceptance of the idea that the neighborhood movie theater is democracy in action, with darkness levelling all distinctions, including those between streetwalker and odalisque.

The West Side beckoned uninhibitedly to an interior where shoes picked up an adhesive of popcorn-studded gum, and nostrils contracted from the odor of disinfectant in the lavatory. In compensation for the theater's other imperfections (which included an occasional rodent scampering down the main aisle), there was the security of belonging to a family where no authoritarian father was present to administer injustice, but only an indulgent earth mother whose smell betrayed her origins but whose womb was capacious enough for all who needed it. Yet the same maternalism that attracted the boy later repelled the adolescent, who forsook the West Side in favor of downtown theaters where an audience was not a family but a collection of anonymous individuals.

In 1943, however, I needed a family, and while I enjoyed an occasional trek to Central City, as downtown Scranton was called, where the theaters had red-carpeted foyers and lighting fixtures shaped like cigarette cases and compacts, my true home was the West Side. I had been a moviegoer for almost two years—an uncritical one but able to recite the names of the stars and record my impressions of the films I saw in a diary, writing in a scrawl as yet unsmoothed by the Palmer Method.

I knew where I had been on 7 December 1941: watching *Sergeant York* with my grandmother and noting later that both she and Margaret Wycherly, who played York's mother, had eyes like dark marbles. I also knew that on 17 July 1943, the bill at the West Side was atypical. In fact, the theater's entire weekend schedule was atypical: there was no change of program.

Generally, the Saturday and Sunday programs were different; sometimes Friday's bill was not the same as Saturday's. On the weekend of 9 July, for example, the West Side had offered three separate features: *The Moon Is Down* on Friday, *I Walked with a Zombie* on Saturday, and *Crash Dive* on Sunday. But this weekend, the same program was scheduled for all three days: *Mr. Big* (my first exposure to Donald O'Connor), and *Prelude to War*. This was not the usual Saturday matinee fare; *Prelude to War*, the main attraction, was shorter than the second feature. Besides, since we were well into the war, no prelude seemed necessary. Although I knew who Hitler was, I no longer joined in the boos and hisses when he appeared on the screen. By now, goose-stepping had become tiresome, and although I had seen *Hitler's Children* two months earlier, the significance of German girls going off to breeding camps escaped me. I had gone to camp too, in the summer of 1942, and I hoped they would not be as miserable.

No one at the West Side on that July afternoon knew that *Prelude to War* had originally been intended for military personnel, not for civilian audiences; that after a White House screening, President Roosevelt had declared, "Every man, woman, and child must see

The movie page of The Scranton Tribune, *17 July 1943*

this film;"[1] that army chief of staff General George C. Marshall and Secretary of War Henry L. Stimson were as eager as President Roosevelt for the general distribution of *Prelude to War*; that commercial release had been delayed for six months because the Office of War Information's Bureau of Motion Pictures found the film biased and superficial;[2] and that the West Side was showing *Prelude to War* for the entire weekend because it was free.

Restless but not unruly, we endured what was really a fifty-five–minute newsreel in an era when the newsreel was part of the bill. But we would have groaned if we had heard that Winston Churchill wanted the entire *Why We Fight* series,[3] of which *Prelude to War* is the first, shown throughout Britain; fortunately for British moviegoers, the Ministry of Information's Film Division intervened.[4]

The 17 July 1943 entry in my movie diary consists of "ugh!" for *Prelude to War* and "kidstuff" for *Mr. Big*. Yet *Prelude to War* leaves its mark the way a summary lecture does in an uninspiring course; if the teacher can at least sum up the material or outline it on the blackboard, the student does not feel cheated.

Prelude has that quality. It claims to provide "factual information of events leading up to World War II"—a valid enough aim. The commercial showing of a government information film, one that received the 1942 Academy Award for Best Documentary, implies that such information had not been imparted; or at least had not been presented within a historical framework. While audiences had been witnessing Axis aggression on the screen for four years, they had witnessed it individually, not collectively; within the context of a particular film, not within the context of post-World War I history. Frank Capra, who directed *Prelude to War* and produced the others in the series, applied the methods of film to the lecture hall; by juxtaposing common features of Italian Fascism, Nazism, and Japanese imperialism, he eliminates the distinctions between blackshirts, brownshirts, and neo-samurai so that the enemy becomes one.

Similarly, the audience becomes a class called to attention by its teacher (narrator Walter Huston) who tosses out a question: "Why are we fighting?" Anyone at the West Side could have answered, but nobody got the chance. It is a rhetorical question, no sooner asked than answered—but answered in word and image. "Is it because of Pearl Harbor? Britain? France? China?" the voice inquires, listing a series of countries, each followed by an image (Britain by a shot of the Blitz, France by German troops marching down the Champs-Elysées). Voice-over and image—offscreen narration combined with music, superimpositions, animated maps, newsreel footage, and graphics—provide the "factual information."

Some of the information, however, is interpretative. The opening and closing images are a parable in pictures: two globes, one white, the other black, revolving in space; the former representing the free world, the latter the enslaved. The narrator has little to show or say of the free world. It is supposedly pluralistic as quotations from the Koran, the *Analects* of Confucius, the New Testament, and the Ten Commandments attest, although "It Came upon a Midnight Clear" on the soundtrack implies that this pluralistic world is basically Christian.

In fact, the whole film seems Christian, which may be due to Frank Capra. Capra's *Meet John Doe* (1941) features a populist Christ figure, and his most representative film, *It's a Wonderful Life* (1946), extols personal sacrifice as humanity's way of imitating Christ. The emphasis on Christianity is also an attempt to convince audiences that the Third Reich is not only anti-Semitic but also anti-Christian. Thus, a shot of a ruined synagogue is followed by several shots of desecrated churches; and for those still unconvinced, the words of the Nazi party's official philosopher, Alfred Rosenberg, fill the screen, predicting the demise of Catholicism and Protestantism. With the Führer as God, religion is superfluous.

Since Hitler's rise would be chronicled in the second of the *Why We Fight* films, *Prelude* focuses on Mussolini and the New Order in southeast Asia. After tracing Italian Fascism to the disaffection, poverty, and inflation that followed the First World War, *Prelude* abandons objectivity for a parody of Mussolini. But Mussolini himself is a parody, so the sight of Il Duce pounding his chest with simian vaunting needs no commentary, certainly not Capra's comparison between fascist theatrics and musical comedy.

Just when Capra seems to be settling for the obvious, he comes up with a surprise. When the chronology reaches 1935 and Italy's invasion of Ethiopia, he abruptly cuts to Japan; he will return to Italy when a related act of hostility can provide the right transition. But first he skips back a few years—to 1931, to 18 September 1931, to be precise: a date the narrator insists we memorize, noting it was then, not on 7 December 1941, that World War II really started. The date marks Japan's invasion of Manchuria; the occasion, a pretext (a rigged railroad explosion). Capra has his transition: Mussolini also invaded Ethiopia on a pretext (a dispute over an oasis on the border of Ethiopia and the Italian Somaliland). Now Capra can cut back to Italy; and since Germany has to be worked into the finale, he combines the three Axis powers into a triptych, showing that it was Japan's quest for raw materials, Mussolini's attempt to restore to Italy its ancient imperial status, and Hitler's cry for *Lebensraum* ("living space") that plunged the world into war for a second time.

The roots of belligerence have been laid bare; all that remains is to show they belong to the same tree. In a three-shot, Hitler, Mussolini, and Hirohito appear together as the narrator warns, "If you see them, don't hesitate." No one thought to ask, "To do what?" Everyone knew.

While Hitler, Mussolini, and Hirohito were not strange bedfellows, they were not triplets, either. Capra makes their lack of individuality seem ludicrous; but that is his point. Sameness is a perennial source of humor, as Pascal has noted. Two faces that are alike will not inspire laughter when they are seen separately; yet together they will. Their juxtaposition—and this is particularly true in the case of comedies involving twins—illustrates the chief source of laughter: the incongruous, the discrepancy between what should be and what is. Human beings reproduce their kind; they do not duplicate themselves. Only machines duplicate. It is the confusion of human with machine, of the original with the copy, that makes mistaken identity and duplication such comic staples. For example, few moments in musical comedy are as amusing, or as devastating, as the party in Frank Loesser's *How to Succeed in Business without Really Trying* (1961) at which everyone arrives wearing the same "Paris original."

What is ludicrous is also vulnerable, and while portraying the Axis powers as an unholy trinity does not make them any less terrifying, it does make them seem more like a temporary menace than a permanent threat. Like the distorted figures that people our dreams and vanish at daybreak, the Axis too will depart when the long night is over.

Yet even before the night had ended, *Prelude to War* found a place on the grid of my memory. Although I must have been as disappointed as anyone else at not getting a real double feature, and probably stifled a yawn as I went blinking into the mellow brightness of late afternoon, I never forgot two points the narrator had made because they were made with such pedantic insistence: 18 September 1931 as the "real" date of World War II, and the Tanaka Memorial (Plan) as Japan's blueprint for conquest. A few years later, I saw *Blood on the Sun* (1945), which dealt with a newspaperman's attempt to uncover the Tanaka Plan. The mention of the plan produced something akin to the charm of recognition; my mind had made its first cross-reference. It was not until much later—in college, in fact—that I learned the truth about the Tanaka Plan: it was spurious. In 1929, however, despite Japan's denial of its authenticity, it was regarded in the United States as the modus operandi of the New Order, beginning with the seizure of Manchuria and China and proceeding to the conquest of the Pacific.

And so the invasion of Manchuria becomes the result of a plan that probably never existed; and a date, 18 September 1931, enters the sacred chronology. Traditional dates are like received ideas: they are transmitted from generation to generation as part of an accepted chronology. Because they reduce an event to a mnemonic, they are a pedagogical blessing; but they also represent knowledge at its most skeletal. Since they are verifiable, they are not questioned; since they are not questioned, they foster imperfect learning by creating the impression that the past can be controlled if its chronology is mastered.

The chronology of World War II is not World War II. Dates are only points on the axis of history; they are not loci. A date bears only a synecdochal relationship to an event, but in no way is it the event. Nor does a sense of chronology necessarily produce historical awareness or the ability to discern patterns, because chronology is sequence, not configuration.

In *Prelude to War*, chronology and configuration are identical, but then, so is everything else: Hitler equals Mussolini equals Hirohito; Nazism equals Italian Fascism equals Japanese nationalism; 18 September 1931 equals 7 December 1941. Although it may have seemed odd that everything tallied, a novice does not ask questions; and as far as the movies were concerned, we were all novices.

We were novices in World War II because we were uneducated; we were uneducated because we were unprepared. Mobilization necessitated a crash course in The Background to World War II. Anything that could be related to the war, was. E.M. Forster's "Only connect" seems to have been Hollywood's motto. Since the war united Americans, the movies reinforced that oneness by coopting such literary techniques as the closing of the circle, the untying of the knot, and selective representation to produce not merely a unified narrative (which would automatically come about from the concatenation of events) but a unified spirit, a single sensibility. When the war was not the basis of the plot, it was worked in by means of tag lines and prologues—the latter often resulting in some strange alliances between present and past.

In 1943, RKO produced *Flight for Freedom*, loosely based on the career of Amelia Earhart. Although the aviatrix in the film disappears in the Pacific in 1937, as did Earhart, *Flight for Freedom* begins

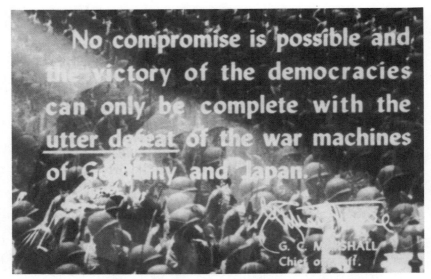

No compromise is possible and the victory of the democracies can only be complete with the utter defeat of the war machines of Germany and Japan.

G. C. MARSHALL
Chief of Staff.

The end title of Prelude to War *(1942). Courtesy National Archives*

with a 1943 prologue in which preparations are being made for a dive bomber attack. Such an attack would be impossible, an offscreen voice assures us, "without her courageous efforts." Thus, the development of the dive bomber, "America's answer to December 7th," is attributed to the achievements of an aviatrix, although the two are unrelated.

So are Nero and Hitler, but in 1944 that did not stop Paramount from rereleasing Cecil B. DeMille's 1932 epic of Neronian Rome, *The Sign of the Cross*, with a prologue in which the crew of a B-17 flying over Rome meditates on the eternal city that had managed to survive Nero, and which will certainly survive Hitler.

There is always a feeling of satisfaction when a plot comes full circle, perhaps because, as Jung has observed, the circle is an archetype of wholeness, and the closing of the circle heals the wounds of fragmentation. Although narrative closure is as old as cyclic epic, its function in a World War II film is more than narrative tidiness; it is emotional reassurance, a guaranteed return to wholeness. In *Air Force* (1943), the crew of the B-17 that flies into Pearl Harbor as it is being bombed takes off at the end to bomb Tokyo—an historical impossibility but a way of making a circle. No war film has ever come full circle more poignantly than *Mrs. Miniver* (1942): the same church in which the vicar announced the outbreak of the war is the one, now bomb-damaged and roofless, in which he explains the nature of the war—"a war of the people."

Prelude to War also comes full circle. The two globes reappear, now labelled "us" and "them." The narrator calls for a choice, as if one were necessary. The Liberty Bell that tolled at the beginning rings out at the end, this time through a gigantic superimposed V for victory.

The victory is really Capra's. By appropriating the conventions of the typical Hollywood film (e.g., linearity, intercutting, montage), he has made a documentary that looks like a feature film; perhaps that is why one still remembers it.

2. The War that Dared Not Speak Its Name

Despite its careful orchestration, Capra's *Prelude* is incomplete; the entire midsection—the years between 1936 and 1939, the period of the Spanish civil war—is missing. Perhaps Capra did not hear the music because it was the music of the "International." Yet to omit the Spanish civil war in a prelude to the Second World War is to reduce a prelude to program music.

Hollywood did not ignore the Spanish civil war, although reaction to it varied from the studios' reluctance to portray it as the class struggle it was, to the rallying around the Spanish Republic of movie liberals who believed that what could not be accomplished in Germany—the defeat of fascism—might be achieved in Spain. Although the Hollywood liberals did not follow the example of Alvah Bessie (as yet not a screenwriter) and join the Abraham Lincoln Battalion of the Fifteenth International Brigade, Lillian Hellman and Dorothy Parker, who were already established screenwriters, visited Spain in 1937, where Parker was moved to write some deeply felt pieces for *New Masses* without a single bon mot.

Coincidentally, Hollywood was wracked by its own civil war at the same time right was battling left in Spain. It was a writers' war, equally political, and no less a confrontation between right (Screen Playwrights) and left (Screen Writers Guild), as each determined to become the screenwriters' bargaining agent.[1] The victory the SWG won in 1938 was a victory for the Hollywood left, although, in retrospect, it seems more a victory for the Hollywood liberals. What happened in Hollywood in 1938, however, was the reverse of what happened in Spain a year later when Franco's victory reduced the Spanish left to impotency—a condition that would prevail for more than forty years.

The concurrence of union battles, the growing threat of Nazism, and the eruption of civil war in Spain enabled members of the film community with a common hatred of fascism to band together in a popular front in which liberals, radicals, Communists, and fellow travellers intermingled. Although political commitment seems inconsistent with the standard view of Hollywood as Lotus Land and Tinsel Town, where moguls make flickers on dream dumps for the booboisie, there was a spirit of liberalism in the movie colony in the mid and late thirties; there were also enclaves of gold within the town of tinsel. This was the time of the exiles, both those from Europe seeking refuge from fascism and those from New York seeking refuge from unemployment by writing film scripts—some finding their métier in the movies, others biding their time between the big novel and the smash play. There was probably no house in America comparable to Salka Viertel's in Santa Monica, where, on a typical Sunday afternoon, Thomas Mann and Igor Stravinsky could be found in discussion with Charles Laughton and Bertolt Brecht.

A round of common activities alleviated the loneliness of being a displaced person in Hollywood. The exiles kept encountering each other, as well as making new friends, at the dinners, rallies, and lectures sponsored by the Hollywood Anti-Nazi League, the Anti-Franco League, and the Motion Picture Arts Committee to Aid the Republic of Spain. Since the head of the Hollywood Anti-Nazi League and the Anti-Franco League was the same person, screenwriter Donald Ogden Stewart, there was no duplication of effort; it was all for the same cause.

Hollywood antifascism was not radical chic; it was radicalism with style—sleek and streamlined before it keeled over in the 1960s and became laid back. Swimming pools and political involvement were not mutually exclusive; if the Hollywood liberals cashed their paychecks before going to a lecture by André Malraux, a reading of *Bury the Dead*, or a fundraiser for the Scottsboro boys, they were doing what liberals have traditionally done: they were trying to understand the basis of their liberalism. As Donald Ogden Stewart, who discovered Marxism at the age of forty-one, expressed it, "My new found philosophy was an affirmation of the good life, not a rejection of it."[2]

Being able to lead the good life made it possible to raise money for those who could not. One of the most successful fundraisers for the Spanish Loyalists, for example, was the Los Angeles premiere on 19 July 1937 of Joris Ivens's documentary *The Spanish Earth*, written and narrated by Ernest Hemingway.[3] The film was also shown at the homes of Fredric March and Salka Viertel.

Although Ivens and Hemingway were pro-Loyalist, and Ivens a Communist as well, neither believed in assaulting the audience with propaganda as if minds were nails to be hammered into alignment. Hemingway's text anticipates *For Whom the Bell Tolls* (1940) in its reduction of the war to an incident that unifies the plot and unites the characters: the dynamiting of a bridge in *For Whom the Bell Tolls*, the irrigating of a village in *The Spanish Earth*.

At first one wonders why so much is made of the irrigation. Superficially, the reason is that the village of Fuentedueña must raise food for the defenders of the Republic; to do so, the land must be irrigated. But there is more, as one learns at the end.

In the opening scenes of *The Spanish Earth*, Hemingway's laconic commentary is interspersed with images of village life, presented with an integrity that is a far cry from the idealized commonality of *Our Daily Bread* (1934), in which a ditch is dug to a rhythm so metronomic that the action seems choreographed. Ivens's peasants are not performing an agrarian ballet; they are working the land for the common good. They have even acquired a common look, with young and old seeming to have sprung from the same earth.

Ivens's images are so meaningful that they require little explanation. The narrator remarks that the village bread bears the union seal; the UGT mark on the loaves is never explained, but that is intentional. If it is an art to conceal an art, then the art of politics lies in concealing the political. What is important is not that UGT is an acronym for Unión General de Trabajadores, a socialist general trade union, not that the villagers seem to be socialists, but that their life is communal and their union is a reflection of that life.[4]

Part of the greatness of *The Spanish Earth* lies in Hemingway's ability to subordinate his narrative to Ivens's images, enclosing them within a text that is never in competition. The text functions as a text should in a documentary—as commentary. *The Spanish Earth* begins, as *Blockade* (1938) does, with a folk portrait. The portrait yields to an animated map showing the road between Madrid and Valencia, the legitimate and wartime capitals, respectively, of the Republic. Once it is understood that the village is between these cities, the road's importance and the village's role become clear. Then Ivens introduces another image, irrigation, combining it with village and road to create an image cluster.

Ivens builds to a climax of images, where war, village, road, and irrigation coalesce. The action moves from Fuentedueña to Madrid, the sound of gunfire marking the transition. The city is the village inverted; while the earth of Fuentedueña is simply upturned, the streets of Madrid look as if they have been maniacally plowed. The blood that stains the streets contrasts painfully with the water that courses through the soil. Ivens planned the documentary as a dialectic, alternating between village and city until the synthesis is reached. Thus rhythm changes with location; anonymous peasants are juxtaposed with historical figures like La Pasionaria and Manuel Azaña, president of the Republic; Hemingway switches from the reportorial style to the reflective for a meditation on death in language so stark that it cannot conceal its nakedness. Finally, the synthesis comes when Ivens cuts from tanks moving across the road to water flowing through the ditches. The connection between war and irrigation reaches a level at once dramatic, aesthetic, and pragmatic: keeping the road open and keeping the water flowing are the same. Everything, then, becomes one: the labor of the peasants in the country is for the good of the city, and the fighting in the city is an attempt to preserve the way of life in the country.

Had the fiction films of the Spanish civil war measured up to *The Spanish Earth*, Hollywood might have had a cycle of which it could be proud. But this was a war in which each side was supported by countries that themselves inspired sidetaking: the Loyalists aided by the Soviet Union, the Nationalists by Italy and Germany. Sympathy for either side could be construed, and usually was, as sympathy for its allies. The sympathizer was slapped with an automatic label: left-wing (or worse) for supporters of the Republic, fascist for *francistas*. The movie industry was in a quandary, hating Communism as much as fascism because both made capitalism unworkable. America's neutrality during the war solved Hollywood's problem: it too would remain neutral. But even a neutral Hollywood cannot ignore a war, for wherever there is war, there is a potential movie.

In the summer of 1937, shortly after the opening of *The Spanish Earth*, Paramount released *The Last Train from Madrid*, advertising it as the first film about the Spanish civil war. The ad is to truth in advertising what the flight of the crow is to distance, for Twentieth Century–Fox could have made the same claim if it had moved faster. In October 1936 Fox was planning its own movie about the war; if the script had evolved as the original writer intended, the first Spanish civil war movie would have been a pro-Franco comedy.

Fox's *Love under Fire* began as an unproduced play by Walter Hackett called *The Fugitives*.[5] An amalgam of pseudohistory and disguised history, *The Fugitives* opens with a prologue, set in 1636, in which a Spanish pirate, Black Jack Peralta, kills his rival for a treasure of diamonds and emeralds. The main action commences three hundred years later, in 1936, as the Nationalists struggle to keep the jewels, known as the Peralta Collection, from falling into Loyalist hands.[6] Hackett has no reservations about identifying factions; he even calls the Loyalists "Communists" and "Reds," which is not entirely accurate, although it conforms to the popular view of the Spanish Republicans. The Nationalists are termed "Royalists," which is probably what Hackett thought the Francoists were. The plot mingles political intrigue and romantic melodrama, uniting them in a happy ending in which the Loyalists get the fake collection and the Nationalists the real one—an obvious way of saying which side is sincere and which is duplicitous.

By 14 October 1936, Kathryn Scola and Darrell Ware had written a screenplay based on *The Fugitives*. Although the plot remains the same (Spain in the throes of a revolution), the closest the screenwriters come to identifying sides is in the line "A Loyalist agent is trying to get the Peralta jewels out of the country, and the Rebels are trying to stop him." The agent is not a "he," however, but a "she." An Englishwoman whose husband died trying to keep Spain a monarchy, she would like to do her share to keep the treasure out of the hands of the faction that is "ruining" Spain—the Loyalists. The Scola-Ware screenplay is pro-Franco in spirit, but certain allegiances are confusing. In a Francoist script, Sarego, the Nationalist general in league with the Germans, should be the hero, but he is really the villain. One suspects the confusion is not the result of the screenwriters' ignorance of the issues but their attempt to keep the audience ignorant of them.

By the end of December 1936, Gene Fowler had written an even more confusing script with the same plot and title. At one point, the hero gives the radio dial a twirl and hears: "Rebels . . . Loyalists . . . Sarego . . . Traitor . . . Win . . . Lose. . . ." "Viva both sides!" he cries, speaking, no doubt, for the intended audience.

By February 1937, *The Fugitives* had become *Fandango* (which sounds more like a criticism than a title). By March, the screenwriter was Allen Rivkin; and the title, under which it was released, *Love under Fire*. On 15 March 1937, Darryl F. Zanuck, head of production at Fox, decided the fate of *Love under Fire*: "Eliminate all references to 'loyalists' and 'traitors,' etc. Refer to all other sides as General so-and-so and his forces."[7]

Gene Fowler, Allen Rivkin, and Ernest Pascal ended up sharing screenplay credit for *Love under Fire*. The hero still flicks the dial, but "Loyalist" and "traitor" have disappeared from the air. The only reference even remotely political is to Spain as "the land of yes and no." Since there is a revolution on, the hero and heroine would like to be on the "safe" side, except that neither knows which side it is—nor does the audience. And what might have been the first American film about the Spanish civil war is only a romance be-

Lew Ayres tipping his hat to Karen Morley in The Last Train from Madrid
(1937), the first American film with a Spanish Civil War setting.
Courtesy MCA

tween a Scotland Yard policeman (Don Ameche) and an unjustly
accused jewel thief (Loretta Young) who meet in Spain.

At about the same time that Fox was struggling with *Love under
Fire*, Paramount was trying to make its nonpartisan Spanish civil
war movie.[8] Since Paramount spent less time agonizing over the
script, it was able to release *The Last Train from Madrid* three
months before *Love under Fire*. Neither studio borrowed from the
other, not would it have been necessary, since both aimed at the
same result: ambiguity. *The Last Train from Madrid* is also an original property—a screen story by Paul Hervey Fox that Paramount
acquired in November 1936. The title tells it all: the story is about
the last train out of Madrid and those lucky enough to board it.
Naturally, everyone wants to leave the besieged capital. Since the
train is headed for Valencia, the city to which the Republican government has fled, one assumes the passengers are all Loyalists. But
in this kind of film, no one is what he or she seems. Although the
captain, "a burly and domineering labor leader," appears to be a Loyalist, he is really a fifth columnist; yet he gives up his life so the

train can leave, which makes him a hero—a Nationalist hero, a Francoist.

For the studios the question was not "What are the characters' politics?" but "Will the picture play Peoria?" The ads touted *The Last Train from Madrid* as "a flaming love drama set against the background of Spain's civil war," promising a screen full of "spies, traitors, deserters, lovers . . . in this first action romance to come out of war-torn Spain." Those believing such hype were not disappointed; the film delivers the promised assortment of characters. But it also offers a lesson in disinterested commitment and neutral involvement, so that, in the event of war, one will be able to serve both the enemy and the resistance. The opening title, appearing after a shot of a smoking cannon, is rhetoric without a cause: "Out of war have come some of the world's greatest dramas—dramas all the more challenging to the imagination because their basis is real. This is such a story—an account of fictional characters caught in beleaguered Madrid fired with one common desire—escape. We neither uphold nor condemn either faction of the Spanish conflict. This is a story of people—not of causes."

But who are these people? First, there is the self-sacrificing captain of the original story, now called Alvarez and given a close friend, Eduardo—a literal blood brother who saved his life in Morocco. Since Eduardo is a political prisoner, he would appear to be a Loyalist, but that is impossible if he is imprisoned in Madrid. Likewise, as a veteran of the Moroccan wars, where he served under Franco, Alvarez should be a Nationalist; yet he is an officer in the Republic. Furthermore, Eduardo is in love with the (Nationalist?) Carmelita, who loves the (Loyalist?) Alvarez.

Then there is Juan, who is in the Republican army, even though he has no great love for the Republic; perhaps it is because he comes from Burgos, the Nationalist capital. Another character is Maria Ronda, a young girl from the Women's Battalion, who wants to see her father before he is executed. There was indeed such a women's battalion in Spain—a Republican battalion. But Maria is hardly a revolutionary (in the original story, she only joins the battalion to eat regularly), and eventually she defects. Furthermore, if Maria's professor-father is to face a firing squad, he must be Nationalist; he is, after all, in Madrid. But, as Marjorie Valleau has observed, "the curious contradiction between Maria's membership in the Republican Women's Battalion and Señor Ronda's arrest—presumably, because he is a Nationalist—is never clarified."[9] Nor can it be unless political identities are revealed, which does not happen.

With nondiscriminatory dispassion, as if adhering to Affirmative

Action guidelines, the screenwriters, Louis Stevens and Robert Wyler, have worked out equal representation for Loyalists and Nationalists, but in such a way that within every Loyalist there is a Nationalist, and vice versa. Of the four who make the train, two—Maria and Juan—are nominally Republicans; but Maria has a Nationalist father, and Juan comes from a Nationalist city. Yet they owe their future to Alvarez who, whatever he is, will not let a blood brother down and gives Eduardo a pass so he can join Carmelita.

In 1937 Paramount was not ready to take a stand, but producer Walter Wanger was. Known in the industry as a liberal, Wanger wanted to do his bit for Republican Spain by making a movie about the war.[10] He first hired leftist playwright Clifford Odets to write the script; when Odets's script proved unsatisfactory, he brought in Communist screenwriter, John Howard Lawson.

Odets seemed to be planning something on the order of his first screenplay, *The General Died at Dawn* (1936)—a romantic melodrama with a war background and proletarian dialogue. Interestingly, Odets never planned to take sides, probably because he knew that such a script would never be approved by the Production Code Administration, headed by Joseph Breen and sometimes called the Breen Office. The administration passed on each film, making certain it adhered to the Production Code; in this case, Article 10 (National Feelings) was pertinent: "*The history*, institutions, prominent people and citizenry of all nations shall be represented fairly."[11]

As it happened, Breen approved Odets's script *The River Is Blue*, provided that, when shooting began, there would be no attempt "to definitely identify any of the combatants with either faction of the Spanish Civil War." When Lawson took over the script, however, Breen did have objections—not about sex but about politics. It is significant that Odets and Lawson came from different backgrounds: Odets from the liberal Group Theatre, Lawson from the radical New Playwrights. Although Odets had been a Communist, he left the Party in late 1935 and recanted in 1952; Lawson remained a committed Communist to the point of writing, in 1953, that the Soviet Union was "dedicating its vast resources to peaceful reconstruction and the cultural enrichment of its people."[12] Thus Lawson's script posed real problems for the Breen Office, which approved it with the understanding that there would be nothing—uniforms, locations, expressions, even songs—that "could possibly be tied in with the actual events that have occurred or are occurring in Spain."

Wanger had no choice but to accept Breen's decision. Furthermore, no matter how liberal Wanger was, he could not afford to antagonize the Roman Catholic Church, which by and large supported the Nationalists, or to imperil the film's distribution abroad; as it was, *Blockade* (1938), as the film was finally called, antagonized the Knights of Columbus and was banned in twelve countries.

In a perverse way, Lawson and director William Dieterle met Breen's demands and still made a movie that was proLoyalist, at least in spirit. Lawson applied the same principle to the Spanish civil war that screenwriters at the time were applying to sex: suggestion. In order to satisfy Breen, who, when he became head of the Production Code Administration in 1934, felt it was his solemn duty to sanitize movie sex so Americans would not be copulating in department store windows, filmmakers resorted to visual metaphors (fires going to embers, tracking shots away from recumbent lovers, rain pelting the windows, and, of course, the slowly closing door) and dialogue disclaimers ("We just sat there," as Fred McMurray says of himself and Barbara Stanwyck in *Double Indemnity*; one knows they did not). To comply with the code, filmmakers invented their own code, and true moviegoers learned how to break it. Thus when they saw *The Woman in the Window* or *Uncle Harry* (both 1944), in which the story turns out to be a dream so the plot can have a moral resolution, they did not have to be told that the endings were concessions to the Breen Office. In fact, most of them would not have known what the Breen Office was. Real movie aficionados did know, however, that the ending was a gimmick, a joke on everyone but themselves; they would ignore the denouement and regard the real plot as everything that preceded it.

Anyone who could decode a movie about adultery or dreamed murder could decode a movie about the Spanish civil war. *Blockade*, however, is slightly more difficult because the plot is wartime espionage with fifth columnists, traitors, double agents, a hero who seems to be working for one side but is really working for the other, and a heroine who is working for the wrong side until she meets the hero and then defects to the right side. If this sounds confusing, it is because there are as many red herrings in *Blockade* as there are in a typical manor house mystery. Even the opening title, "Spain. The Spring of 1936," is intentionally misleading. To paraphrase the Frank Loesser song, spring was indeed a little late that year since the war began on 18 July. Furthermore, while *The Last Train from Madrid* is set in a real city, *Blockade* is set in the mythical Castelmare, which is not even a Spanish name.

Everything is designed to confound the curious, including the hero's politics. In an idyllic opening imitative of *The Spanish Earth*, Marco (Henry Fonda) is extolling nature, looking like a shepherd in a landscape painting where the light pours down from the sky in shimmering cones. Suddenly the modern world intervenes in the form of a car driven by Norma, a cool blonde played by the quintessential lady spy, Madeleine Carroll; it is fascination at first sight.

Norma is one of the world's rootless; she has been everywhere but belongs nowhere. Yet she is deeply moved by Castelmare's monastic tranquility. If Castelmare seems more like a shrine than a town, it is because it is Catholic. Everyone pauses for the Angelus, and later, everyone crowds into a Catholic church to pray for the arrival of the relief ship. If Castelmare is supposed to evoke Bilbao, and the film's title the Nationalist blockade of Bilbao in April 1937 to prevent food supplies from reaching it, then such religious activity is completely natural. The usual distinction between the anti-Catholic Republicans and the Catholic Nationalists did not apply to the Basque town of Bilbao, which was pro-Republican as were most of its clergy whom Franco considered heretics. In fact, the Basques saw no contradiction in being Catholic and Republican.

Since Lawson could not identify Castelmare as Bilbao or Marco as a Basque, he made Marco's religion and politics one by implying he is a Catholic Republican. Marco's, then, is the right side, Norma's the wrong. But when she sees the misery that the blockade is causing, she converts to Marco's side; with her conversion there is only one side represented, which, while unnamed, is clearly the Republican.

The other, more sophisticated way in which Lawson made *Blockade* pro-Republican was through historical displacement, in which a fictional event is substituted for a factual one without effacing it, so that some vestige of the original incident remains. Historically, the British ship the *Seven Seas Spray* broke the blockade on 20 April 1937 when it brought food to the starving people of Bilbao, who cried out, "Long live the British sailors! Long live liberty!"[13]

In *Blockade* there is also a supply ship, which, like everything in the film, is of unidentified origin. However, its arrival evokes memories of a film of well-known origin, Eisenstein's *Potemkin* (1925). Those knowing the film will make the necessary connection, thinking not of Britain but of the Soviet Union because to a hard-line Communist like Lawson, the Soviet Union was the only world power championing the Spanish Republic, Britain, France, and the United States being neutral.

In *Blockade*, when the people of Castelmare see the ship, they go out to greet it, behaving as the citizens of Odessa do when they see the Battleship Potemkin. The act of comrade helping comrade is portrayed iconographically so that history (the *Seven Seas Spray*) is displaced by film (*Potemkin*), and fact (Soviet support of the Republicans) by fiction (a Soviet supply ship). Although the text is neutral, the subtext is Republican and the iconography Soviet.

Lawson knew that unless the viewer is knowledgeable in the art of film quotation, allusions and *hommages* remain locked within the frames. To reach everyone, Lawson made his side (or rather sides—Republican Spain/Soviet Union) the side of peace. Told he can now find some peace, Marco looks into the lens and replies, "Peace? Where can you find it? Our country has been turned into a battlefield. There is no safety for old people and children. Women can't keep their families safe in their houses; they can't be safe in their own fields. Churches, schools, and hospitals are targets. It's not war; war is between soldiers. It's murder, murder of innocent people. There's no sense to it. The world can stop it. Where's the conscience of the world?"

Appeals to conscience are difficult to ignore, particularly if they come from Henry Fonda, whose delivery was convincing enough to win an endorsement for *Blockade* from the California Council of Federated Churchwomen and the National Council of Jewish Women. The Ohio Knights of Columbus, however, denounced his plea as Marxist propaganda, historically false and intellectually dishonest. Apparently, the Knights did not realize that the Spaniards in the movie are meant to be Basque Catholics (which is not historically false); or perhaps they did and, like Franco, resented it.

When the war that dared not speak its name came to an end on 31 March 1939, Paramount, that unpredictable studio, was the first to utter it in the opening title of *Arise, My Love* (1940): "It is Spain and the summer of 1939. The Civil War is over. Of the soldiers of fortune who came from all over the world, only a few remain, waiting to be written off, in a military prison near Burgos."

It seemed that the lost chord had finally been restored to the prelude, but marked "piano." Paramount advertised *Arise, My Love*, which is overtly interventionist, as "the gay, glorious story of a war correspondent and a war ace." The ace is an American who had flown for the Republic; the correspondent, a female journalist who, by masquerading as his wife, saves him from Franco's firing squad and gets a scoop at the same time. Then the film takes a serious turn as the couple leave Burgos and walk right into World War II. Although *Arise, My Love* is basically a romance, the fact that the action begins in Spain had as much to do with politics as it did with plot construction. The flyer regards his efforts in Spain as "palooka preliminaries . . . for the main event." After three years of not even calling the war by its rightful name, Hollywood made a connection—one that historians have continued to make—between the war that ended in March 1939 and the one that began that September.

It was a connection that became a convention. When screenwriters were not using Spain as the missing link, they were using it as a political label. To establish a character as a left-winger, all that was required was some reference to his having fought in Spain. In *Paris Calling* (1941), Randolph Scott, whose home was really on the range, explains why he is a Yank in the RAF: "I flew in Spain against Franco, in China against the Japs." That he should be flying against the Nazis is understandable. When in *Gung Ho!* (1943) Colonel Evan Carlson (a more congenial role for Scott) asks a group of volunteers why they want to become Marine Raiders, the answers range from hatred of the Japanese to hatred of fascism; as one recruit puts it, "I fought in Spain. I fought in Greece. This fight is all the same—fascism." Similarly, in *The Cross of Lorraine* (1943), one prisoner of war criticizes another for advocating political tolerance: "I used to hear that in Spain, too, when the fascists attacked Madrid."

The movie Americans who fought for Spain had no particular look; they could be anyone from John Garfield to Gary Cooper. Certainly no movie brigader has ever resembled Alvah Bessie—unshaven, cigarette dangling from his lips, and looking totally convinced that what he was doing was right. And no movie character has ever evoked that magnificent young Italian George Orwell immortalized in *Homage to Catalonia*—the one who wore his cap pulled down "fiercely" over one eye and who clasped Orwell's hand in a vigorous expression of solidarity.

An ex-Loyalist could look like a Brooklyn longshoreman (Orson Welles in *The Lady from Shanghai*, 1948) or a scrapper from the Lower East Side of New York (John Garfield in *The Fallen Sparrow*, 1943); he might wear a sailor's cap and a navy blue turtleneck; his eyes might have a knifelike sharpness or they might be cool to the point of world weariness, full of cynicism that only a new cause or an old flame could dispel (Humphrey Bogart in *Casablanca*, 1942). On one occasion he was a benign liberal whose eyes twinkled with brotherly love (Gary Cooper miscast as Robert Jordan in *For Whom the Bell Tolls*, 1943).

The coolest Spanish civil war vet of them all did not wear a zippered jacket and cap, but a trenchcoat and pinched-brim Fedora—Rick Blaine (Bogart) of *Casablanca*. Shortly after he makes his first appearance, he announces with uninflected indifference, "I stick my neck out for nobody." Yet there was a time when he was sticking it out for everyone—for the Ethiopians in 1935, for the Spanish Republicans the following year. Although Rick dismisses his altruistic past, he was in Spain for the same reason most of the volunteers were—"for the sake of an ideal, no matter what motive prompted them to seek one."[14] When Hugh Thomas, the leading historian of the Spanish civil war, wrote "let not posterity impugn the sincerity of these men,"[15] he was clearly thinking of men like Rick.

Orson Welles created a role for himself in *The Lady from Shanghai*—Michael O'Hara, who fought in Spain and who glowers when he hears someone boast of having served on a pro-Franco committee. His radicalization in Spain explains why he has become a unionist and why he is repelled, and momentarily blinded, by the "bright, guilty world" of the rich—a world in which the arch capitalists shoot it out in a hall of mirrors that seem to reflect their images to infinity until their myriad selves shatter in an explosion of glass.

Hollywood studiously avoided references to the International Brigades because they were formed by the Comintern; 60 percent of the brigaders were Communists before they volunteered, and 20 percent became Communists afterward.[16] However, two films that came out in 1943, *The Fallen Sparrow* and *Watch on the Rhine*, while they did not use the phrase "International Brigade," came close with "Brigade."

If, in *The Fallen Sparrow*, screenwriter Warren Duff had said something, no matter how obliquely, about the Abraham Lincoln Battalion, in which the hero served, the film might have been a superior antifascist thriller instead of a muddled anti-Nazi melodrama. The plot, set in November 1940, involves a Spanish civil war veteran (John Garfield) who, after two years of torture and imprisonment in a Nationalist jail, returns to the United States to discover that his best friend has been murdered. Once the plot has developed into a manhunt, a popular form of the antifascist film, the war in Spain could be connected with World War II since the hero's tormentor in Spain is his friend's killer. A link could also be forged between Spanish fascism and Nazism; but neither connection is made because any explanation as to why a German is torturing an American in a Spanish prison in 1938 is lacking.

The resolution hinges on a banner the Nazi is determined to present to Hitler; it is not an ordinary banner but the banner of the hero's brigade—another opportunity to associate Franco's Spain with Hitler's Germany. But the opportunity is lost because the brigade is never identified. When the hero calls the banner "the symbol of the three thousand men who were my friends," one would have to know he is referring to the thirty-three hundred volunteers who comprised the Abraham Lincoln Battalion in order to understand the reference. Only then would the hero's politics be apparent, as would the meaning of the last line: "There'll be brigades forming again"—good word play, but not enough to make the brigades the precursors of the Allied armies.

When Dashiell Hammett adapted Lillian Hellman's *Watch on the Rhine* for the screen, he made her protagonist, Kurt Müller (Paul Lukas), a brigade leader and even included an early scene in which Kurt's young son boasts of his father's having fought in Spain. In the play it is clear that Kurt fought for the Loyalists, but Hellman left it at that because she was trying to avoid giving Kurt a political label. Her point is that Kurt fights fascism anywhere, including Washington, D.C., where he and his family are based at the time of the action. It was undoubtedly Hammett's Marxism that prompted him to make the addition, thereby doing what the Communist press thought Hellman should have done in the first place: make Kurt a Communist. But the reference to the brigades is gratuitous; it was more important to Hammett than it is to the plot. One only wishes Hammett had been the screenwriter for *The Fallen Sparrow*, where clarification was needed.

Hollywood seems to have caught Spanish civil war fever in 1943; after discovering the missing music to World War II's prelude, Hollywood was playing it in all keys. The reductio ad absurdum would have been to make the prelude real music and use the war in a musical, which is nearly what happened.

Warner Bros. had been planning a remake of Sigmund Romberg's operetta, *The Desert Song*, since 1936, but script and casting problems kept delaying production. Finally, in August 1941, screenwriter-producer Robert Buckner and Charles Grayson prescribed "A New Cure for *The Desert Song*," in which they argued that the film could be made if the plot were updated without the story line's being altered.[17] Thus, the action could still be set in French Morocco, but in 1939; the Riffs of the operetta would be part of a slave labor force the Germans had conscripted to build a railroad across the Sahara to Dakar; and El Khobar, the Red Shadow, would be their renegade leader, now anti-Nazi rather than anticolonial.

Warners accepted the prescription, and by March 1942 Buckner had a script ready that even went further than the "modern background" that had been promised. The Red Shadow had also been modernized; he is now a veteran of the Spanish civil war. Having fought for the Republic, he is the perfect champion of the enslaved Riffs. But he is not sanguine about his experience in Spain. In the second revised temporary script (24 March 1942), he says, "I've been around here since the Civil War in Spain. It turned out we were on

Irene Manning and Dennis Morgan, the first and presumably last Loyalist Red Shadow in The Desert Song *(1943).*
Wisconsin Center for Film and Theater Research, courtesy MGM/UA

the wrong side, me and a few other fellers from the States with great ideals and lousy leaders. *. .*." Perhaps the Red Shadow—or Buckner—experienced the same disillusionment that Orwell did with the Communists' conduct of the war; hence the reference to the "lousy leaders." At any rate, in the final shooting script (1 May 1942) and in the actual film, the Red Shadow says only that he came to Morocco from Spain "one jump ahead of a fellow named Franco."

Buckner, who produced *The Desert Song* and shared screenplay credit with the director, Robert Florey, must have realized that leftists, repentant or otherwise, have no place in operetta; thus the film skips over the hero's politics, and takes only one swipe at Vichy in the form of an allusion to Vichy water's looking like eyewash. *The Desert Song* was topical, as planned, but apolitical. It is now one of those lost films, unrentable and supplanted by the 1954 version with Kathryn Grayson and Gordon MacRae. If one remembers the 1943 *Desert Song*, it is for the scene in which the heroine sees the chain gang of Riffs stagger by and offers an iced drink to one of them;

he takes a sip and passes the glass to the others.[18] This act of sharing is as political as *The Desert Song* cares to be.

As if three movies about ex-Loyalists were not enough for 1943—four if one includes *Casablanca*, which most Americans would have seen that year—Paramount released its eagerly awaited version of *For Whom the Bell Tolls*.

In October 1940, a few days after Scribner's published *For Whom the Bell Tolls*, Paramount purchased the film rights: the studio that had made the first fiction film of the Spanish civil war was now about to film the most celebrated work of fiction about the war. It was not that Paramount had become audacious after *Arise, My Love*, which, for all its interventionism, scarcely caused a political ripple. Paramount wanted an epic on the order of *Gone with the Wind*; thus it purchased the novel for its resident epic maker, Cecil B. DeMille, whose association with the studio had begun in 1932 and would last for the rest of his career. With DeMille as director, there was no doubt as to who the screenwriter would be: his alter ego, old flame, and now permanent member of his staff, Jeanie Macpherson.[19] Reading that Paramount had bought the novel and assuming it was for DeMille, Macpherson wired the director on 26 October 1940, informing him that when he returned from New York, she would be ready to discuss the project.

Within a month, Macpherson had written a nine-page "analysis" that also listed the problems involved in filming Hemingway's novel: lack of action, excessive brutality, and "a very slim little plot." "This book is the HARDEST book in the world to make into a Picture," she warned. The politics of the war did not seem to bother her, perhaps because she was not completely familiar with them; she alluded to the episode in which the "Fascists line up the villagers and push them over the cliff," while it was really the Loyalists who did it. Yet Macpherson knew that each side was being helped by other countries (perhaps having inferred it from the novel) and felt audiences could learn "that the destruction resulting from this Spanish Civil War was brought about by outside influences *playing upon* and encouraging inner dissensions, and political factions of the country itself." However, it is hard to imagine Macpherson developing the theme of Soviet and fascist intervention; what primarily appealed to her was the "spiritual" relationship between Jordan and Maria, which she compared to "the piping of a shepherd's flute in the midst of the thunderous bombing of war!"

It is always tempting to speculate on what the fate of a movie project would have been, had the studio's original intentions been realized. If Macpherson had written the screenplay, the film would have been a tragic romance; to her, "mud-flower" love whose "clean, sweet fragrance cuts across the stench of bloody battlefields" was the heart of the novel. She even suggested that the film open with Jordan's seeing Maria for the first time just before the war, so that at their next meeting her altered appearance, especially her shorn head, would make her unrecognizable. Under DeMille's direction, *For Whom the Bell Tolls* would have been to the Spanish civil war what his *Story of Dr. Wassell* (1944) was to be to World War II: lushly photographed hagiography. In the tradition of *The Last Train from Madrid*, there would be a nonpartisan foreword, this time spoken, and, if DeMille had his way, by James Stewart as Jordan: "Civil War—who shall say which side history shall be sympathetic with. It is friend against friend—brother against brother—each convinced he is fighting for the right and welfare of his country." These words, which DeMille scribbled on his memo pad on 30 January 1941, mark the end of his association with the film.

The subsequent history of *For Whom the Bell Tolls* reveals that Paramount was planning something apolitical but nothing as ambiguous as *The Last Train from Madrid*.[20] The Spanish civil war was over; 1941 was not 1937. Besides, all the characters were Republicans; identifying them as such was not the problem, nor was the war. The problem was the nature of the war—a clash between right and left. Paramount had to find some way to get around that fact and reduce the war to the perennial confrontation between good and evil; to present it as a war, not a civil war, but one in which Spain was the battleground and fascism the belligerent.

After DeMille became involved in a Latin American epic (which was never filmed), Sam Wood inherited the project. Wood, whose rabid anti-Communism may have shortened his life,[21] was hardly about to glorify the Spanish left: "It is a love story against a brutal background. It would be the same love story if they were on the other side."[22]

Clearly Wood was what the studio wanted. However, Louis Bromfield, the original screenwriter, was not. Bromfield was so conservative that he wrote a script that was too bland even for Paramount. His first draft (10 September 1941) is as faithful an adaptation as an author would wish. Rather than invent, he simply quoted verbatim, stopping short only of Hemingway's "thees" and "thous." Bromfield's only original contribution consisted of clarifying the ending so there is no doubt that Pilar and Maria reach Gredos. On the other hand, there is no motivation for Robert Jordan's being in Spain. How can there be when not one "Fascist," let alone "Loyalist" or "Nationalist," is used?

Bromfield must have been told to establish identities, because in his revised script (7 October 1941) he acknowledged that Maria is "the daughter of the leading Republican of the town." But that is as far as he went. Bromfield was too uninventive to write a script that would retain Hemingway's basic plot and enable Paramount to find an audience for the film by portraying the Republicans as proto-Allies fighting the Germans. The fact that Bromfield inserted one "Republican" into his revision suggests that Paramount knew something was lacking.

The studio tried to remedy that lack by replacing Bromfield with Dudley Nichols, who, in addition to being an infinitely better screenwriter, was also a liberal. Nichols's script of 21 May 1942 is sprinkled with "Fascists" and "Republicans," not to mention Popular Front philosophy. When one of the guerrillas asks Jordan why he is fighting for Spain, Jordan answers that he is also fighting for the United States: "It isn't only Spain fighting here, is it? Looks like a rehearsal for another world war. Fascist countries are just trying out their new weapons here so they can get the jump on the democracies when they're ready to upset the apple cart."

The sentiments are Nichols's alone; Hemingway's Jordan never speaks like a thirties liberal. A typical Hemingway male, Jordan speaks laconically or poetically, as the occasion requires, but not with such political frankness. Hemingway's Jordan internalizes his politics, knowing that to be less insular, less of an "island," he must experience a oneness with the Spain he loves, not by embracing the whole country, but by embracing first a side, then the group that personifies it, and finally the woman who redeems it.

Hemingway was not trying to place the Spanish civil war within the context of a world war that had just begun and in which the United States was not yet involved. Nichols was, and Jordan's speech is another attempt to see Spain as part of a complex of events that resulted in the Second World War. Nichols rewrote Jordan's speech, and in the revised final script (20 July 1942), Spain became a pawn in the struggle between fascism and Communism: "I believe another world war's beginning to boil up here. Germany and Italy on one side, Russia on the other—and the Spanish people in the middle of it all. The Nazis and Fascists are just as much against democracy as they are against the Communists. They're making your country a proving ground for their new war machinery. . . . so they can get the jump on the democracies and knock off England, France and my country before we get armed and ready to fight."

Spain indeed was in the middle of a struggle between the forces of fascism and Communism, but those forces existed within Spain it-

Gary Cooper and Ingrid Bergman as Robert Jordan and Maria in For Whom the Bell Tolls *(1943). Courtesy* MCA

self, and each force was abetted by a stronger force from without. Nichols's Jordan, whose speech appeared in the film's first release but was later cut, ignores the fact that the war was a civil war, viewing it only as the curtain raiser to World War II with Spain providing the setting and Italy, Germany, and the Soviet Union providing the props. As for the brigaders, they are "like fellows who see a fire starting outside their own yard and try to put it out before it spreads and burns down everything," seeming more like forest rangers than left-wing patriots.

Jordan's simile was dropped from the film, but Paramount, never one for waste, salvaged it for the souvenir program that was given out at the premiere.

For Whom the Bell Tolls opened in July 1943; a month later, Paramount's former president and then chairman of the board, Adolph Zukor, was quoted in *Time* magazine (2 August 1943) as saying the film has "no political significance." Zukor was right; virtually all of the "Fascists" in the shooting script had become "Nationalists" on the screen so that Franco's Movimento Nacional would not bear the stigma of fascism. Audiences, long accustomed to hearing the word, associated it primarily with Nazi Germany. The one instance in which "fascist" was retained, Pilar's account of Pablo's slaughter of the "local fascists" (whom she also called Nationalists), could have been an oversight, but probably represented a tradeoff in which Nichols was allowed to keep one "fascist," for Hemingway's sake, if he changed the rest to "Nationalist."

Regardless, the film was a great popular success; only those who had read the novel were disappointed. Yet even they would have to admit that many of the original episodes were retained: Pilar's monologue on the killing of the Civil Guards (done as flashback with voice-over narration), Maria and Jordan in the same sleeping bag (but photographed in such a way as to make it uncertain whether they are both in it), and Maria's shattering account of her father's execution by the Phalangists and her subsequent humiliation at their hands, including the shaving of her head and the gang rape in her father's office. The film does not ignore the Soviet presence in Spain, either. Karkov, the *Pravda* correspondent ("I am from Stalin," he says emphatically) appears, along with General Golz. For the film, André Marty's name had to be changed to André Massart. Hemingway loathed Marty, the French Communist and commander of the International Brigades, whom he portrayed in the novel as vain, arrogant, and paranoid on the subject of spies. It is Marty's suspicious nature that prevents Jordan's message from reaching Golz in time and so causes the debacle at the end. Hemingway managed to get away with using Marty's real name, but Hollywood, always fearful of an invasion of privacy suit even from abroad, settled for a name change.

What is missing in the film is Hemingway's balanced view of the Loyalists. In the novel, although Jordan is fighting for the Republic, he knows that the Loyalists are far from perfect. The guerrilla band itself is a Loyalist microcosm—ill-equipped and disorganized, desperately in need of outside aid. Pablo, the former leader, is now a horse thief and a drunkard; the new leader, Pilar, is a woman meant to be a follower. For the guerrillas, the Republic is an earthly paradise, a socialist myth they have embraced at the expense of their religion, which is replaced by communal rituals and amenities ("comrade," "thou"). Like Republican Spain, they are living out a dream—a dream with a tragic ending.

Since Hemingway was pro-Loyalist but not an apologist for the Republic, he could express the Nationalist view, as he does in a moving episode when Jordan reads a letter he has taken from the body of a Nationalist soldier; in it, the dead man's sister lauds her brother for "doing away with the Reds to liberate Spain from the domination of Marxist hordes." The episode was not even considered for the film. With Hitler's invasion of the Soviet Union, the Reds had become allies. But the primary reason for the omission was that there could be no indication that the war in the film is a civil war. Thus, what is depicted on the screen is not much different from a typical combat film: machine guns sputter, bombs burst, tanks make paths with their treads, and a bridge is dynamited. Those knowing nothing of the Spanish civil war would assume they were watching a World War II movie.

And if they saw it in the autumn of 1943, they would have even greater reason to think so. Before *For Whom the Bell Tolls* went into its second release, Paramount decided to excise about thirty minutes from the film, believing its length might be a handicap outside the major cities. Presumably Sam Wood was authorized to make the cuts. It was an easy matter: all an editor had to do was carry out the command that was penciled on the release dialogue script of 13 September 1943: "take out political dialogue."

Wood had no love for the Spanish Republic to begin with. Consequently, in the version that most Americans saw there is no explanation for Jordan's fighting in Spain, no reference to German and Italian planes, no flashback dramatizing Pablo's killing of the Civil Guards, and no Karkov and Massart. The Communists posed a special problem: unlike the Germans and Italians, they were more than references; they were characters. Golz was kept since it is to him that Jordan's desperate message is sent. But the scenes with Karkov and Massart were deleted, which meant that the names of the actors who played them—Konstantin Shayne and George Coulouris, respectively—were removed from the credits. This is a striking reversal of precedent; usually an actor ends up on the cutting room floor before the opening of a film, not after it.

In *The Glass Menagerie* (1945), Laura observes of the unicorn that has lost its distinguishing mark, "Now it is just like all the other horses." So it is with *For Whom the Bell Tolls*, which is like all the other antifascist films. Even watching it today, one forgets that the setting is the mountains of Spain in 1937 and not the hills of Yugoslavia in 1943.

In *Confidential Agent* (1945), the Nationalists are fascists again, but for a good reason: the setting is not Spain. Although the film, based on Graham Greene's *The Confidential Agent* (1939), is about the Spanish civil war, the entire action takes place in England where the war is being reenacted in microcosm as a Nationalist (L.) and a Republican (the hero D.) try to purchase coal for their respective sides from an English mine owner who will sell to the highest bidder. Greene's "entertainment," as he dubbed it, is a left-wing thriller with a Communist hero. Robert Buckner, who wrote and produced the film version for Warner Bros., could no more retain the hero's politics than he could his letter name. Thus D. became Denard (Charles Boyer); K. and L., Licata and Contreras, respectively. Marie, the villainess, had her surname changed from Mendrill to Melandez, probably because it sounds more Spanish, although "Melendez" would be more authentic. And in case anyone thought Charles Boyer was playing another Frenchman, Else (Wanda Hendrix), the Cockney maid, immediately greets Denard with, "You're Spanish, aren't you? So is Mrs. Melandez."

Greene regarded the film as one of the more faithful adaptations of his work, which it is as far as plot is concerned.[23] Yet in some respects the film is more specific than the novel, in which neither the war nor the participants are ever mentioned by name. By leaving the war unnamed, Greene equated it with the dark conspiracy that is at the heart of so much spy fiction. In this novel, however, the conspiracy is real, so real that it casts a pall over England and presages the gathering storm over Europe. Greene intended that the factions in Spain have British counterparts who, in turn, prefigure the Allies and Axis of World War II.

Greene had interwoven politics and melodrama so successfully that Buckner had a job trying to disentangle them. In the novel, D. is a man of paradoxical character, a professor of medieval French

Charles Boyer as Denard, observing how war ages the face in Confidential Agent *(1945). Courtesy* MGM/UA

who becomes a Loyalist agent and a willing killer for the Spanish Republic. Even more paradoxical, D.'s motives are essentially religious: If the Catholic Church supports Franco, it is, as D. believes, because church rule is ecclesiastical fascism, resulting in wealth for the few and poverty for the many. If the Church represents enlightenment and civilization, D. prefers barbarism. Buckner knew that such ideas could not be expressed on the American screen in 1945, and that he could never explain D.'s actions to a mass audience. Given a Production Code that regarded entertainment as the primary function of motion pictures, he and director Herman Shumlin still did a creditable job.

Both had more than a casual interest in Graham Greene's work.[24] The Virginia-born Buckner had planned to be a doctor, but diphtheria forced him to pursue a different career, newswriting, which led to the publishing world and then to Hollywood. While on the editorial staff at Doubleday, Doran, Buckner was instrumental in getting the house to publish the American editions of Greene's *The Man Within* (1929) and *The Name of Action* (1931). Shumlin, the noted Broadway director who had staged and produced Lillian Hellman's first five plays, was attracted to *The Confidential Agent* for another reason. Shumlin, who if not a Communist was certainly a fellow traveller, was a member of Contemporary Historians, the Popular Front group that produced *The Spanish Earth*. According to a Warner Bros. publicity release, Shumlin had wanted to film *The Confidential Agent* as soon as he read it in 1939 because he sympathized with its politics. But in 1939 Shumlin was in New York staging Lillian Hellman's *The Little Foxes*; three years later he came to Hollywood to direct his first movie, the screen version of another Hellman play that he had staged in New York, *Watch on the Rhine* (1943). That film's antifascist theme made him the logical choice for director of *Confidential Agent*. Warner Bros. purchased Greene's novel on 24 December 1944 on the strength of Mrs. Jack Warner's enthusiasm for it and Shumlin's interest in directing the screen version.

Confidential Agent is in the tradition of the Warner Bros. melodrama with its foggy streets, men in trenchcoats and fedoras, and women with voices coarsened by the tar of unfiltered cigarettes. Cinematographer James Wong Howe provided the fog and shadow that were part of the studio's signature, but it was Buckner who made the film conform to studio politics (antifascist, but also anti-Communist) and genre. He did essentially what Dudley Nichols had done with *For Whom the Bell Tolls*, reducing the Spanish civil war to a clash between democracy and fascism, so that instead of being a left-wing thriller the film is an antifascist melodrama. Thus the film is pro-Loyalist only in the sense of being antifascist, not in the sense of justifying the Loyalist cause, which is too closely identified with Communism.

The treatment that Buckner wrote in early 1945, however, suggests that originally he was thinking along the lines of the novel, intending to make both sides guilty of atrocities and to have the hero admit he has killed for the Loyalist cause. Buckner also planned to place the Spanish civil war within a global context by juxtaposing newspaper headlines: SPANISH LOYALISTS BOMB GERMAN CRUISER/JAPS SINK U.S. GUNBOAT ON YANGTZE. The headlines would have formed an interesting chiasmus: Loyalist victory/U.S. loss, German loss/Japanese victory. The democracies were aligned against the Axis, but they were not winning, as was indeed the case in 1937. The chiastic headlines do not appear in the final shooting script, much less in the actual film. Furthermore, Denard does not kill, and the Loyalists, who become the precursors of the Allies, do not commit atrocities. Nor did all the information that Buckner requested of Dr. Herman Lissauer, the scholarly head of the Warner Bros. research department, find its way into the script. Buckner was particularly interested in the war news of 16–23 October 1937, the time covered in the film. The four pages of headlines that Lissauer compiled would have provided a historical framework for the plot, but Buckner decided to minimize history and emphasize melodrama. It was enough to imply there were fascists in England; it would be foolish to press one's luck with the Production Code Administration.

Since *Confidential Agent* is set in England and portrays the Loyalists only as antifascists (not as atheists or Communists), the Breen Office had no major objections. In fact, Breen was so concerned that "w.c." be changed to "washroom," that the blasphemous "thank Gawd" be deleted, and that Mrs. Melandez's motive for suicide be morally justified that he was oblivious to Buckner's sly inclusion of some of the novel's left-wing philosophy. The plot hinges on Denard's attempt to buy coal from Lord Benditch, Rose Cullen's father. Since moviegoers would find it difficult to understand how a Cullen could be the daughter of a peer, Buckner makes it clear that, until 1936, Lord Benditch was Joe Cullen, worker. Once Cullen had risen above the working class, he betrayed it, the same year the Nationalists betrayed the ideals of the Spanish Republic.

Socially, Lord Benditch is on a par with the Spanish aristocrats, who supported Franco against the Republic because they wanted to bring monarchy back to Spain. As an industrialist who crushed socialism in the Midlands by closing the pits and weakening the unions, Benditch recalls the German coal and steel magnates who endorsed Nazism because they feared Communism.

If Benditch's willingness to aid Nationalist Spain is a historical metaphor for the insidious cooperation between Hitler and German industrialists like Emil Kirdorf and Fritz Thyssen, Rose's line in the film, "But the war's in Spain, not here in England," is both ironic and prophetic. A Loyalist and a Nationalist are both in England to buy coal. Buckner clearly understood Greene's historical metaphors and clarified them in the Midlands sequence. In the novel, Bates, the trade unionist, is so disheartened by the failure of socialism and the closing of the mines that he cannot rally the miners; he suspects the coal will go to the Nationalists, despite Benditch's claim that it will be shipped to Holland. Bates stands for Britain's demoralized Labour party, which failed to persuade the government to aid Republican Spain. In the film, Buckner has given Bates a son, and a speech in which Bates reveals that his son is fighting in Spain to prevent German bombs from falling on England.

Eventually, the bombs will fall; meanwhile there will be a run-through in the Midlands, just as there was one in Spain. But in the Midlands, the left does not fight the right; the left fights its own. When Denard begs the miners not to dig coal for fascists, they turn on him. The final irony is that the Nationalists also fail to obtain the coal. Once the newspapers print the story of the proposed sale, Lord Benditch cancels it because it is a violation of British neutrality. The failure of the transaction is Greene's attempt to offer a fictional explanation for a historical event: the British government's embargo on shipments of war material to Spain. Greene has invented a situation that could account for such an embargo, and a climate of opinion that could create it: fear of violating that "absolutely rigid neutrality" that Churchill urged (although there were those in the government who might have aided the Nationalists if they had been able to circumvent their country's policy of nonintervention).

Buckner went as far as he could with Greene's concentric arrangement of events in which the lesser is enclosed within the greater, the symbol within the symbolized, and England within Spain. A few moviegoers in 1945 might have picked up the parallel between British capitalism and Spanish fascism, but the majority wanted a film that lived up to its ad: "Watch Her Lips Answer The Call When Charles Boyer Whistles For Lauren Bacall! They're Burning With Yearning In Warners' Screen Scorcher!"

For them, Buckner provided a happy ending. Although both the novel and the film end with D./Denard and Rose on a tramp steamer bound for Spain, Greene implied D. would be killed upon arrival. By comparison, Buckner's ending is euphoric. Rose appears on deck, announcing in a voice as deep as the shadows from which she has emerged, "And then I fall for an idealistic fool who's trying to get himself killed;" to which Denard replies, "You restore my faith. One day I know we must win."

A 1945 audience would take the last line as a reference not to Spain but to World War II. In December 1945, when *Confidential Agent* was released, we had won our war, but the Spanish Loyalists had not won theirs. However, it doesn't matter. By historical displacement, the Loyalists have become the Allies, and although Charles Boyer and Lauren Bacall are off to bleeding Spain, they too undergo displacement: they sail into a war that concluded six years ago and out of one that has just ended. Missing both, they experience neither.

Even after World War II was over, some felt that the prelude should still be heard with the restored section played forte. Lillian Hellman was one of them. In 1946, when she wrote the screenplay for her anti-appeasement drama, *The Searching Wind*, she set one of the scenes in Madrid during the Spanish civil war—something she had not done in the play, where the heroine's profession of schoolteacher made it unfeasible.[25] In the film version, Hellman made the heroine a journalist; thus she could not only place her character in Spain but also have her berate her ambassador-lover for failing to report that Italian and German planes are killing civilians. To Hellman, and to many liberals of the thirties, Spain was the acid test of the democracies' ability to fight fascism—a test they failed by remaining neutral. In 1946 Hellman still believed Spain was the crucial link in a chain that began with Mussolini's march on Rome in 1922 and ended with the Munich agreement in 1938. The dates Hellman chose for her prelude (1922, 1928, 1936, 1938) were by no means arbitrary, but they were, in 1946, fairly standard.

Spain had become so synonymous with Ernest Hemingway that when Casey Robinson wrote the screenplay of *The Snows of Kilimanjaro* (1952), he included the war, although Hemingway's short story, written in 1934, has nothing to do with it. Robinson conceived Harry (Gregory Peck) not just as a Hemingway figure but as a proto-Hemingway, and the film not as an adaptation of a Hemingway story but as a retrospective of Hemingway themes (macho writer, lost generation in Paris, bullfights, safaris, and, of course, the Spanish civil war). Thus, Robinson sent Harry off to Spain, but with no enthusiasm for the "lousy civil war" (Hemingway would have said "bad,"[26] not "lousy," but then Harry really isn't Hemingway). Actually, the only character in the film who is at all committed to Spain is Cynthia (Ava Gardner), Harry's ex-mistress, who becomes an ambulance driver for the Loyalists and dies repenting her induced miscarriage (so that Twentieth Century–Fox could receive absolution from the Legion of Decency).

Eight years later, Ava Gardner had an opportunity to play another Spanish civil war heroine, this time for MGM where she was under contract. Since the studio needed a vehicle for her, it purchased Bruce Marshall's pro-Franco novel, *The Fair Bride* (1953), the story of a prostitute and a priest thrown together by the war. Because of the subject matter, which MGM considered sufficiently controversial to warrant a consultant from the Catholic clergy, the studio decided to advertise the film version of Marshall's novel, *The Angel Wore Red*, as "the startling love story of a scarlet woman," which made the heroine and the title color coordinated.[27]

It was not just the religious aspect of the plot that created problems; difficulties persisted even after the prostitute became a "cabaret girl." Nunnally Johnson, though an excellent screenwriter, had no feeling for the subject matter; in one version, he had the chaplain "taking" confessions instead of "hearing" them. Moreover, Johnson was indifferent to the politics of the war, even as they were reflected in a pro-Franco novel.

The Spanish civil war has been variously interpreted as a conflict between right and left, fascism and freedom, Catholicism and Communism, and the godly and the godless. Marshall portrayed it as a holy war between the Catholic Church and Communism, emphasizing that it began on 19 July, the feast of St. Vincent de Paul. Yet the novel is not a simple case of Church—*si*, Kremlin—*no*. The very first incident in both novel and film is an argument between a young priest, Don Arturo (Dirk Bogarde), who is about to leave the priesthood because of the backwardness of the Spanish clergy, and his bishop, who is more concerned with dress regulations for women than with the growing disaffection of the faithful.

The Fair Bride is the work of an intelligent writer who, unable to resolve his own doubts about the war, expressed them in his novel. Although Marshall's doubts did not affect his love of the Church, the fair bride of the title, they did affect his attitude toward Spanish Catholicism. The story calls for a Graham Greene, who can create drama out of the paradox of a priest who breaks his vows but becomes a better human being for his association with a prostitute. But Marshall was so troubled by the Church's role in the war that he allowed the action to drift into allegory, or to stagnate in pools of introspection.

Once Arturo joins that circle of searching priests who have lost their faith in the Church only to find it in women, Marshall must find a Magdalen for his fallen Christ and a plot for both of them. He picked a relic as a plot pivot: a finger of St. John of the Cross that, if it falls into Loyalist hands, will mean the end of Catholic Spain.

For the most part, Johnson's screenplay duplicates the novel, though some characters have been dropped and others added, and the finger has been changed to a phial of the saint's blood (which seems less obscene). The tortured introspection has vanished, and the only paradox in *The Angel Wore Red* is the familiar one of the fallen woman who achieves salvation by sacrificing her life for the good of others. The film, then, is one of faith rather than religion. The relic's return to the Nationalists even makes an agnostic correspondent wonder whether the age of miracles is really over.

However, a film of faith is no more bound by the strictures of history than a novel of religion; consequently, Johnson felt no obligation to give any more details than Marshall did. In the novel, even the setting is unspecified: sometimes it seems to be Madrid, other times Barcelona. Likewise, the film's opening title is minimally informative: "1936. A city in Spain about to experience the cruellest of all wars—a Civil War." Those to whom 1936 was just another year probably thought the film was about Spain during a Communist takeover when Catholics were being subjected to wholesale persecution. Soviet flags are flying everywhere; soldiers address each other as "Comrade" and their superiors as "Comrade General" or "Comrade Commandant." A godless mob storms a cathedral, destroying the high altar and leaving behind a heap of rubble and a burning crucifix.

The Angel Wore Red is a Cold War film, just as *The Fair Bride* is a Cold War novel. By stressing the Communist presence in Spain, the desecration of churches, and the killing of priests and nuns, Johnson had nothing further to explain: the "godless atheistic" Communists are at it again. For authenticity's sake, "Franco," "Nationalist," "Socialism," and "Socialist" are uttered—once each; repetition breeds confusion. By following Marshall's simplified view of a war in which the Communists are the villains, Johnson even refers to the Communists (meaning Loyalists) as "rebels," although the Nationalists were the ones who did the rebelling.

The war was still a bête noire to everyone, including Franco, who denied MGM permission to shoot *The Angel Wore Red* in Spain, although the film was implicitly Francoist in the sense that it was anti-Communist. The war that once dared not speak its name was now the war that dared not be filmed—not in 1960, not in 1964.

Columbia had a similar problem with Spain when it wanted to film *Behold a Pale Horse* (1964) there. This was understandable: the script portrays the Francoists in an unflattering light, yet it also implies that Spain would not have been any better off with a Loyalist victory. There is a major difference, however, between *The Angel Wore Red* and *Behold a Pale Horse*: the latter takes place twenty years after the war has ended. But the blood is still bad. *Behold a Pale Horse* argues that the war has never really ended; two of its survivors, the Loyalist Manuel (Gregory Peck) and the Nationalist Vinolas (Anthony Quinn), reenact it twenty years later.

If audiences of the late thirties and forties required an expository prologue for a Spanish civil war movie, those in 1964 needed a roll-up title of the *Star Wars* kind. Although it scarcely matters, *Behold a Pale Horse* has a prologue, the most elaborate one in a Spanish civil war movie, combining voice-over and newsreel footage: "In 1936 one thousand years of history exploded in Spain. The forces of Nationalism joined together against the forces of the Republic. Soon the whole world found itself involved in this struggle. The whole world looked toward Spain. In 1939 the Spanish Civil War came to an end. There were the men who lost, crossing the border into France and exile."

The prologue is accurate, the way a grade school history text is accurate, but still vague. Since the language is so cautious, one must look to the visuals to appreciate director Fred Zinnemann's attempt to find a solution, perhaps a personal solution, to the mystery of a war that refuses to rest peacefully in history's crypt. To show that one side is the diametric opposite of the other, and therefore its reverse image, Zinnemann used the same symbols, but antithetically, for both: a bull grazing contentedly in the fields (Loyalist)/the bull of the corrida (Nationalist); the Loyalist crucifix the young Paco rejects/the crosses the Francoists proudly wear around their necks; the simple bed on which the ex-Loyalist Manuel lies/the couch too small to accommodate the ex-Nationalist Vinolas and his mistress.

Unlike the paradoxes in *The Fair Bride*, those in *Behold a Pale Horse* are not meditative; they are dramatized realities. A priest, administering the last rites to Manuel's anticlerical mother, tries to console her with "The Lord giveth and taketh"; "Mostly taketh" is her curt response. Through a kind of transvaluation, a common form of paradox, this gaunt, unforgiving woman becomes an avatar of the Madonna, just as her son, the limping revolutionary, becomes a scapegoat Christ, sacrificed so a corrupt regime can remain in power. Yet the Loyalist Christ is far from perfect. Like his mother, Manuel is vehemently anticlerical. An anarchist turned terrorist, he strikes a priest with such force during a bank robbery that the priest becomes brain damaged. On the other hand, Vinolas, an adulterer who makes love to his mistress in a room adorned with crucifixes, is not much better. One shudders to think of a Spain ruled by either or by what either represents. At the end, Vinolas is shot in the knee, thus inheriting Manuel's limp—Zinnemann's way of saying that all war does is pass afflictions from one side to the other. No civil war ever ends; once the survivors have gone, their descendants take up the struggle, repeating it in miniature or microcosm.

The mean between the extremes is Father Francisco (Omar Sharif) who (like Lilly in another Zinnemann film, *Julia*, 1977) represents the compromise between political apathy and revolutionary fervor. Yet *Behold a Pale Horse* is not Father Francisco's story any more than *Julia* is Lilly's; it is the story of opposed doubles—each unyielding, each unforgiving. The story does not end; it only concludes with the victor's receiving the wounds of the vanquished.

Hollywood has been unable to make a film about the Spanish civil war with the same directness with which it made movies about

World War II, when nothing was too good for uninformed audiences: prologues, forewords, maps, introductions by prominent figures. The Spanish civil war provokes animosity from those who cannot separate the Loyalist cause from the Soviet Union, and ambivalence in those who may be sympathetic to the Republic but find that when they have separated the dream (a socialist republic) from the reality (Loyalist atrocities, Communist attempts to undermine the revolution, disharmony and disorder within the Loyalist ranks), it is the dream to which they are sympathetic.

Unless that ambivalence is resolved (and as anti-Soviet paranoia increases, it hardly seems likely), it appears doubtful that Hollywood can ever make an honest film about the war. As the twentieth century draws to a close, the events that occurred before its midpoint will start acquiring a golden patina that will be hard to remove but easy to polish. One thing the Spanish civil war does not need is refurbishing. What it will get, if it gets anything, is uncertain.

3. Hollywood as Premature Antifascist

Although Hollywood claimed to be neutral on Spain (but really wasn't), it never even pretended to be neutral on fascism.[1] In fact, Hollywood began its war on fascism before fascism began its war on democracy. Initially, it was an undeclared war, and as in all such wars, the date for the commencement of hostilities is disputed. Film historians customarily speak of *Confessions of a Nazi Spy*, which was released in the spring of 1939, as the first anti-Nazi movie. But every war, even one waged by Hollywood, has its prelude.

Nineteen thirty-three was not only the *annus mirabilis* of Adolf Hitler and Franklin Roosevelt; it was also the year of Hollywood's awakening to fascism. For it was in 1933 that the industry began to reflect on what could happen to America if, like Italy and Germany, it became a dictatorship. Hollywood did not embark on a series of "what if" films; there are not even enough to constitute a genre. But such films did appear sporadically; some were astute, others naive. For the most part, they were fretful ruminations, parables disguised as fantasies with telltale signs of sleep interrupted, particularly fuzzy thinking.

That a liberal like Walter Wanger and a conservative like Cecil B. DeMille would each make such a film in the same year—one warning against fascism (Wanger's *Gabriel over the White House*), the other justifying it (DeMille's *This Day and Age*), and both lending themselves to such misinterpretation that many found the antifascist film fascist, and the fascist film antifascist—indicates how politically confused filmmakers, critics, and audiences were.

Gabriel over the White House portrays the transformation of a conservative, Herbert Hoover–type president into a Rooseveltian liberal. At the beginning of the film, he is dismissing unemployment as "a local problem" and recommending "the spirit of Valley Forge" as a means of weathering the Great Depression. After an auto accident, however, he inaugurates a New Deal, eliminates unemployment, puts through legislation preventing foreclosures, and brings about world disarmament—all in such record time that he suffers a heart attack. This brings about a return to his former self, but before the president has a chance to repudiate his efforts, he dies.

The president is a dictator—benign, but still a dictator. To launch his New Deal, he ignores the constitution and acts unilaterally. When a senator accuses him of setting up a dictatorship, he replies, "Then it is a dictatorship based on Jefferson's definition of democracy—a government for the greatest good of the greatest number." The senator's assessment is correct; the president's approach to crime is to have criminals executed by a firing squad; his solution to red tape is to cut it and get back to "first principles—an eye for an eye."

Gabriel over the White House has no solution to offer a nation in the throes of a depression; it depicts an America subject to Fortune's caprice, where any turn of events is purely accidental; it hints that the other side of the New Deal is the New Order; it warns of dark messiahs, Janus-faced saviors showing a fascist profile at one time, a democratic profile at another. But the film itself is Janus faced; it also implies that a benevolent dictatorship can keep a country from going fascist. Since the film has it both ways, it was taken both ways—as profascist and antifascist. Although Wanger resolved to be less ambiguous in the future, he made the same mistake in *The President Vanishes* (1934), which he produced at Paramount the following year; end and means are again confused as a president attempts to put down fascism by fascist means.

There is no confusing end and means in DeMille's *This Day and Age*, in which boys take the law into their own hands to rid their town of a gangster. The end (the gangster's removal) justifies the means (kidnapping, trial, and punishment, all in the name of Americanism). The nature of their Americanism, which borders on Old West vigilanteism, is reflected in the kidnap code, the jingoistic "Yankee Doodle Dandy." In appearance and behavior, however, the boys could not be more representative of Nazism if they had been coached by members of the Hitler Youth. In fact, their torchlit tribunal recalls the gathering of the Hitler Youth on midsummer eve. In their barbarism ("This is a court of justice, not of law"), their contempt for reason ("We haven't got time for any rules"), and their vaunting of masculine superiority ("It takes men to produce men"), the boys need only brown shirts to complete the Nazi image.

Given DeMille's right-wing politics and his penchant for sensationalism, it hardly seems likely that he was trying to educate Americans about the evils of fascism.

Whether a film is an antifascist or a fascist parable, it creates fear; when it lacks a consistent viewpoint, it creates confusion. Hollywood had declared war, but on what? On a force that was alive in the land and that had to be conquered by force; on a force that could not be named because it consisted of so many disparate elements: Father Couglin's anti-Semitic radio sermons, the Silver Shirts, the Klan, the demagoguery of Huey Long—all of which thickened the miasma produced by the Great Depression.

Even in 1936, after Mussolini's invasion of Ethiopia and the re-militarization of the Rhineland, Hollywood's treatment of fascism still showed the effects of a limited awakening: an unclear head and blurred vision. *Fury* (1936), a much better film than *Gabriel over the White House* or *This Day and Age*, is still ambivalent about mob violence. It goes further than most antifascist films of the thirties, however, by emphasizing a feature of dictatorships that is often overlooked: their self-proclaimed infallibility. In *Fury*, even when there is proof that the hero is innocent, he is not acquitted: the state does not err. Again the parallel with Nazi Germany is unmistakable and, in fact, is strengthened by the direction of Fritz Lang, who had fled Germany in 1933.

Unfortunately, *Fury* never reaches the climax to which it seems to be building. The hero's experience should have left him disillusioned about humanity, even misanthropic. But instead he sermonizes, though admitting his thoughts are "all jumbled up"; and while he excoriates the mob that tried to lynch him, he wonders whether "maybe it's done them some good." The dubious possibility that the mob may have learned something undermines the denunciation and, ultimately, the film.

Hollywood's thinking was also "all jumbled up"; it had declared war on what it perceived to be democracy's foe—a foe that was anomalous because it was the product of too many strains, domestic as well as foreign, to qualify for a one-word designation. In the absence of le mot juste, Hollywood resorted to parable, in the hope that an American mob clamoring for a victim would evoke a European country clamoring for a scapegoat.

It is understandable, then, that the first antifascist films appeared in the form of parables and fantasies. Parable and fantasy are extralogical: in parable, what matters is the point, not the detail; in fantasy, the credibility of the world created by the fantasist, not of the real world. The industry rarely ignored a world event, and the rise of fascism was too significant to dismiss. But in the mid thirties, it could not be realistically dramatized. Apart from its being imperfectly understood, there was the possibility of antagonizing Italians who admired Mussolini for getting the trains to run on time, and Germans who lauded Hitler's restoration of national pride. There was also the Production Code, which required that all nations be treated fairly (although that would soon change), to be considered.

Undiluted history is poor box office, but history ignored is poor strategy. The answer was metaphor, allusion, parallel.

In 1933, the industry, even if it could have, would not have embarked on a cycle of antifascist films. Financially, it would have been suicide; the antifascist film is political, and the political is rarely good box office. Even when the industry became overtly antifascist at the end of the decade, there were enough isolationists in America to prompt the studios to adopt Augustus's motto and "make haste slowly." Actual war would change the situation, for with war comes combat, heroism, and romance—the old movie staples. But war was still in the future; meanwhile, allusion was all.

In 1933, if the industry had any policy apart from making movies that make money, it was to provide a depression audience with a product realistic enough to command belief and utopian enough to justify their paying to see it. While Hollywood did not close its eyes to the depression, it did not fix its gaze on it, either. Although some thirties films are uncompromisingly grim (*I Am a Fugitive from a Chain Gang*, 1932; *Make Way for Tomorrow*, 1937), in most of them the uglier aspects of depression life were filtered out on the principle that where there is want, there is hope; and where there is hope, there is an upbeat ending. Some of the screwball comedies also admit the existence of a depression. They do not play it up, however; they merely allude to it, showing the unemployed riding the rails (*It Happened One Night*, 1934), living in a Hooverville (*My Man Godfrey*, 1936), and fighting for free food in an Automat (*Easy Living*, 1937), in a scene that made sense only during a depression and is therefore more frightening than funny.

Like allusion, metaphor is safe. Busby Berkeley choreographed a menacing "Lullaby of Broadway" in *Gold Diggers of 1935*, combining motifs from the Odessa Steps massacre in *Potemkin* with precision tapping to suggest what might happen if the nation began marching to the beat of a different drummer, whether to the rhythm of the "International" or "Die Wacht am Rhein."

Left-wing screenwriters, whether they veered to the extreme left or remained merely left of center, preferred something stronger than allusion: they preferred to make a symbolic connection or draw a meaningful parallel between a fascist and a familiar type such as a warlord or a gangster. While *Gabriel over the White House* pictures in science fiction terms what can happen under a dictatorship, *The General Died at Dawn* (1936) shows what does happen; comparison of the two illustrates the difference between a film of political caution and one of political commitment. Written by Clifford Odets, *The General Died at Dawn* is the story of an American gunrunner, O'Hara (Gary Cooper), out to stop a Chinese warlord, General Yang, perhaps a caricature of Chiang Kai-shek, whom the left despised for his anti-communism. Yang epitomizes the fascist dictator just as O'Hara does the American freedom fighter who fights wherever he finds oppression. Odets, who as a playwright went from anticapitalism (*Waiting for Lefty, Awake and Sing*) to antifascism (*Till the Day I Die*), made Yang the embodiment of both capitalism and fascism; Yang is, as O'Hara puts it, "Yang, Inc." O'Hara, on the other hand, is the true proletarian who envisions a world where "everyone will walk on earth without fear of poverty." When O'Hara claims that, in opposing Yang's dictatorship, he is being thoroughly American, he is echoing the sentiments of those who were fighting fascism before 1 September 1939 or 7 December 1941.

Screenwriters of the left often tend to politicize material, for example, organized crime, that ordinarily does not strike others as political. But to a leftist, particularly to a Communist, organized crime is another form of exploitation. It was treated as such in one of the best premature antifascist films, *Marked Woman*, which Robert Rossen, who became a Communist in 1937 (the year *Marked Woman* was released), coauthored with Abem Finkel.[2] *Marked Woman* does not reduce fascism to a submerged metaphor that surfaces with the right parallels; fascism permeates the entire plot, which is based on the 1936 vice trial of "Lucky" Luciano.[3] In the film, the prostitutes, euphemistically called "hostesses," are not just manipulated by the syndicate; they are exploited by it and subjected to threats and extortion. Initially, Mary (Bette Davis), the heroine, allows herself to be exploited; but a mobster's manhandling of Mary's kid sister, which results in the girl's death, causes Mary to turn state's evidence even though her face is slashed in retaliation.

Unlike other premature antifascist films, *Marked Woman* lacks a tidy resolution. There is no hope for the Marys of the world; at the end, instead of rushing into the arms of the waiting district attorney, she and the other hostesses disappear into the fog.

Until Hollywood was ready to mount an all-out offensive against fascism, the antifascist film could only draw analogies between totalitarianism and such American equivalents as terrorism, mob violence, vigilanteism, and the criminal underworld. It was usually the screenwriter who forged the parallels, but the right director could do it with images, as Fritz Lang did in *You Only Live Once* (1937), in which it is visually possible to associate the police who hound an innocent man and his wife to their death with the Gestapo.

Such associations were not the prerogative of radical writers and sensitive directors, nor were they the preserve of the major studios; soon they would filter down to Poverty Row where studios like Republic turned out the movies that made up the second half of the bill on Saturday afternoons. If, in the late thirties, Saturday matinee audiences sensed something different about the varmints in some of the Republic westerns, if the villains seemed alien to the range, if they were neither outlaws nor desperadoes, it was because they were fascists in disguise.

It was logical that Republic would take an antitotalitarian stand. Herbert J. Yates, who headed Republic from 1935 to 1956, determined that his films would foster the virtues of "patriotism, conservatism, self-reliance and justice" whether they were set in the present or, as was often the case, in the Old West.[4] Yates would be the first to agree that the fundamental things apply, especially in Middle America, the South, and the Southwest—Republic's chief markets—where the fundamentals were important. Since a typical audience consisted of the young and the undiscriminating, the message had to be brief, easily grasped, and neatly summarized: traditional values are the abiding ones, villains are always punished, and people are naturally cooperative. It was the spirit of cooperation, particularly as it existed on the frontier where homesteaders banded together against rustlers and outlaws, that the studio promoted so zealously in the low-budget westerns that were its specialty.

For all of Yates's patriotism, which was so intense that during World War II he asked his directors to show the flag on the screen whether the script called for it or not, the studio was "governed first and foremost by the profit motive."[5] And profits could start dwindling if every oater were set in the 1880s and '90s. The solution was an occasional western with a contemporary twist.

Perhaps the most familiar sagebrush cliché is "law and order," a phrase that is to the western what "follow that cab" is to a private eye movie. The blackshirts in Italy, the brownshirts in Germany, and the Silver Shirts in America were as contemptuous of law and order as the outlaws, the crooked sheriffs, and the shady realtors—the traditional heavies of the western.

Fascist thugs are heavies, too—born heavies who also intimidate and terrorize. Thus they would be at home on the range. The West was populated by so many kinds of badmen, from bandits to goon squads, that it could easily accommodate a few more. As one might expect of an anomalous enemy, the newcomers were a hybrid: a cross between outlaw and gangster, henchman and saboteur.

In 1937, Republic came out with the eighth of its popular Three Mesquiteers series, *Range Defenders*.[6] Like the studio's other western heroes, the Mesquiteers were not subject to time; they could mete out justice in either the postbellum or post-Versailles West. When they went modern, they tackled such problems as veterans' rights and conservation. *Range Defenders* updated the perennial clash between the Mesquiteers and the lawless through a contemporary plot about a sheepman's efforts to keep the farmers from voting for their candidate for sheriff.

The updating, while not unanticipated, was still unusual. Screenwriter Joseph Poland drew parallels between fascism in Europe and totalitarianism out west. Ranches are confiscated, and black-shirted bullies abuse the elderly. The community is described as an "armed camp" where a sheepman and his "guerrillas are strong armin' the ranchers, grabbing their land and water rights." Although villains have worn black shirts in the past, their dress on this occasion is eerily apt. They sport sleeve badges similar in design to the circular ss Civilian Dress Insignia (white lightning flashes on a black background). In its own ingenuous way, *Range Defenders* evokes a fascist society where voting day is marked by the presence of guards, the erection of barricades, and the violation of civil liberties.

In many theaters, *Range Defenders* would have been on the same program with a Republic serial. While the major studios had been making military preparedness films during the thirties by spotlighting different branches of the armed services, Republic did its bit with serials—*Undersea Kingdom* (Navy, 1936), *Coast Guard* (1937), and *The Fighting Devil Dogs* (Marines, 1938). Whether feature or serial, the purpose was the same: to show America's readiness to confront the enemy, even though the enemy was never named. The next step was to hypothesize, to ask: What if the enemy were in our midst? What if the enemy were the owner of the local refinery or mine?

In 1938, the Mesquiteers, one of whom is now John Wayne, tangle with bona fide enemy agents. A year can make an enormous difference: Austria and Czechoslovakia were still intact in 1937; they were not in 1938. War had become less remote. Thus, *Pals of the Saddle* (1938) is even more topical—an espionage western; the hero who formerly headed outlaws off at the pass now heads enemy agents off at the border. The plot takes its point of departure from the bombing of Guernica, Anschluss, and the annexation of the Su-

The Nazi-inspired henchmen of Range Defenders *(1937), two of whom sport Hitlerian mustaches. Wisconsin Center for Film and Theater Research*

detenland. The first image to appear on the screen is a spinning globe in flames, over which one word is superimposed: WAR. Then come war's concomitants: soldiers on battlefields, bursting shells. Next, a succession of headlines: CONGRESS PASSES NEUTRALITY ACT.... WAR SUPPLIES FORBIDDEN NATIONS IN CONFLICT. ... NEW POISON GAS FOUND.

Pals of the Saddle takes a sizeable bite out of Europe's crumbling cake but leaves America's intact. Like a loyal American, the film acknowledges our neutrality act (or rather, acts—there had been three). But neutrality is not commercial; on the other hand, a neutral country infiltrated by agents from a belligerent nation trying to obtain an important chemical—one "found only in the salt beds of the Southwest that will revolutionize modern warfare"—is "boffo," as *Variety* would say. Thanks to John Wayne and the heroine, a government agent with a pistol-compact, the important chemical "monium" stays where it belongs.

In 1939, as the world moved closer to war, so did Republic—with an attack on unpatriotic and opportunistic Americans in *In Old Monterey*, starring Gene Autry in his thirty-second film. When America's "Singing Cowboy" reminded people that it could happen here "and will happen unless we have a fighting force so superior that no one will dare attack us," who would not sell his land to the army for maneuvers and bomb tests?

The screenplay of *In Old Monterey* was completed by mid June, six months before the outbreak of World War II. It seems like another military preparedness film, except that the military is now preparing for something—for war, as the headlines montage indicates at the beginning: WAR THREAT SWEEPS EUROPE. . . . WORLD POWERS INCREASE ARMAMENTS. . . . CONGRESS SPEEDS PLANS FOR US DEFENSE.

Accompanying the headlines is the sound of gunfire; all this in old Monterey, no less. Yet that is the point: the title has nothing to do with the film, and the title song, warbled by Autry at the fadeout, is a placebo for audiences who have witnessed a boy's tragic death, his tear-drenched funeral, and—the pièce de résistance—crotchety George "Gabby" Hayes, Autry's sidekick, singing "Columbia, Gem of the Ocean."

This time, Republic was fingering the icing on America's cake, and then smoothing it over. The studio had never gone quite so far before, but then neither had the Third Reich. Superficially, *In Old Monterey* is a military preparedness film that combines a salute to the service with a service-oriented plot; but it is also a civilian preparedness film that presents the people's response to military defense. Thus it would provoke neither isolationists nor Middle Americans since it is not arguing for war but for a defense system so strong that war will be unthinkable. Such a system, however, requires sacrifice, particularly from property owners who may have to evacuate their land—with compensation from the government—so the army can test high-power explosives. At first, the ranchers resist: "It's just as bad as if there was a real war goin' on," one complains. Then Autry shows them film clips of the Spanish civil war (of all things) and the Japanese bombing of Shanghai: "This is the bombing of Shanghai, China where 100,000 innocent people lost their lives. . . . Here is a city in Spain being bombed, with the same terrible toll of the civilian population." What Autry is advocating is not quantity of defense but quality: "not more men, more guns and more equipment, but better men, guns, and equipment." Better than whose, one might ask? But one didn't; the enemy was still anonymous.

The enemy, like the fifth column, can be within our ranks. The film makes this point in its subplot (borrowed from *Trail of the Lonesome Pine*, 1936), in which a boy is killed when the mine owners, in an attempt to pit the locals against the government, blow up a ranch house, making it seem the work of the army. What happens in the film is the reverse of what happened in Germany, where industrialists willingly cooperated with Hitler; in *In Old Monterey*, private enterprise is the culprit, as it is in *Pals of the Saddle* and in scores of other westerns. The film does not even bother to argue for an alliance between industry and the military; as long as people cooperate, rugged individualism will vanish, and greedy industrialists will get their comeuppance.

Again in 1939, and two films later, Autry is *South of the Border*, tangling with agents from "some belligerent nation . . . stirring up trouble, hoping to gain control of American oil concessions" in Mexico and setting up a submarine base there. Although the enemy is unnamed, a radio message, "Notify U-Boats, Obtain Oil Tonight," makes it obvious which belligerent nation is fomenting revolution down Mexico way—"U-boat" being a deliberately unsuccessful attempt at camouflage. Again the theme is topical, the sentiments patriotic, the resolution musical, and the aftertaste one of spun sugar.

The neighborhood theater that played *In Old Monterey* or *South of the Border* on a Saturday afternoon in 1939 might also have shown a chapter of the Republic serial, *Dick Tracy's G-Men*. If so, in addition to watching Autry justifying war games to keep the peace or discovering U-boats off the Mexican coast, one could hear Dick Tracy equate espionage with the bubonic plague. In the serial, the head of a spy ring is characterized as a "rat, gnawing at the foundations of democracy . . . carrying germs of plague and disease." Such a rodent obviously "had to be exterminated." In the final chapter, Tracy reads the riot act to the country without a name: "I sincerely hope his [the villain's] execution . . . will serve as a warning to any other spies or troublemakers who might think America is easy pickings."[7] Understatement was not Republic's forte, nor was elegance of expression. Tracy's peroration was aimed at the Cracker Jack crunchers.

For all its tough talk, a Republic film was never political; it was really the voice of America, affirming whatever America's position happened to be: prewar neutrality (with a defense buildup, just in case), wartime unity, and postwar anti-Communism. For example, in the fall of 1938, stories about Nazi spies in America began appearing in the press; Republic had spies operating out west, though their nationality was never specified. In its own way, Republic accomplished in 1938 what Warner Bros. achieved a year later in *Confessions of a Nazi Spy*; it sounded an alert that Warners made into an alarm.

In the spring of 1939, an exhibitor planning to show *Confessions of a Nazi Spy* had a choice of eighteen mats for newspaper ads, with leads such as

The Picture That Calls A Swastika A Swastika!

I'll Talk! I'll Talk! I'll Tell You Everything
> Who gives us orders . . .
> What we're after . . .
> How we work . . .
> Who pays us . . .

Nazi Spies in America? That's got nothing to do with me! He'll learn differently when he sees *Confessions of a Nazi Spy*.

What do you know about the man next door? Where does he get his orders? To whom does he report? How many others like him are there in the United States . . . spying, stealing, taking photographs, betraying America? It's your American right to know! It's your American privilege to see!

Over there you wouldn't be allowed to see this picture![8]

While the ads differed in degree of luridness, they had one element in common: they carried the name of Leon G. Turrou as technical adviser.

In 1939, most moviegoers would not have associated the name of Leon Turrou with the FBI agent whose work on the Lindbergh case had led to the conviction of Bruno Hauptman for the 1932 kidnapping of Charles Lindbergh's son; but they might have known him as the G-man who had unmasked a German spy ring in 1938, only to be dismissed from the FBI for violating his oath of confidentiality when he sold a series of articles based on the case to the *New York Post*. On 20 June 1938, three days before the series was to begin, Turrou submitted his resignation to J. Edgar Hoover, citing health and family as reasons. Attorney General Joseph B. Keenan refused to accept the resignation, and Turrou was "dismissed with prejudice" to prevent his returning to the FBI.[9] A restraining order prevented the series from beginning on schedule; it was not until December that "Confessions of a Nazi Spy," as the series was called, appeared in print.

The fact that "Confessions of a Nazi Spy" had been halted did not deter Warner Bros. from proceeding with plans to film it. Warners purchased the film rights on 23 June 1938, the very day the first installment was to appear in the *Post*. The project was a natural one for a studio that excelled at transforming sensational news stories into movies that managed to retain the semblance of authenticity without slipping into pure documentary. Robert Elliot Burns's experience on a Georgia chain gang had formed the plot of *I Am a Fugitive from a Chain Gang*; "Lucky" Luciano's conviction on the evidence of prostitutes had provided the inspiration for *Marked Woman*. Warners would not even have needed the Turrou articles; the newspaper accounts alone could have furnished the plot, as they often did. Yet the studio was determined to make the film, using either the articles or the case on which they were based. By 10 September, seven weeks before the series finally appeared, a treatment had already been completed by Milton Krims, who would eventually become one of the screenwriters.

When the series began on 4 December 1938, the *Post*, with an air of vindication, stressed the need for "an expansion of the intelligence branches of our military and naval establishments." Even the White House was not immune to espionage, as the series would have shown had the Department of Justice not intervened and demanded certain deletions before publication could commence. Apparently, in January 1938, ship designer W. Starling Burgess had had a confidential talk with President Roosevelt about the need for using an aluminum alloy in the manufacture of American warships. Within hours, the Germans knew of their conversation. Furthermore, only three official sets of blueprints existed for the destroyer that Burgess had recommended to the president. The original set was at the New York offices of the naval architects Gibbs & Cox, the Navy Department had the second, and Burgess had the third. The Department of Justice forbade any reference to Burgess's talk with the president or any allusion to the possibility that Gibbs & Cox had been infiltrated by German agents.

These deletions did not detract from the drama of the case, which, like any spy caper, seems an affront to credibility. In accounts of espionage, what appears to be a blatant disregard for verisimilitude is really a configuration of events that is so logical it at first seems unreal, then implausible, and finally invented. In the film, even the Turrou figure has to admit that "it all seems so unreal."

The cast of the Turrou case could have stepped out of the pages of a Helen MacInnes thriller instead of a newspaper: the gray-haired Jessie Jordan of Dundee, Scotland, who forwarded mail between Nazi agents in America and German intelligence in Europe; Guenther Rumrich, U.S. army deserter, who was such a rank amateur that he tried to obtain fifty blank passports by posing as the nonexistent Under Secretary of State Weston; Jenni (Johanna) Hoff-mann, hairdresser on the German liner *Europa*, who was implicated by Rumrich; Dr. Ignatz Theodor Griebl, Yorkville obstetrician, womanizer, and naturalized American in the army reserves, who fled to Germany, leaving behind a "who's who" of American Jews and liberals compiled for a future pogrom; Kate Moog Busch, a nurse and Griebl's mistress, who, as the papers said, "has many friends in high places" (she knew Admiral James F. Halsey, and had once been President Roosevelt's nurse; such connections were among the dele-tions the Justice Department required) and who was to be ensconced in a Washington apartment-salon to pry information from unsus-pecting government officials and military personnel. The motifs were also in the grand tradition of espionage: encoded match books, plane designs concealed in a violin case, and a bizarre (but unat-tempted) plot to kidnap an American colonel.

For all their efforts, the spies obtained nothing of strategic impor-tance. Their activities were the stuff of melodrama, not tragedy, for they lacked the stature of tragic protagonists and the complexity of Cambridge moles like Guy Burgess and Anthony Blunt. The mo-tives of the German spies were simple, ranging from nationalism to disaffection, from love of power to love of money. But monolinear figures are perfect for the thriller where characterization is only an encumbrance to the plot. And since the case was incomplete, a writer could speculate on the fate of those who had returned to Ger-many—especially the fate of Griebl, who had left unexpectedly for Germany in May 1938 after making a full confession to Turrou.

As it happened, the actual case turned out to be more interesting than the film version. Yet the first draft screenplay, called *Storm over America*, had promise. If the events it dramatizes seem more like installments in a series, and their arrangement more temporal than causal, it is because the screenwriters settled for a semi-docu-mentary approach that skipped from one locale to another and re-duced the plot to episodes. Lacking in the script is the configuration that results when all the pieces interlock, as they do in *Five Fingers* (1952) where, at the end, there are no gaps in the puzzle. While the screenwriters were clearly trying to arrange the events as links in a chain, they were missing the initial link: It was not Griebl who was the central figure in the case, or even Rumrich, but master spy Wil-liam Lonkowski (alias William Schneider, Willie Meller, William Lonkis). It was Lonkowski who, with the aid of Griebl, set up a spy base in Montreal; Lonkowski who made Senta de Wagner, the pro-prietor of a Hempstead, Long Island liquor store, a courier for his spy ring; Lonkowski who enlisted spies to work as mechanics at

Roosevelt and Mitchel airfields in Long Island. Lonkowski was the thread of continuity in a patchwork conspiracy.

Still, *Storm over America* has a wonderful recklessness about it. Loud without being shrill, it does not hide its bias beneath the veneer of art. Most of the spies appear in the script under their actual names, a situation that changed when the studio realized it could be hit with an invasion of privacy suit. (Kate Moog Bush, however, is always called Erika Woolf in the various drafts; as a material witness with "friends in high places," she could hardly be called by name.) In a scene in Yorkville's nonfictitious Vaterland Cafe, Griebl urges his fellow Bundists to annihilate "this subhuman minority of beasts, this small clique of depraved monsters who by their shrewd, slimy machinations control 90% of the government, almost 100% of the banks, industries, railroads, mines, even the newspapers. . . ." There is also a peroration-type ending that makes fascism an international concern. A Nazi general predicts the conquest of South America, extolling the progress German intelligence has made everywhere but in the United States where the agents "bungled" their mission. Regardless, "any nation that dares stand in our way will be destroyed. It is not for nothing that every young German is taught to sing . . . tomorrow the world is ours." Dissolve to hobnail boots pounding the soil. THE END.

There would be no anti-Semitic diatribe in the final version, and audiences would be spared the hobnail boots. However, the production files of *Confessions of a Nazi Spy* reveal that Warner Bros. was thinking in terms of a no-holds-barred film. Reading through the memos, one can only imagine what it was like at the studio in December 1938 when everyone associated with the project got so caught up in the spirit of espionage that they started behaving like spies themselves. Dr. Lissauer, head of the research department, was so excited about making an anti-Nazi movie that he informed Robert Lord, the associate producer, of the rumor the German-American Bund was spreading that Jewish firms were discharging their gentile employees to make room for Jewish refugees. Presumably Lissauer thought that bit of information could be worked into the script, which originally was to contain an indictment of the Bund. Director Anatole Litvak asked Lissauer to procure a copy of the Nazi publication, *Instructions for Our Friends Overseas* (#7) (which, as Lissauer discovered, was only available to Bund members). Milton Krims, who would write the screenplay with John Wexley, commuted between Hollywood and New York to attend Bund meetings—in disguise, of course. Irving Deakin of the story department managed to crash a bon voyage party on the *Europa* and get some shots of the ship's interior. However, Deakin could not provide the ship's authorities with a plausible reason for photographing the wireless room. Still, he was able to obtain copies of the Bundist periodical, *Junges Volk*, as well as photos of Bundist youths at Camp Siegfried. When Yorkville restaurant owners refused to allow their establishments to be photographed, Deakin shot what he could surreptitiously, including the interiors of the Vaterland and Hindenberg cafes which served as models for the nameless restaurant in the film.

The nature of the memos that the project generated suggests that the studio's primary considerations were legal. But memos cannot tell the complete story; they cannot recreate the anxiety that existed between 22 December 1938 and 18 March 1939 when the film was being shot; they do not say that Robert Lord carried a gun for self-protection; they do not express Jack Warner's fear of anti-Semitic reprisals.[10] Finally, they cannot explain why Warner Bros. made the first explicitly anti-Nazi movie.

Warner Bros. was the logical studio to make *Confessions of a Nazi Spy*. First, German belligerency was not an unfamiliar subject to the brothers Warner. In 1917, when the brothers were still in distribution, they had obtained the rights to *War Brides*, in which Nazimova portrays a woman who kills herself rather than breed children for an unidentified country whose army looks suspiciously Teutonic. In 1918, the brothers had produced *My Four Years in Germany*, which combines newsreel footage with staged action (a practice that was also common during World War II) and includes scenes in which the enemy, now unmistakably German, "beat and kill prisoners of war, send spies to America, launch the Russian Revolution, and plan to divide America among Mexico, Japan and themselves."[11] Even more virulent was their 1918 production *Beware*, which traces German aggression back to Attila, thus anticipating the World War II habit of linking the present with the past by explaining the rise of Nazism in terms of the failure of Versailles.

Having attacked the Kaiser prior to America's entry into World War I (*War Brides* opened on 5 April 1917, the day before the United States declared war on Germany), Warner Bros. was not about to wait for World War II before attacking Hitler. Furthermore, as sons of Polish Jews who fled their homeland because of anti-Semitic pogroms, the brothers had a personal interest in exposing Nazism—first in America, then in Europe. Finally, Jack Warner would never forget what had happened in 1936 to one of the studio's employees, Joe Kauffman, in Berlin: "Like many an outnumbered Jew he was trapped in an alley. They [Nazi hoodlums] hit him with fists and clubs and then kicked the life out of him with their boots and left him dying there."[12]

Thus Warners ignored death threats, the German consul's displeasure, Hitler's wrath, and a possible isolationist boycott. Jack Warner and Hal Wallis, then executive producer at the studio, were committed to making as topical an exposé of Nazism as possible. And what would be more topical than a movie that used the spies' real names? It is amazing that Wallis wanted to use actual names, yet there are memos to that effect, and Wallis has admitted as much in his autobiography.[13] Even in the treatment and drafts, the characters, except for Kate Moog Busch, are called by their real names. Because the spies had already been indicted, Wallis thought their names could be used, in addition to the names of the liners *Bremen* and *Europa*. Either he did not realize or he had forgotten that prisoners could sue for libel.

Morris Ebenstein of Warner's legal department had to caution Wallis that there was the possibility of a libel suit or even a court injunction against the film if names were used without consent. Ebenstein was even concerned about advertising; the ads could be provocative but not damaging. Strictly forbidden were any allusions to the film's being a "picturization" of a recent spy trial, or, for that matter, of any trial; any admission that the characters were real, particularly the character played by Edward G. Robinson, modelled on Turrou; and any acknowledgment that the Turrou articles were the basis of the movie. On the other hand, publicity releases could state that the film was inspired by recent spy trials in New York, Los Angeles, and the Panama Canal Zone; that Turrou was the technical adviser; and that the espionage and spy-smashing methods depicted in the film were authentic. An invasion of privacy suit, then, was not the studio's sole concern: Warners did not want to antagonize the FBI, especially after Turrou's dismissal.

With fictitious names, the aura of authenticity would have to be achieved by different means. For a time, Wallis considered doing away with the credits, thereby giving the film the appearance of a newsreel. In view of the importance that writers, in particular, attach to screen credits, strong opposition might have been expected from Krims and Wexley; yet they agreed to waive credit if everyone else did. Even the star, Edward G. Robinson, claimed he would abide by the studio's decision regarding his billing: any size billing or none at all. Finally, a compromise was reached: the title at the beginning and all other credits at the end.

Given the studio's penchant for forewords, one could envision *Confessions of a Nazi Spy* opening with one of those scroll-like pro-

Dr. Kassel (Paul Lukas) addressing the New Jersey chapter of the Hitler Youth at Camp Horst Wessel in Confessions of a Nazi Spy *(1939). Wisconsin Center for Film and Theater Research, courtesy* MGM/UA

logues, with the print moving up the screen at a pace calculated to make audiences read every sacrosanct word. Ebenstein suggested a foreword to Wallis that was a cross between a disclaimer and a deposition: "While the particular characters and events in this photoplay are fictional, the espionage methods revealed therein are true and the methods of detecting the spies are also true." Wallis replied that a foreword claiming the characters and events were fictitious would garner "the biggest laugh of the picture." There would be no foreword, Wallis decreed; instead, there would be voice-over narration with the commentator speaking "clear, sharp and loud."[14]

For a property deemed so controversial that Wallis allowed only a limited number of scripts to be issued, and those "kept under lock and key," the result is rather disappointing. Frank Nugent of the *New York Times* remarked that anyone who had followed the case would find nothing new or startling in the movie. After all, *Confessions of a Nazi Spy* premiered four months after the Turrou articles; furthermore it never lived up to its title.

The concern over possible lawsuits, the frustration of submitting scripts to the White House only to have them come back blue-pencilled, and finally, the realization that what had been envisioned could never be filmed resulted in a gradual diminution of drama. The plot still retained its basis in fact, but not all the facts could be used, and even those that could were deliberately altered to prevent a total identification of the person with his or her film counterpart. Thus, instead of fact, there remained only the evocation of fact. Jessie Jordan became Mary McLaughlin. Ignatz Theodor Griebl was renamed Karl Friedrich Kassel; now a reserve officer in the Navy, he resides at the impossible address of 704 E. 84th St., not at the often-cited 56 E. 87th St. At least he has not moved from Yorkville. Rumrich, now Schneider, changed boroughs—from the Bronx to Brooklyn, where he could check on troop movements at "Fort Wentworth" (really Fort Hamilton). Johanna Hoffmann turned into Hilda Kleinhauer; she is still the ship's hairdresser, but the ship is no longer the *Europa* but the *Bismarck*. Many of these alterations—in names of persons and places, in addresses, in locations—were innocuous enough. But Camp Siegfried, where German-American children disported themselves like Hitler Youth, experienced a truly damning name change: Camp Horst Wessel, after the German pimp who gave the Nazis their official song and the Third Reich its second anthem. Although it was agreed at the outset that Kate Moog Busch would appear under the name of Erika Woolf, Warners was so conscious of her White House connections that her once significant role was reduced to a walk-on. Since she appears in only one scene, who she is, or even what she is, is never made clear.

As a spy thriller, *Confessions of a Nazi Spy* lacks the chief ingredient of the genre—suspense. The semi-documentary format and suspense are not mutually exclusive, as *Boomerang* (1947) and *Call Northside 777* (1948) have shown; but in these films, the events unfold as part of the plot in which they cohere, not as isolated incidents in a case that is being dramatized. In these films, the case is the plot; in *Confessions*, the case is the film because there is no plot. Chronology replaces narrative, with the events seeming more like entries in a diary than interconnected episodes in a plot.

Furthermore, the most powerful parts of *Confessions*, the narration and the montage, have nothing to do with the spy trial. One will recall that Wallis wanted voice-over narration instead of a foreword. In the film, the narrator first appears in silhouette, then fades to an off-camera voice that grows progressively graver as the time of Anschluss, the annexation of Sudetenland, and the Munich pact draws nearer. The montage confirms the narration: an animated map traces the route of the "vitriolic and scurrilous propaganda" emanating from Germany. In a series of wildly expressionistic canted shots, passersby are bombarded with pamphlets streaming down from the sky, bearing such titles as *The President Is a Communist* and *Tomorrow the World Is Ours*. At the end, there is a stunning montage of newspaper headlines superimposed on actual newsreel footage showing the latest Nazi victories. The montage was easily updated when the film was rereleased so the fall of the Netherlands and Norway could be added.

Confessions of a Nazi Spy concludes as a movie, not as a newsreel. Renard and the district attorney are in an old-fashioned greasy spoon where two blue collar types decry the "nerve" of the Nazis for spying on the United States. "The voice of the people," the district attorney observes. "Thank God for such people," Renard retorts to the approving strains of "America the Beautiful" on the soundtrack.

Thus Warner Bros. succeeded in making the first overtly anti-Nazi American film. *Confessions of a Nazi Spy* was, in fact, the first film to mention Hitler. Nor does the film shrink from referring to the concentration camps: A woman passenger on the *Bismarck* deplores the existence of such camps in her homeland; Kassel fears he will be sent to one if the Gestapo discovers he has confessed to the FBI. The film also indicts the German-American Bund as a racist organization committed to undermining the Constitution; it even includes a scene intentionally reminiscent of the 22 February 1938 Bund rally at Madison Square Garden where anti-Bundists (in the film, an American Legionnaire and a patriotic German-American) were beaten and ejected. One also has to admire the ingenious introduction of Goebbels through an unbilled appearance by Martin Kosleck, who always played Nazis with such bureaucratic stolidness that their ruthlessness seemed to be a cover-up for their mediocrity.

At least *Confessions of a Nazi Spy* identifies the enemy, which is more than the first Spanish civil war movies or the cryptofascist

ones did. When *Confessions* errs, it errs on the side of the angels—
by putting propaganda before plot. Espionage is melodrama, and
melodrama involves sweetly done treachery and finely spun intrigue, neither of which is present in the film, as one of the witnesses in the case, Senta de Wagner, observed. Writing to Warner
Bros., she criticized the way "grand material, ready to be woven into
another triumph for your studio" has been turned into "rags." That
the film was a bad weaving job was not her only complaint: "Inge-
nuity, charming intrigue, particularly finesse, the fundamentals of a
spy tale—it was all missing." [15]

Such finesse would have been out of place in *Confessions of a
Nazi Spy*, but it would have been appropriate in another espionage
film that Warners was contemplating even before it became interested in the Turrou articles. The film that became *Espionage Agent*
(1939) started out as "Career Man," an original screen story by Robert Buckner about a foreign service official who discovers his wife
has been a spy.[16] The subject had great potential: it would be what
Senta de Wagner and scores of moviegoers wanted. Although an outline based on Buckner's story was ready by 13 January 1938, the
treatment was not completed until mid November. Casting and
script problems caused further delays; at one point, James Hilton
was brought in but received no screen credit for his contribution. By
the spring of 1939, when *Confessions of a Nazi Spy* was about to be
released, Jack Warner was growing impatient: "If we intend to make
a story of this kind we must get it in real quick because the world is
changing so fast; if we wait too long this is going to be very old
news." [17]

Warner also wanted a "good, hot title," which the film lacked even
within a month of its opening. Wallis considered *I Spy* but finally
chose *Espionage Agent*, although as late as 24 August *Neutrality
Zone* was being considered because neutrality was constantly in the
news. On 8 September 1939, President Roosevelt proclaimed a state
of "limited national emergency," while at the same time stressing
neutrality as the United States' official position; equally ambivalent
was the stand taken in *Espionage Agent*.

At least *Confessions of a Nazi Spy* does not equivocate; *Espionage
Agent* does, maintaining that "we don't want to take sides" but lamenting that "we are where we were twenty years ago [1918] and up
against the same kind of spying." Consuls in the film are taught how
to use code machines because America is "infested . . . with spies
and enemy agents"; then they are told that Americans just "want to
be left alone." All this agonizing occurs in the context of a "lady
with a past" movie: an American woman, unsuccessfully pursuing

a stage career in Europe, decides that working for the Nazis is preferable to starving. However, she does not reckon on her employers' expecting her to continue working for them after she returns to America and marries a consular official.

Because it took eighteen months to develop from original screen story to completed film, *Espionage Agent* reflects the uncertainty that kept increasing in America. The film, which advocates counterespionage as well as neutrality (with a mobilization plan, just in case), mirrors an America that had witnessed the passage of three neutrality acts in three successive years—1935, 1936, and 1937—during which President Roosevelt kept calling for increased defense spending and rearmament. *Espionage Agent* was like America: living in peace but thinking of war.

Espionage Agent was not a success; its opening, September 1939, was ill-timed. Had it been filmed in 1938, as planned, it might have succeeded. Then *Confessions of a Nazi Spy* would have been its successor, rather than the other way around; together they would have made an interesting set of variations, fictional and factual, on the theme of espionage in prewar America.

It seems unlikely that *Confessions of a Nazi Spy* influenced Republic's decision to make *In Old Monterey* and *South of the Border* in 1939. Republic, which had made *Pals of the Saddle* in 1938 without being influenced by anything except the headlines, probably thought it was time for Gene Autry to get involved in national defense and so cast him as an undercover agent in *South of the Border*. However, *Confessions* definitely influenced another 1939 "first"— the first American fiction film to portray life in Nazi Germany, produced a year before the major studios mustered up the courage to go inside the Third Reich.

The film was *Hitler, Beast of Berlin* (although few saw it under that title); the studio was another one on Poverty Row, specializing in even lower budget movies that Republic—PRC, or PDC as it was known in 1939. PRC's only concern was to make movies fast and cheaply. In 1938, Ben Judell had formed PPC (Progressive Pictures Corporation), turning out a series of exploitation films; in 1939, PPC became PDC (Producers Distributing Corporation) and a year later, PRC (Producers Releasing Corporation). While the initials changed, Judell didn't. Seeking to capitalize on the success of *Confessions* as well as on the war in Europe, he authorized an "A picture budget" for *Hitler, Beast of Berlin*, which went into production two weeks after the invasion of Poland.

The industry was unprepared for Judell's film, even though Hobe

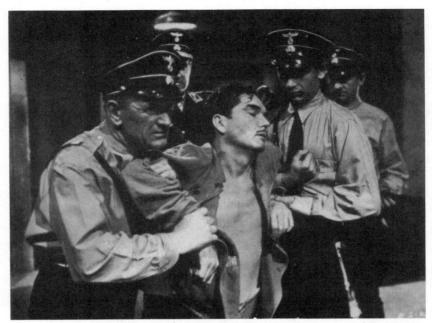

The torture of a resistant (Ronald Drew) in Beasts of Berlin *(1939), the first American film to portray life in Nazi Germany*

Morrison, the *Variety* reviewer, felt it had nothing new to say. Morrison may have been correct, but he was speaking as a critic who had already seen the powerful Russian film, *Professor Mamlock* (1938), which graphically portrayed Nazi anti-Semitism right down to the "Jude" scrawled across Mamlock's surgical robe. But *Professor Mamlock* would only have been seen in cities with theaters that played foreign films; and even in such cities, foreign films were still rarefied fare. To the average moviegoer, Judell's film said much that was new; and it might have said more if it had not encountered censorship problems.[18]

The film that had been scheduled for release on 15 October 1939 was not the film that was shown in New York a month later; on 18 November, a cut version opened at the Globe Theater on Times Square with a new title—*Beasts of Berlin*. In the intervening month, New York and New Jersey had banned the film, probably fearing a Bundist backlash. Furthermore, the Motion Picture Producers and Distributors Association (MPPDA) denied it the Production seal, presumably because it violated Article 10 of the Code, which required fair representation of "prominent people and citizenry of all nations" (although that changed when the prominent people became the enemy).

Realizing that few exhibitors would show a movie that ran afoul of the MPPDA, Judell was forced to make cuts, change the title, and then change the revised title, so that by 1940 it was known as *Goose Step*, the title of Shepard Traube's original story on which the movie is based. And in 1943, the title was changed again to *Hell's Devils* when it was rereleased to capitalize on the fame of one of the actors, Alan Ladd, who had gone on to become a major star.

Beasts of Berlin is a far more intelligent film than its title(s) indicate. The reason is the creator—the Broadway producer-director, Shepard Traube, whose most successful production was *Angel Street* (1941). Traube, who both wrote and directed *Beasts of Berlin*, was not a typical Poverty Row filmmaker.[19] He was already established in the theater when he went to Hollywood in the mid thirties.

Except for the opening title, which tautologically denies that the film evidences "hatred, prejudice or bias to any class" (except, as it should add, toward the class known for its hatred, prejudice, and bias) and the contrived happy ending, *Beasts of Berlin* is the first American film to make the necessary connection between the failure of Versailles and the rise of National Socialism and to portray the natural antagonism between National Socialism and Communism. Although the plot would soon become a commonplace, in 1939 the activities of the anti-Nazi underground were still new.

Despite its A picture budget, the film has a sleaziness that neither money nor its lack is responsible for: it is a perfect illustration of the production's fitting the theme. *Beasts of Berlin* reduces Nazism to pulp. Since there was no time in the shooting schedule for art, faces were often filmed against a background of darkness which eliminated the need for a set, evoking something more fearsome than any set could: a world of disembodied, ghoulishly lit faces peering out of the void.

Although *Beasts of Berlin* imitates some of the effects used in *Confessions of a Nazi Spy* (headlines, newsreel footage, propaganda raining from the sky), it is able to take a much stronger stand against Nazism because the action is set not in America but in Germany. While *Confessions* only mentions Hitler and alludes to the camps, *Beasts* shows Hitler (in a newsreel shot) as well as the inside of a barracks where the prisoners sleep in bunk beds and wash in a common trough.

In *Beasts of Berlin*, it is also possible to ascertain the religion and politics of the underground members—something even later films fail to do. The underground is a mixture of Jews and Catholics, Social Democrats and Communists. When the hero is asked how long he has been a Communist, he replies that he is a Democrat (i.e., Social Democrat), although it is apparent from the "comrade" greeting used by some of the members that there are Communists in the movement. Yet it makes sense that, as a Social Democrat, the hero works with Communists and is sent to a concentration camp, since the camps were initially intended for political prisoners, chiefly Communists and Social Democrats. "The concentration camps are full of people like us," the hero remarks to another inmate.

The inmates of the concentration camp also include Catholics and Jews, the latter called non-Aryans as they would be until 1941. When asked whether he is an Aryan, the hero answers that he is a Catholic. A bearded scientist, clearly Jewish, is forced to say, "I am swine." The Nazis brutalize Catholics as well, even priests. In one scene they strip a priest of his cassock, although they cannot stop him from saying Mass for the inmates.

Beasts attributes the appeal of National Socialism to the Germans' desire for unity and their wish to see their country restored to its pride of place. However, the film also implies it was an obsession with unity that led to the persecution of those able to distinguish between unanimity of belief imposed from without and unity of spirit arising from within.

In spite of having been shot in less than a week, *Beasts of Berlin* manages to include character types, motifs, and situations that recur in films throughout the war: the committed resistance leader and the apathetic friend (the Alan Ladd character) won over by his example, the failure of Versailles, fascism versus Communism, "non-Aryan" for "Jew," an underground that prints anti-Nazi literature, the torture of political prisoners, and the bull whip as the indispensable Nazi prop.

And a little child shall lead them. PRC did.

4. Hollywood as Neutral Interventionist

When Harry Warner returned from abroad on 4 September 1939, the day after Britain had declared war on Germany, he proclaimed grandly, "That which we fought the British to obtain we will have to fight with them to retain"; shortly thereafter, his brother Jack, speaking on behalf of the studio, announced, "America is neutral, and we are Americans. Our policy is one hundred percent neutrality. There will be no propaganda pictures from Warner Brothers."[1] On 9 September 1939, Herbert J. Yates was quoted in the *New York World Telegram* as saying that Republic would "veer away from pictures of war."

Although duplicity in studio heads is not unknown, this was not the usual case of forked-tongued rhetoric. The brothers Warner were sincere—Harry in supporting Britain, Jack in committing the studio to neutrality. But it was a special neutrality, a Rooseveltian neutrality—a defensive neutrality. In his own way, Jack Warner meant what he said about propaganda films; he might have said, in fact, that Warner Bros. never made propaganda films in the usual sense. If propaganda is manipulation by word or image, then Warners did not so much manipulate audiences as confirm what audiences already believed but could not articulate, thus effecting a coinciding—rather than an imposing—of visions. By dramatizing the mass convictions of a people, Warners enabled moviegoers to project their feelings onto the same screen on which the studio projected its own.

Veering away from war is not the same as avoiding the subject altogether. In 1940, Republic veered away from the war and into *Three Faces West* (originally called *The Refugee*: its new title was chosen to sound less bleak). The movie is about an Austrian refugee doctor who finds his calling in the American dustbowl where his fastidious daughter learns to rough it with some help from John Wayne, who proves considerably more appealing than her Nazi fiancé. Yet even Republic could not resist the plight of beleaguered Britain, veering back again for a look at women in war in a film appropriately entitled *Women in War* (1940).

When Jack Warner announced "no propaganda pictures," he was saying, in effect, that he would not jeopardize American neutrality; but since American neutrality was already in jeopardy, what he really meant was "no pro-war pictures" (but not "no anti-Nazi films" or "no pro-Allied films"). As the "Roosevelt studio," Warners was willing to defer to the president, who, in the late summer of 1939, genuinely wanted to keep America out of war. Thus Warners put off making *Underground*, which it had purchased in April 1939 as an original screenplay, although by 8 September producer-screenwriter Robert Lord had reshaped the script to include the recently declared war.

When *Underground* finally came out two years later, it seemed derivative and anticlimactic after MGM's *The Mortal Storm* (1940) and Fox's *Four Sons* (1940), both of which dramatized the destructive influence of Nazism on family life. In the summer of 1941, there was nothing unusual about the story of two brothers (one a Nazi, the other a resistant) and their professor-father. Yet *Underground* poses some interesting moral questions that the others do not. *Underground* features the brother who renounces Nazism, as does *The Mortal Storm*, but here Kurt, the converted brother, must still pretend he is a Nazi. When his resistant brother Eric is captured, Kurt, knowing Eric will be killed anyway, betrays him to the Nazis, thus putting himself above suspicion. At least Eric can go to his death confident that Kurt will continue his work in the resistance.

Although delaying *Underground* represented a temporary concession to Roosevelt, the industry as a whole did not back off from making films with an anti-Nazi background in 1939–40. And if Hollywood made only a limited number of such films, the reason—at least in 1939—had little to do with fear of losing the German market. That might have been a factor earlier (e.g., in 1936), but even then it was never the deciding one. The German market had no influence whatever on Warners' decision to make *Confessions of a Nazi Spy* or subsequent anti-Nazi movies. Warners had closed down its German branch in 1936 after Nazi thugs had killed one of its Jewish employees.[2]

By 1936, it was also evident that the German market was shrinking. The 1936 *Film Daily Year Book* (p. 1177) reported that Germany's official policy was to import American "super films" but "to exclude average American films from competition with the German product." That same year, the German Ministry of Propaganda issued the *Decree concerning the Exhibition of Foreign Films* (12 July 1936), which set the number of import permits at 105 and denied permits to companies making films injurious to German prestige or at variance with the Aryanism of the Third Reich.

In 1936, some studios, especially MGM and Paramount, would have been influenced by the *Decree*. Paramount maintained facilities in Germany until 7 September 1941 when they were closed by government order; MGM closed its German offices on 14 August 1940.[3] But even Paramount would have been more influenced by American popular opinion than Nazi policy. During the next two years, with Germany banning even Shirley Temple films as a baneful influence on the young, the studios must have realized they would be doing little business with Germany. The number of American films shown in Germany shrank from sixty-four in 1933 to thirty-six in 1938.[4] The 1939 *Film Daily Year Book* said of Germany, "Because of exchange regulations and other factors, few American films are shown here" (p. 1107); the reason was that, as of 1938, "the German market, as far as the U.S. product was concerned, ceased comparatively to exist" (p. 65). It could hardly come as a surprise that, on 17 August 1940, the Third Reich announced a ban on American films, although for economic reasons they continued to be shown until at least early 1941.[5]

What concerned the studios most, however, was not the German market, or even the war in Europe. (The European war might have prompted studios to abandon some of their more controversial projects, change titles, or defer filming; but the number of films affected was negligible because the number planned was never large to begin with.) Hollywood's main problem was discerning the country's mood. America's rhythm was off, and the industry was having difficulty monitoring the fluctuations. Thus production either lagged or, in the case of *Beasts of Berlin*, moved at the rate of silent frames projected at sound speed.

Hollywood attempted to adapt to the nation's arrhythmia. Peace was no longer the interval between wars; it was the interval between the fall of countries. Sighs of gratitude during the infrequent lulls became just sighs when the lulls were over. It was hard for anyone, much less Hollywood, to tabulate the number of times the scale had tipped; nor did it matter where the imbalance lay. The trays had bounced up and down so many times that the scale was worthless.

Time marched erratically, and what was affirmed one day was, if not denied the next, then considerably modified. On 21 January 1938, the House passed a $553 million naval bill; within a week,

President Roosevelt had requested another $800 million for defensive purposes. America was on the defensive, but not at war. Three days after war erupted in Europe, Roosevelt, in a special broadcast, reaffirmed America's neutrality. Three days later, on 6 September 1939, he announced that the United States Navy would patrol the Atlantic and the Caribbean; as a result, 116 destroyers were reconditioned.

With the passage of the 1939 neutrality act, a neutral America lifted the embargo so arms could be shipped to England and France. The time was then right for Warner Bros. to amend its own declaration of neutrality. Since the studio had no anti-Nazi film to release in 1940, it rereleased *Confessions of a Nazi Spy* with additional footage showing the latest Nazi conquests as well as the invasion of little Finland by "communist Russia," thus equating Stalin and Hitler (but only for a time) and making Nazi espionage in America the prelude to Nazi aggression in Europe. "No propaganda films," but instead Naziphobia balanced by Anglophilia. In the late summer of 1941, Warners' *International Squadron*, a tribute to the RAF, was in the theaters along with *Underground*. Although set in World War I, *Sergeant York* (1941), released about the same time, reduces the dilemma of isolationism versus intervention to pacifism versus arms bearing. As Alvin York learned, sometimes it is necessary to take lives in order to save them. So much for Warners' 100 percent neutrality. Like Rooseveltian neutrality, it was 40 percent promise, 60 percent preparation.

Warners' policy can be summarized by the title of an address Harry Warner delivered to his six thousand employees on 5 June 1940: "United We Stand, Divided We Fall." While the speech itself was rambling and the thoughts were often lost amid anecdotes, Warner cleverly took a number of seemingly unrelated topics—the employment situation at the studio, Nazism and Communism (scarcely distinguishable), religious and racial prejudice, the folly of appeasement—and united them into a vision of what he believed a studio should be: a family of individuals from different races and religions—but not politics—sharing the same moral convictions. When he denounced Nazis and Communists as equally totalitarian and swore he would hire neither, he inadvertently set the stage for the blacklist that began seven years later. At the same time Warner criticized the free world for doing nothing about the persecution of the Jews and chided his European colleagues for thinking that, even up to 1 September 1939, they could still do business with Hitler.

Although Warner did not exactly encourage intervention, it would be hard to imagine his protesting America's entry into the war; he probably would have echoed Roosevelt after Pearl Harbor: "We are all in the same boat." Warner did, however, advocate supporting the Allies both because he felt they deserved support and because he wanted to prevent a repetition of their fate. America, he argued, must learn from Europe's mistakes and put up a united front against fascism, which was precisely what the European democracies had failed to do.

Warner also used the occasion to paint a picture of healthy employment at the studio, no doubt in answer to a charge in the October 1939 issue of *TAC: A Magazine of Theatre, Film, Radio, Dance* that Warners, along with MGM and Fox, had cut personnel and instituted layoffs in compliance with a "fake neutrality" that called for major revisions in production. *TAC* also accused the studio of circumventing neutrality by making the pro-British *Espionage Agent* and planning jingoistic fare like *The Fighting 69th* (1940) that would appeal to England and France, from which Hollywood was still deriving profits.

It was a foolish accusation. If the United States had declared war on Germany in 1939, the flood of war films that inundated the country after Pearl Harbor would have begun two years sooner. In the fall of 1939, the number of films with a war background would not have come close to filling any studio's coffers. Furthermore, when such films were being planned, the question was not whether to treat the subject of Nazism but how to treat it: within the context of a recently declared war or in a pre-1939 setting. The latter was the safer course, particularly for a conservative studio like MGM.

MGM was interested in making a movie of Phyllis Bottome's 1938 anti-Nazi novel, *The Mortal Storm*, as early as March of that year, when the book was synopsized for Louis B. Mayer.[6] But the studio moved slowly, recalling what had happened two years earlier: it had announced its intention to film Sinclair Lewis's *It Can't Happen Here*, only to renege when the MPPDA advised against it on the grounds that such a film would antagonize the fascist governments of Italy and Germany. *Three Comrades*, with its discreetly anti-Nazi overtones, was about as adventuresome as MGM was willing to get; and even those overtones might not have been heard if Joseph L. Mankiewicz, the film's producer, had not made them audible.[7] They were clear enough to the German consul, who, after seeing the film in Los Angeles, requested MGM to identify the anomalous but inferably Nazi thugs as Communists. When Mankiewicz threatened to resign from MGM if the change were made, the thugs remained unnamed Nazis.[8] But the studio took no chances with *Idiot's Delight* (1939), retaining some of the pacifism but none of the antifascism of Robert E. Sherwood's play, and even lightening the apocalyptic ending.

There were others at MGM like Mankiewicz who were not intimidated by Nazi ire and who believed, like William Dozier, that a film version of *The Mortal Storm* "fits in with today's headlines of Nazi persecutions."[9] To elicit support for the project, Kenneth MacKenna touted the novel as "the story . . . of the effects upon a family group of the German policy of intolerance and persecution" and attributed the book's appeal to the "popular consciousness of world problems."[10] Making a film that would reflect popular consciousness and indict intolerance and persecution meant making an accusatory film with wide appeal—not the easiest goal to achieve, especially for a studio that shied away from controversy. Yet by February 1939, Mayer was persuaded that it could be done; what probably convinced him was the plot's revolving around a family, one of his favorite subjects.

It was the plot, however, that was the major hurdle. After about a week of shooting, Victor Saville took over the direction from Frank Borzage, who, in addition to having personal problems, had found it difficult to relate to the subject matter. As a Jew, Saville felt he could identify with the characters better than Borzage. Saville was also *The Mortal Storm*'s producer, yet he chose not to be credited for either role. In the spring of 1940, when the film was completed, he decided to have his name removed from the credits; as a Briton, he feared isolationists would use his connection with *The Mortal Storm* as proof of a Hollywood-based conspiracy of Europeans trying, through their films, to involve America in the war. Saville was proved right the following year when that accusation was made.

In addition to posing problems for Borzage, the plot of *The Mortal Storm* created difficulties for the screenwriters. The family in the novel is half Jewish and half Christian. Rudi and Freya Roth, the children from Professor Roth's first marriage, are Jewish; Roth's stepsons through remarriage are Christian. The novel portrays the polarizing effect of National Socialism on the Roths: the stepsons embrace Nazism, Professor Roth is interned in a concentration camp, and Freya's Communist lover is murdered. Interestingly, the movie version ends more tragically than the novel (usually, it is the other way around). But the movie version also evidences the kind of trade-offs that occur during production.

The shooting script that Phyllis Bottome saw in February 1940 is far more outspoken than what reached the screen. Although she praised the script, she questioned the frequent use of "non-Aryan," noting that "'Jew' was always used by proud and self-respect-

Mrs. Roth (Irene Rich) visiting her husband (Frank Morgan), who wears his race on his sleeve in The Mortal Storm *(1940). Courtesy MGM/UA*

ing Jews of themselves."[11] The script also contains a scene in which Rudi, not realizing he is Jewish, begs his father to say he isn't. That scene does not exist in the film because, in the transition from script to screen, Rudi is made less of a character and therefore less of a Jew. Even Freya's Jewishness is downplayed. While "Jew" occasionally appears in the script Bottome read, it is not used once in the film; instead, "non-Aryan" is substituted throughout.

Like any popular art form, film must make concessions. It is understandable that Bottome was annoyed by "non-Aryan," although that designation persisted in films throughout 1940 and did not disappear until 1941. The reason for "non-Aryan" in the 1939–40 films is obvious: while most audiences could accept an anti-Nazi film, not everybody could accept one that was also about Nazi anti-Semitism. The closest *The Mortal Storm* gets to issues of race is the "J" on Professor Roth's sleeve in the concentration camp scene. "Non-Aryan" is safe; not everybody would understand its meaning, and those who did, if they were anti-Semitic, would not react to it as they might to "Jew." While there are known anti-Semites, there are few known anti-Aryans.

As compensation, though not enough to restore what has been lost, there are scenes in *The Mortal Storm* that are not in the original novel: a book burning, a classroom rebellion against Professor Roth, and Freya's death. On the other hand, Freya's lover ceases to be a Communist and instead is turned into a pacifist. This is courage tempered by caution.

Naturally, *The Mortal Storm* would have been a stronger film if it had adhered to the novel. Freya's leaving Germany, as she does at the end of the novel, would be preferable to her being shot while she and her lover are attempting to ski to safety. It was not enough for Freya to die; her death required a palliative, which Saville thought he had found in Minnie Louise Haskins's "Gate of the Year," recited at the fadeout by an offscreen voice: "Go out into the darkness, and put your hand in the hand of God. That shall be to you better than a light, and safer than a known way." It is like a recessional—a walk with God through the mortal storm. If there were no atheists in foxholes, there were precious few in Hollywood for the duration. Rarely had so much prayer been heard outside of a cloister.

The Mortal Storm continued a tradition that started with some of the classic World War I films (e.g., *Four Sons, All Quiet on the Western Front, Grand Illusion*): the tradition of the "good German," or in the case of brothers, the good brother. At the end of *The Mortal Storm*, one of the stepsons renounces Nazism, the falling snow covering his footprints in an exquisite example of natural symbolism.

Escape (1940) followed *The Mortal Storm*; shooting commenced on 16 July 1940, just three months after *The Mortal Storm* was completed. It too is based on a novel—by the pseudonymous Ethel Vance, whose real name supposedly could not be disclosed for fear of Nazi reprisals, although that may have been a publicity gimmick. *Escape* is the reverse of *The Mortal Storm*: it is the old MGM artifice as distinct from Saville's moderately realistic look. There is also nothing controversial about *Escape*; it would appeal to anyone because it is about love, all kinds of love: mother–son, man–woman, aristocrat–commoner, Nazi general–Bavarian countess; even the ultimate, sacrificial love in which a child, probably Jewish, gives her passport to a needy American.

The plot concerns an eminent German actress (Nazimova), imprisoned in a concentration camp and about to be executed because, while in the United States, she harbored "renegade citizens of this country." The country is never named, but it is obviously Germany;

the camp is never identified, but it is clearly Dachau; the city within driving distance of the camp is never called by its true name, but it is Munich.

If it seems hard to believe that the same studio that produced *The Mortal Storm* also made *Escape*, it should be remembered that no studio could commit itself to one kind of film, even to one kind of anti-Nazi film. It is not that, with *Escape*, MGM was reverting to a fairy tale version of Nazism; it is simply that MGM was making a different kind of anti-Nazi film, as it would continue to do during the war years by introducing the theme into various types of movies, including musicals (*Rio Rita, Cairo*).

Since *Escape* is set in the Bavarian Alps, it conjures up the world of operetta. Thus the concentration camp resembles a Victorian hospital ward, with cots instead of bunks. *Escape* is also set in operetta time—in the bygone year of 1936, so current events do not make sport of the script. A dictator is in power, but except for a single "Heil, Hitler," his name is never uttered. His admirers call him "savior," Hitler's honorific among German schoolchildren. Although "Ein Volk, Ein Reich, Ein Führer" is emblazoned on an office wall, there are no storm troopers, only political police who scrutinize passports and behave robotically.

The country may be unnamed, but it is the country of the fittest. "Are we the fittest?" the countess (Norma Shearer) wonders. "Don't you read the newspaper?" is the Nazi general's (Conrad Veidt) rejoinder. In this unnamed country, everybody plays Wagner—the symphony orchestra, and even the Nazi general, who no sooner sits down at the piano than he breaks into the "Liebestod" from *Tristan und Isolde*. Nevertheless, the unnamed country is not beyond censure. "This place isn't a country; it's a Coney Island madhouse," Robert Taylor exclaims, exasperated by the futile attempts to locate his mother. Once, and only once, the anti-Nazism is gestural: "I've had it up to here," Taylor shouts, raising his arm in a contemptuous "Heil."

Among the characters in *Escape* is the "good German," a doctor who helps Taylor rescue his mother because he was once one of her fans. The doctor must have seen her in *Romeo and Juliet* because the scheme he concocts is straight out of Shakespeare's play: a sleeping potion that produces the semblance of death so the son can come to the camp and claim his mother's body.

To enable mother and son to leave Germany, the countess persuades one of her wards to relinquish her passport. Once the girl discovers it is for an American, she gladly consents. The girl's name is Maria; although her name is more evocative of the New Testament than the Old, her looks are strikingly Semitic. At least in *The Mortal Storm* there is a "J" to go by; *Escape* is more circumspect.

Although the escape is the climax, it is not the resolution. What begins as an anti-Nazi film concludes, not as a pro-Nazi one, but certainly as one that is not unsympathetic to the doomed love of the Nazi general for the storybook countess. As the general, Conrad Veidt may not qualify for the "good German" role, but he is far from being the "evil Nazi." He is too genteel. If Norma Shearer is meant for anyone, it is for him—not for Robert Taylor, whose love for his mother leaves no room for her. Shearer is so soignée, Veidt so cultured, and their manners so faultless that they make a natural couple. At least he can love her on her own terms—with an erotic decorum that transforms passion into posture. But that love cannot be. When he learns of her complicity in the escape, he expires—a well-groomed man collapsing in the arms of an elegantly gowned woman.

If Fox seemed bolder than MGM, it was because Darryl F. Zanuck, vice president in charge of production, became an interventionist in 1939.[12] But even a progressive studio like Fox could not bombard the public with anti-Nazi films, one more sensational than the other. Like any studio, Fox had to insure a film against irrelevance as well as insure an audience for the film. Again, this meant using Nazism in various contexts, with the genre determining the way the subject would be handled. Ultimately, anti-Nazism would be incorporated into every type of film, but that would not happen for two more years. Still, even in late 1939, Nazism was no longer the exclusive property of the "serious" film, whose audience might be more discriminating but also more susceptible to boredom and sensitive to repetition. Thus Nazis were portrayed differently in different films. In a series film like *Charlie Chan in Panama* (1940), the Nazis could be spies, agents, or saboteurs, while in a romantic melodrama like *The Man I Married* (1940) they are drawing room villains.

Like other heroes, Charlie Chan eventually had to face the enemy, and did (about the same time as the Lone Wolf but earlier than Ellery Queen). He had already encountered spies in Paris in *Charlie Chan in City of Darkness* (1939), set at the time of the Munich agreement, but those were spies without a country. By 1940, the series had become a little more adventuresome. While *Charlie Chan in Panama* does not use "Nazi," it leaves no doubt that Ryner, the master spy, is German.

It was the setting of *Charlie Chan in Panama* that gave the film true relevance. Although it was released in February 1940, John Larkin and Lester Ziffren had a treatment ready by August 1939, pitting Charlie Chan against spies in the Panama Canal Zone. The authors were obviously influenced by the Canal Zone's first espionage case in December 1938, when Hans Heinrich Schackow was charged, along with thirty other Germans, with photographing Canal Zone fortifications.

When the film opened, the critics appreciated its timeliness, summed up in the closing line, which Chan delivers as if it were a Confucian analect: "Intelligent defense of nation best guarantee for years of peace." The defense of the canal was a matter of grave concern, and the film, which involves a plan to blow up the Pacific Fleet, mirrored the anxiety that existed in Washington. When war broke out in Europe, there were several hundred Germans and Austrians in the Canal Zone. On 5 September 1939, President Roosevelt issued an executive order requiring ships entering the canal to submit to inspection and to the removal of personnel, if necessary.

In a revelation (one that will be repeated in *The House on 92nd St.*, 1945), Ryner turns out to be a woman, Kathi, from that well known but unnamed country. Yet the screenwriters cleverly identify the country by having Kathi masquerade as a Czech refugee, who, at one point, tells Chan she is afraid of returning to her homeland where she faces "death or the concentration camp." In a rejoinder that, even in 1940, must have sounded like the punch line of a sick joke, the inscrutable Chan replies, "Why? Map of Europe has lost your native country."

Kathi's native country was not lost at Fox, however. In the fall of 1939, about six weeks after the war began, Zanuck became interested in remaking *Four Sons*. At first he planned to retain the World War I setting but then decided the film would be more topical if set in the thirties. Thematically similar to *The Mortal Storm*, *Four Sons* concerns a family in the Sudetenland, which was part of Czechoslovakia but predominantly German. The family's dilemma mirrors that of the Sudetenland itself. One son regards the family as Czech; another, as German. Of the four, only one resists Nazism, thereby becoming the "good German."

Zanuck proceeded cautiously with the filming of *Four Sons*, preferring human drama to the drama of history and rejecting screenwriter John Howard Lawson's attempt to give the plot a chronological perspective. Lawson was too historical for Zanuck: "The personal story has been submerged to give prominence to the march of events," Zanuck complained. "It must be the other way around." He also felt that Lawson's continuing along this line would result in the "loss of 50% of the story's value as entertainment."[13] It is clear that Zanuck stood for entertainment, film's primary function as defined by the Production Code. Entertainment could encompass Nazism, but not necessarily its history. He ordered Lawson to shift the emphasis from the events to the characters and "milk the personal story for all its values." Consequently Hitler's name received only one mention, and the village lost its pristine simplicity as it was moved into the twentieth century. Zanuck wanted another *Grapes of Wrath*, and urged Lawson to strive for that film's "honesty and simplicity." There was no similarity between *Four Sons* and *The Grapes of Wrath*, and Lawson knew it; Lawson also knew that working within the studio system would occasionally require him to sacrifice truth for effect or suppress it altogether.

What Lawson wanted would never have worked in 1940. To present a balanced picture of the Sudetenland, he wanted to show that there were Czechs who welcomed the annexation to the point of greeting the Germans effusively as they marched in. While there was indeed such a display of enthusiasm, it was by no means universal (although in a film it could be construed as such); and to show it would only deflect sympathy away from the Czechs, whose tragedy was supposed to be milked for all it was worth. Hence, the annexation of the Sudetenland as shown in *Four Sons* is nothing more or less than Anschluss. When one of the sons hears of it, he cries, "They'll wipe us off the map. It'll be Austria all over again."

Four Sons received mixed reviews, although Lawson was commended for keeping anti-Nazi propaganda to a minimum, and Zanuck was credited with making the first film to show the beginnings of the war, which was more or less true. But it was Lawson who made it possible; even though he had had to dismantle his chronology, he had still kept the action in the 1936–39 period, so that the plot included a bit of everything: Anschluss, the annexation of the Sudetenland, and Poland, but not enough of any one to make the film the historical tragedy he envisioned.

Zanuck was more audacious with *The Man I Married*, released three months later. The subject lent itself to audacity. The film was supposed to be called *I Married A Nazi* and was announced as such, thus confusing some isolationist senators who were compiling a list of propaganda movies. The "I" is Carol (Joan Bennett), an American; the "man," Eric, her German-born husband whom she accompanies on a trip to the Fatherland in 1938. With the action set a year before the war, Carol evolves from a scatterbrain, who believes concentration camps "are not half as bad as they say they are," to a woman with enough convictions to leave the man she married.

There is some vicious parody in *The Man I Married*. At one point,

Hitler is called "Schicky," and the guffaws in the audience only confirmed what William L. Shirer had written in *The Rise and Fall of the Third Reich*: "I have heard Germans speculate whether Hitler could have become the master of Germany had he been known to the world as Schicklgruber. . . . Can one imagine the frenzied German masses acclaiming a Schicklgruber with their thunderous 'Heils?' 'Heil Schicklgruber'?"[14]

The Man I Married seems to have been the first American anti-Nazi film to use "Jew" rather than "non-Aryan," which was rapidly acquiring the status of a euphemism for private parts or basic functions. However, it was not quite so daring a feat as it seems because the word is spoken in German, not in English. When Eric learns his mother is Jewish, he mutters, "Jude, Jude, Jude" in a state of shock. Eric has no choice but to allow his son to return to America with Carol, who bids her husband farewell in one of the best examples of alliteration in film: "Heil, Heel!"

The taboo would only be broken when "Jew," not "Jude," was heard in an anti-Nazi context. This happened the following year in United Artists' *So Ends Our Night* (1941), a tragic tale of political exiles and refugees shuttling from country to country to avoid deportation. A German breaks off his engagement when he discovers his fiancée is a "Jewess," who will make him a "defiler of his race." Later, the fiancée (Margaret Sullavan) is called "a dirty, filthy Jew" by a police officer. While "Aryan" and "non-Aryan" are also used in the film, they appear in a painfully ironic context. A young German refugee (Glenn Ford in his first important role) is puzzled that there are refugees who are "100% Aryan" while he himself is "only 50%." It is the refugee who is 100 percent Aryan that sacrifices his life for those who are not.

As a distribution company for independent producers, United Artists had no signature of its own, only the signature that filmmakers who, for various reasons, chose not to—or could not—work within the Hollywood system, gave it. Formed in 1919 by Charlie Chaplin, Douglas Fairbanks, D.W. Griffith, and Mary Pickford, United Artists had released all of Chaplin's films since *A Woman of Paris* (1923); in 1940 it released his first "talkie," *The Great Dictator*, Chaplin's dual awakening to sound and fascism.

At the end of *No Time for Comedy* (1940), the wife of a playwright, who has failed in his attempt at serious drama, tells her husband to try satire and take as his target those who praise dictatorships. Chaplin, who never dealt with the abstract, attempted the concrete: a satire not of dictatorships but of a dictator—the ultimate dictator, the great dictator.

Chaplin began *The Great Dictator* in January 1939. Abandoning it temporarily, he returned to it at the end of the year, completing it in March 1940. The tragic course of events that caused him to make the film in the first place also caused him to halt, and then resume, production. Although Chaplin's intentions were admirable, the film is not subtle enough to be good satire; instead, it is a humanitarian pastiche of history and fiction. *The Great Dictator* recalls *Lysistrata*, in which Aristophanes took a contemporary situation—the Peloponnesian War—and built a fantastic plot around it. Like *Lysistrata*, *The Great Dictator* is also utopian, though the poet Aristophanes would never have written an ode to brotherhood in the homiletic style of Chaplin's climactic speech.

The premise of *The Great Dictator*, however, is undeniably clever: a barber, a World War I veteran, develops amnesia after Versailles and awakens twenty years later, in 1938, to discover "Jew" painted on the door of his shop—the taboo word written but rarely spoken. The implication is that in 1918 the world went into a deep slumber and awakened in time for Anschluss. Yet that point, which other films have also made, is never developed. Instead, Chaplin reached into the comic treasure chest and came up with an old bauble: mistaken identity. The barber, a Hitler look-alike, is mistaken for the Führer.

Since Chaplin has always made his films universally intelligible, he simplifies the story by resorting to a perennial, but not very subtle, source of humor: the transparent or telltale name: Tomania (Germany), Austerlich (Austria), Bacteria (Italy), Adenoid Hynkel (Adolf Hitler), Benzino Napoloni (Benito Mussolini), Double Cross (Swastika)—the last being the best. Intermingled with all this transparency are realistic scenes of Jews being mistreated and harassed. But the realism is short lived, and the film ends as wish fulfillment: Hannah, the Jewish girl who befriends the barber, returns to Austerlich while the barber, again mistaken for Hynkel, delivers a radio address, claiming he has no designs for conquest and pleading for a "world of reason." His last words are spoken to Hannah: "Look up, Hannah! The soul of man has been given wings and at last he is beginning to fly. He is flying into the rainbow—into the light of hope. Look up, Hannah! Look up!"[15]

But Hannah is in Austria, hardly the other side of the rainbow for a Jew in 1938. And the speech, sincere but overlong, demands suspension of disbelief that Chaplin knew could not be given willingly. It is not the barber speaking to Hannah; it is Chaplin speaking to the world. The barber's fate has been relegated to the background; what becomes of him is no more important than what becomes of

Chaplin in the title role of The Great Dictator *(1940). Note the "double cross" armbands.*

Hannah. They no longer matter; only the message matters, or rather, the heart of the message. The details are irrelevant.

In *Lysistrata* (which was produced seven years before the Peloponnesian War ended with Sparta's defeat of Athens) the Spartans and the Athenians are reconciled at the end; it is an ironic resolution as saddening as it is ahistorical. But in *The Great Dictator*, released two years after Anschluss, a promise that Austerlich will not be invaded is not even ironic; it is sweetly sad.

In reviewing *Foreign Correspondent* (1940), which United Artists released about six weeks before *The Great Dictator*, the critics did not have to separate the filmmaker from the film, praising the one while expressing reservations about the other. *Foreign Correspondent* was praiseworthy on all counts: as a Walter Wanger production, an Alfred Hitchcock film, and a contemporary espionage thriller. Wanger had his own production unit at United Artists from 1936 to 1941. Often indifferent to budget and easily seduced by the topical, Wanger was enough of a liberal to do for Europe what he had tried to do for Spain; this time he was less constrained by public opinion.

Wanger wanted to make a movie supporting the British war effort. Hitchcock, who had come to America to direct *Rebecca* (1940) for David O. Selznick, felt uneasy about being in a country that was at peace while his own was at war. Their shared concern resulted in *Foreign Correspondent*, a transformation of Vincent Sheehan's *Personal History* into a thriller, featuring a protagonist who would soon become as familiar as the battling district attorney or the scoop hunter—the apathetic lad who wakes up to fascism.

The film's anti-isolationism is clear from its dedication "to those who saw the clouds of war while we were seeing the rainbows." However, it takes more than corrective lenses to acclimate the eye to shades of grey after its exposure to the spectrum. Thus *Foreign Correspondent* moves gradually, as does the hero, from indifference to commitment. The action begins on 13 August 1939, and as 3 September approaches, the correspondent's education nears its final stage, reaching completion as a headline fills the screen: ENGLAND DECLARES WAR ON GERMANY.

Although *Foreign Correspondent* bears the mark of the liberal Wanger, it also carries the signature of Alfred Hitchcock. It is a Hitchcockian "people are not what they seem" movie, in which an avuncular gentleman is a murderous agent, and the heroine's father, Stephen Fisher, is a tweedy villain (rather like the Scotsman in *The Thirty-nine Steps*, 1935). But the film also invites comparison between Fisher and Sir Oswald Mosley, head of the British Union of Fascists. In one of those scenes that World War II history buffs relish, Fisher muses on the German genius, looking transfixed as he calls his favorite people "cunning, unscrupulous," and then adds, dreamily, "inspired."

At the end, the correspondent, with the everyman's name of Jones, broadcasts to a still neutral America, telling it to keep the lights burning (and, by inference, to keep the ammunition coming): "Keep those lights burning, cover them with steel, build them in with guns, build a canopy of battleships and bombing planes around them and, hello, America, hang on to your lights; they're the only lights in the world."[16]

Foreign Correspondent is not the strongest of the anti-isolationist films; that distinction belongs to Paramount's *Arise, My Love*. It may seem less odd that Paramount made *Arise, My Love* the same year it made the first "Road" movie, *Road to Singapore* (1940), if one remembers that in the years before Pearl Harbor, each studio did something atypical (world events encouraged it) but not entirely out of character. Headlines-conscious Republic anticipated the Battle of

Britain in *Women in War* (1940); Universal, which had made the definitive World War I movie, *All Quiet on the Western Front*, made the first film about the French resistance, *Paris Calling* (1941); Columbia, whose penchant for sea movies goes back to *Submarine* (1928), released the British-made *U-Boat 29* (1939) and then produced two sea melodramas of its own: *Escape from Glory* (1940) and *The Phantom Submarine* (1940).

On the other hand, none of these films is exactly representative. A more typical 1940 Republic film is *The Carson City Kid*; a more representative 1941 Universal movie is *The Wolf Man* (although *Paris Calling* did have the kind of international cast that Universal assembled for its horror films); more illustrative of the Columbia product is the series "B" movie (e.g., *Blondie, The Lone Wolf*).

Similarly, *Arise, My Love* is both typical and atypical of Paramount. It is typical in the sense that it illustrates the studio's specialty: romantic comedy with a sophisticated air. What is not typically Paramount is the interventionist theme. Since Paramount still had distribution facilities in Germany when *Arise, My Love* was being filmed (24 June–15 August 1940), the studio decided to shoot scenes with anti-Nazi dialogue in two versions: one for the foreign market, one for the domestic.[17] The decision, however, was unnecessary: two days after *Arise, My Love* was completed, the Nazi government imposed its ban on American films.

A romantic comedy with an interventionist plea can work if the plea, implicit in the title, is part of the plot. Billy Wilder, who wrote the script with his collaborator Charles Brackett, knew from his days in Vienna and Berlin that opera is the other side of operetta. Thus he planned the script as an operetta that darkens into opera, beginning with a character straight out of operetta—the masquerading lady—and then letting the action waltz its way into opera. After the lady (a reporter who saves an American pilot from execution by posing as his wife) doffs her disguise, the film becomes a romantic odyssey, slightly screwball but always affecting, that takes the couple, Gusto and Tom, from Spain to Paris, sets them afloat in the mid Atlantic when the *Athenia* is torpedoed, and reunites them in the forest of Compiègne in June 1940, just as France capitulates to Germany.

The original shooting script of *Arise, My Love* was stronger than the actual film, but only slightly. En route to Berlin, Gusto does her "homework" by reading *Mein Kampf*. Originally, she was to say, "The whole thing's a little confusing. Take the Russo-German pact. Hitler and Stalin tucked in bed together." Then she was to quote

Hitler on the Russians: "the scum of humanity." The dialogue was deleted; instead, Gusto throws *Mein Kampf* out of the train window—an action that says more than any dialogue can.

There were other reasons for not bringing in the Russo-German Nonaggression Pact that had to do with plausibility, not politics. First, the script implied that Gusto had read about the pact in *Mein Kampf*, which is impossible. Also, the pact was signed a week before the invasion of Poland, which was just about to occur as Gusto and Tom were setting out for Warsaw (which, of course, they do not reach). The scene on the train must therefore be devoid of anything suggesting war before war is declared.

Yet it is amazing what was retained. Although *Arise, My Love* does not include a single "non-Aryan," it does contain a reference to a correspondent who requests gefilte fish at a Nazi reception. Tom's reaction to Hitler's mustache ("I don't know what it is about that guy that gets me. Maybe it's his mustache . . .") was deleted, but his conception of the Führer was not. When he tells the general of the prison at Burgos to say good-bye to Adolf, the general is confused. "Adolf's a rat," Tom explains and then describes how he taught the rat to "heil" with its paw.

In a more covert way, Wilder criticized isolationists and appeasement. Surprisingly, Breen overlooked Tom's remark that he wasted his abilities on "palooka preliminaries" in Spain "just before Hitler and Chamberlain warm up for the main event," which implied that not only the Spanish civil war but also the Munich pact heralded the Second World War.

Wilder was also not above criticizing Europe. "We in Europe—we are sick," a French maid laments. "We think we've cured one war; then it starts all over again, and worse." But Paris, Wilder's beloved Paris, is beyond criticism. When an editor looks down from his window at the Nazis marching down the Champs-Elysées, he quietly bids farewell to the three sisters: liberty, fraternity, equality. At Compiègne, where Gusto is covering the armistice, a Nazi officer requests that because of the gravity of the occasion she dispense with lipstick. Her reply, "My lips will be as white as chalk," would, under other circumstances, have been a fine pricking of pomposity. Wilder respected the gravity of the occasion in his own way, by undermining his wit so that even a smile is unthinkable.

Arise, My Love builds cumulatively to the fall of France, starting with some anti-Hitler jokes, proceeding through screwball romance to a shared political conscience, and ending with an interventionist prayer. The ending of the film is even more anti-isolationist than that of the shooting script, in which Gusto buoys up Tom's spirits by telling him that he will at least be able to train fliers even if he cannot fly himself. She says much the same in the film but she also reminds him that the prayer he used to say at takeoff, "Arise, my love," can no longer be private: "Tom, remember your prayer. This time we have to say it to America: 'Arise, my love. Arise, be strong, so you can stand up straight and say to anyone under God's heaven: "All right, whose way of life shall it be—yours or ours?"'"

America is the beloved that must rise, and not merely into the wild blue yonder like Tom's plane. What *The Great Dictator, Foreign Correspondent,* and *Arise, My Love* have in common is imagery and dialogue about lethargy and political naiveté (the amnesiac barber, the blasé correspondent, the news-hungry reporter, the pilot of fortune who calls himself a "confused liberal")—each film becoming progressively more vocal in its insistence on a wake-up call for America.

In September 1941, at a Senate subcommittee hearing to determine whether Hollywood was propagandizing for the war in Europe, D. Worth Clark of Idaho asked Nicholas Schenck, president of Loew's, Inc., "We are at peace, are we not?" Schenck hesitated before answering. "Not exactly," he finally said. "We are at peace in some way."[18]

That way consisted of preparing for our own war and following Britain's through national defense and pro-British films.

When MGM's homage to the navy Hellcats, *Flight Command,* appeared at the end of 1940, the critics sensed it was more than just another military preparedness film. The *Los Angeles Times* (17 December 1940) even said it was probably "the first feature of its type" and, as such, "has exceptional news value in the light of events today." With the fall of France and Belgium, and the Blitz in its third month, any film calling the United States Navy "America's Maginot Line" hardly revealed a nation at peace. Implied was the belief that America's Maginot Line would prove more effective than France's if it were tested. In the meantime, the United States would speak peace but think war, which is exactly what happens in *Flight Command.* After two weeks of war games in the Pacific—two weeks of planes running out of gas, crash landings, flares, and urgent communiques—one Hellcat remarks, "We must be at war and don't know it."

MGM knew it, and so did Paramount. Paramount's *I Wanted Wings* (1941), although set in 1938–40, opens with an oxymoronic foreword stressing peace but anticipating war: "Birthplace of man's wings, America today watches her skies with grave concern, for in these skies of peace the nation is building the upper battlements of its defense." The ambivalent note struck by the foreword, with its uneasy yoking of opposites, carries over into the opening scene—a mock air raid that a radio announcer, also mingling and mangling imagery of peace and war, justifies by implying that the former is possible only if the latter is not considered impossible: "Although no fires sweep the gutted streets of a murdered city . . . no terror or sorrow fills the upturned eyes of helpless civilians . . . these realistic maneuvers are a convincing guarantee that Americans—soldier and citizen alike—intend to be prepared."

The promilitary nature of *Flight Command* and *I Wanted Wings* was obviously enhanced by the defense mindedness of screenwriters who were in the military themselves: the former was coauthored by Commander Harvey Haislip; the latter was based on the book by Lieutenant Bierne Lay, Jr., who also collaborated on the screenplay. In each film, the preparedness theme is couched within a familiar plot: the know-it-all who learns to be part of the team (*Flight Command*), the interconnected destinies of three men (*I Wanted Wings*).

Warners' *Dive Bomber* (1941) is even more of a peacetime war movie. Although it was released a few months before Pearl Harbor, in it the United States is clearly on the brink of war. Cadets are told they are in the navy "to fly and fight." Fliers need a pressure suit to prevent "two kinds of blackout—our kind and the kind they're having in London now." An aviator with a heart ailment laments being grounded just as "the main event is about to start." And the entire film is a paean to those who "defend our country in the stratosphere."

The movie industry was behaving just as it had in 1915 when, two years before America's entry into World War I, "the public underwent a barrage of preparedness pictures which, with few exceptions, were antipacifist as well."[19] These 1915–17 films also anticipated the 1939–41 cycle in theme (espionage, the vulnerability of the Panama Canal, topical allegory, jingoism), character (the converted pacifist, the heroine spy, the enlightened scatterbrain, the raping Hun), and approach (naming the enemy only after 1917, but before then making the identification embarrassingly easy).

Just as American World War I films eulogized France, those of World War II virtually lionized England, for reasons ranging from topicality to a studio head's belief in Britain. Herbert J. Yates was not an Anglophile like Harry Warner or Darryl F. Zanuck. But he was shrewd enough to know that Britain was box office. Thus he was able to get an edge on the majors and put *Women in War* into release in May 1940, more than a year before Fox came out with *A Yank in the* RAF.

There was drama in beleaguered Britain, the human drama of a nation that spoke our own language; a nation suffering—and surviving—an ordeal that we had been spared. There was also romance.

Invasions inhibit romance, but blackouts encourage it. It is during a London blackout that Ilona Massey meets George Brent in *International Lady* (1941). It is in a bombshelter that Madeleine Carroll and Fred MacMurray meet in Paramount's *One Night in Lisbon* (1941), an Anglo-American romance that is more Anglo than American. At one point, MacMurray, initially a chauvinist, confesses to a British diplomat, "It's funny about England, and the way Americans feel about you. It's like being related, in a way. You know how you feel about relatives. They do a lot of things that irritate you; but when it comes right down to it, you are related. You speak the same language, you have the same ideals, and you have the same plans for the future."

The speech has a charming ingenuousness about it; it is the kind of admission that heralds the end of parochialism. That ingenuousness, however, does not obscure the film's theme: America's need to support Britain in her war with Germany. But in keeping with the traditions of romantic comedy, Anglo-American cooperation is reduced to a sweet pun. As MacMurray and Carroll are about to kiss at the fadeout, MacMurray says, "Nothing is more important than England and America hold fast to each other."

Madeleine Carroll was back at her old stand in *My Favorite Blonde*, which, although it was not released until 1942, was written in August 1941. Paramount was evidently planning to capitalize on Madeleine Carroll's identification with Britain, widely known because of her appearances promoting "Bundles for Britain," by casting her again as a British agent, this time pairing her with Bob Hope in a parody of *The Thirty-nine Steps* (in which she had costarred six years earlier with Robert Donat). Now it is Carroll whose life is in danger, and Hope finds himself in Donat's situation—stumbling into a gathering where he has to address a group he has never met (mothers) on a subject of which he is ignorant (child care).

Since one of the screenwriters of *My Favorite Blonde* was British-born Frank Butler, it is no surprise that there is a pitch for Britain, naturally coming from Madeleine Carroll, in the form of a parable delivered in language that a vaudeville ventriloquist (the Bob Hope character) can understand. Carroll explains to him what war is like for the British, without referring to the Luftwaffe or the Blitz, but to the "little people who sit home at night and wait—wait for a lot of little boys to fly over in expensive toys and drop death on their homes and children, all in the name of a new order—a new, distorted version of justice, humanity, and civilization."

Hope interprets her words in the only context in which they make sense to him—American democracy, in which "the little guy . . . is still free to tell the big guys how to run the show." To preserve that freedom, the little guys of America must aid the little people of England.

Twentieth Century–Fox had planned to salute Britain even before Paramount did. In October 1940, Zanuck had an idea for a film set against the backdrop of the Battle of Britain. It was to be a companion piece to *A Yank at Oxford* (1938), but this time, the Yank would be in the Eagle Squadron, the u.s. unit of the RAF. The screenplay was to go through many changes before emerging as *A Yank in the RAF*. On 25 October 1940, when Zanuck dictated the plot outline, it was *The Eagle Squadron*, "about a fellow who never knew how to take orders"[20]—in short, a "cocky youth reconstructed by the military" movie. At the time, Zanuck was thinking of a film based on the life of Billy Fiske, the American sportsman and pilot who joined the RAF and was killed in an air raid. But since the film was intended as a vehicle for Tyrone Power, a tragic ending was unsuitable; it would mean Power's fans would not see him get the girl.

Nevertheless, Zanuck pressed on. Within less than two weeks, George Bruce had written a treatment expanding Zanuck's outline into a wartime romance between a Yank in the RAF and an ambulance driver. The American flier was made a malcontent who quit his job as test pilot because his company refused to remedy defects in plane construction. Zanuck replied that charging an American aircraft manufacturer with making defective planes would not set well with audiences who, for the past decade, had been seeing movies hailing advances in aviation. A week later, Bruce submitted a revised treatment that still left Zanuck unsatisfied. The approach was nowhere near the paradigm, *A Yank at Oxford*, which Zanuck had screened for Bruce because it was "an excellent example of the American in England—and his relationships with Englishmen."[21]

Although Zanuck always exercised personal supervision over his films, he regarded this one as his own creation to such an extent that when it was finished, the credits included "based on an original story by Melville Crossman"—a pseudonym Zanuck frequently used. Nothing escaped Zanuck's attention, even the names of the characters. The hero went from Pete to "Dizzy" to Steve to Tim; the heroine from British to American. Zanuck was still holding out for a tragic ending, even though it now might mean a different actor in the lead—a James Cagney type, perhaps.

By December 1940, Zanuck had further revised his concept of the film, now seeing it as a drama with some light moments. But he still had no script.

Karl Tunberg and Darrell Ware were commissioned to write the screenplay, but Zanuck was no more impressed with their 7 January 1941 script, now called *The Eagle Flies Again*, than he had been with Bruce's treatments. His reaction reveals one of the reasons for making the film: to show that "England stands as the last bulwark of freedom,"[22] something Zanuck genuinely believed. He wanted the British to believe it, too. Thus on 16 January 1941 he sent a plot summary to the Air Ministry in London, promising the film would be "a visual document to inspire all civilized people with the hope that Freedom, Liberty and our way of life may prevail . . ." and that far from being propaganda, it would be "entertainment." The Yank would still die, but his death would be uplifting—uplifting entertainment since he would be dying for England.

The British replied within two weeks: the Yank must not die. A dead Yank in the R A F would hardly inspire other Yanks to defend the last bulwark of freedom. Also, if the Yank lived, he could get the girl, and Tyrone Power could play the role originally intended for him.

By the end of February 1941, Tunberg and Ware had finally presented Zanuck with a script he liked; now called *A Yank in the* R A F, it had, as Zanuck noted enthusiastically, "charm" and "characters slightly offbeat."[23] What was really offbeat was not the characters but the casting of Betty Grable as the love interest. This, clearly, was entertainment. But through all its permutations, the film's purpose remained the same: Darryl F. Zanuck's homage to the few to whom "so many owed so much."

A Yank in the R A F had no sooner gone into production than Zanuck launched another tribute to Britain, *Confirm or Deny*, a newspaper melodrama in which a scoop-hungry American gets a crash course in ethics from his British betters. Discovering Hitler's plan for the Battle of Britain, the newsman (Don Ameche) is ready to tell the world until the British, who also know of the planned attack and need time to prepare for it, convince him he will be endangering their country.

The genesis of *Confirm or Deny* reveals much about Zanuck's Anglophilia. Although Jo Swerling was a highly competent screenwriter, Zanuck was appalled by his first script (21 March 1941). He reminded Swerling that a film about Germany's plan to attack Britain could not be set in the spring of 1941, months after the Battle of Britain began. Yet even when the time of the action was pushed back to September 1940, the critics still found the film passé.

Swerling had also planned a tragic ending for the newsman and the British heroine. Although that too would change, Zanuck was not as upset about their dying as he was about their not dying for England. Zanuck considered himself Hollywood's Anglicist, the one who knew more about England than the English. Thus he was genuinely offended by Swerling's insensitivity. The characters were either "stupid or heels," Zanuck complained; their delineation "would certainly find disfavor with the British Foreign Service . . . and would certainly not promote the feeling that exists between Great Britain and the United States." If Swerling were a true Anglophile, he would not have an RAF pilot dying in a hotel basement without a doctor. The pilot "would be in the best hospital in London," Zanuck insisted. Furthermore, such a faux pas "would give Churchill good grounds for believing the worst about our industry."[24]

Zanuck's fear of imperilling Anglo-American relations resulted in a film in which Britain is more of a bastion of integrity than a bulwark of freedom. If the British seem superior to the Americans in *One Night in Lisbon* and *My Favorite Blonde*, it is because an embattled people always appear more valorous, and therefore worthier of praise, than a people not yet tested. *Confirm or Deny*, however, praises the British for being morally superior, contrasting British integrity with American opportunism. There is no doubt that Zanuck believed Britain was a moral center, but that belief was considerably strengthened by his desire to be Britain's ally in the eyes of the world and certainly in the eyes of Churchill. Motives are never pure, only more pure than base. Thus Zanuck sincerely felt Americans could learn from Britain. He had always been an Anglophile, even as a child. It was his mother's British ancestry that fascinated him, not his father's Swiss parentage.[25] When World War II finally came to America, Zanuck, who had been commissioned as a reserve lieutenant colonel in the Signal Corps almost a year before Pearl Harbor and was later raised to the rank of full colonel, accompanied British commandos in a 1942 raid on the German-occupied French coast.

As a filmmaker, Zanuck expected his Anglophilia to be profitable as it had been in *Lloyds of London* (1936), *Suez* (1938), and *A Yank at Oxford*. What he hoped would be profitable for Americans he also hoped would be profitable for Twentieth Century–Fox. *A Yank in the RAF* was profitable in both senses, *Confirm or Deny* in neither. Because Zanuck was so determined to glorify Britain, he missed the humanity in Britain's finest hour. MGM was able to discover that humanity, immortalizing it in *Mrs. Miniver* (1942), because MGM was a studio devoted to something far more significant than England's moral leadership: the family.

By the summer of 1941, Hollywood's violation of American neutrality seemed to warrant investigation. On 1 August 1941, two isolationist senators, Gerald P. Nye of North Dakota and Bennett Champ Clark of Missouri, introduced a resolution calling for "a thorough and complete investigation of any propaganda disseminated by motion pictures and radio or any other activity of the motion-picture industry to influence public sentiment in the direction of participation by the United States in the present European war."[26]

Thus Senate Resolution 152 was born, authorizing a dual inquiry into film propaganda and film monopoly. There was nothing especially subtle about linking propaganda with monopoly. The Big Eight—Paramount, MGM, RKO, Warner Bros., Twentieth Century–Fox, Columbia, Universal, and United Artists—clearly constituted a monopoly. Furthermore, five of the eight—Paramount, MGM, RKO, Warners, and Fox—were vertically integrated, exhibiting their own films in their own theaters. Since the eight made most of the anti-Nazi films, which Nye and Clark believed were intended to draw America into war, breaking up the monopoly by proving that the eight and their subsidiaries were in violation of the Sherman Anti-Trust Act would also put a stop to Hollywood's warmongering. (It would almost put a stop to Hollywood seven years later when the monopoly charge was revived and the studios were ordered to sever production from exhibition and distribution.)

The same mentality that saw anti-Nazi films as the result of monopolistic practice and vertical integration also saw a connection between anti-Nazi films and those who made them—"foreigners" in a Hollywood that, in Nye's words, "swarms with refugees and British actors"; a Hollywood dominated by men with "non-Nordic" surnames like Cohn, Goldwyn, Schenck, Katz, Mayer; a Hollywood of Jews.

On the evening of 1 August 1941, the ubiquitous Senator Nye was in St. Louis, speaking in the municipal auditorium at a rally sponsored by the rabidly isolationist America First Committee and addressing an audience as uninformed as himself. Hollywood, he announced to their loud approval, was "glorifying war, telling about the grandeur and heavenly justice of the British Empire," because if Britain lost the war, Hollywood would lose the British market.[27] The crowd cheered Nye as he identified each culprit, using an inflection for names like Cohn and Silverstone that was later interpreted as Jew baiting. The crowd even booed the name of Darryl F. Zanuck, perhaps because it thought Zanuck was either Jewish or one of those "foreigners." As an anti-Semitic, antimonopolistic Anglophobe, Nye was at least consistent in his prejudices, believing that a Jewish monopoly, with a vested interest in Britain, was making anti-Nazi and pro-British movies. Perhaps the best commentary on Nye's speech was the presence of Father Coughlin's followers across the street, distributing copies of the Reverend's anti-Semitic weekly with the paradoxical title *Social Justice*.

The following month, the subcommittee on Senate Resolution 152, chaired by D. Worth Clark of Idaho, began hearings, which lasted from 9 to 26 September. Except for the testimonies of Nicholas Schenck, Zanuck, and, particularly, Harry Warner, the hearings were a monument to ignorance, in which Nye and his cohorts revealed, under the guise of fact finding, their own biases as well as their lack of knowledge about the industry they were investigating.

More disturbing than their ignorance was their lack of embarrassment about it. It was as if knowing something about the movies were sinful; ignorance, which the self-righteous have often invoked as a sign of integrity, became the sole qualification for passing judgment. And prejudice became just prejudice, as Christ's anger was just anger.

After Bennett Clark accused Warners of making more "hate-producing films than any other company in America," Senator McFarland of Arizona asked if he had seen any of them. Clark replied, "No. I have not seen any of them. I am not going to see any of them" (p. 81).

Nye's filmgoing habits were equally eccentric, or perhaps he felt that not having seen a film made him a better judge of its content. Nye kept referring to *I Married a Nazi*, not knowing that Fox had changed the title even before its release to *The Man I Married*. When McFarland asked Nye what he found so objectionable about the movie, Nye answered that he had "not reviewed a picture in a long, long time" (p. 57) and suggested a screening to refresh his memory (although it must be difficult to remember what one has not seen).

Never at a loss for words, except the wrong ones, Nye meant to say that he had not thought about ("reviewed") *I Married a Nazi* ("a picture") for a while. Naturally—he had never seen it, even under its correct title. Later he admitted he might have confused it with *Confessions of a Nazi Spy*: "For the life of me I could not tell you which was which" (p. 60). Yet, as Harry Warner reminded him, when

Nye saw *Confessions* at a special screening in Washington 11 May 1939, it left enough of an impression for him to say that "anyone who truly appreciates the one great democracy upon this earth will appreciate this picture" (p. 345).

The bigotry and anti-Semitism that partially motivated the investigation revealed themselves in references to "non-Americans," "those born abroad," "alien or refugee actors," and especially Nye's put-down of Chaplin: "a great artist, not a citizen of our country." Sometimes prejudice was cloaked by ingenuousness, as in D. Worth Clark's wondering whether movies like *The Mortal Storm*—which, of course, he had not seen—might "create unity among the various groups in the United States" (p. 323). But the only group that could conceivably be united by *The Mortal Storm*—even if the film had such rallying power, which it did not—would be Jews. In effect, Clark was saying that films about Jews, which were precious few to begin with, might unite them and strengthen the Hollywood-Anglo-Jewish monopoly.

The true nature of the investigation did not escape the press. A *Washington Post* headline called it by its rightful name: "Witch Hunt on Capitol Hill." Generally, the dailies defended the movie industry's right to freedom of expression and praised the studios for dramatizing the menace of Nazism. Ohio's *Dayton News* even accused the subcommittee of Nazi tactics; Massachusetts's *New Bedford Mercury* questioned the Senate's right even to finance such an investigation; *The St. Louis Dispatch* called the proceedings a "farce"; New York's *Auburn Citizen Advertiser* suggested that if there were to be any housecleaning, it should start in Congress, not in Hollywood.

The industry survived the investigation and emerged as the scapegoat of fanatics who were behaving as undemocratically as the Nazis in the movies. At the next inquisition six years later, when the subject was not anti-Nazi but pro-Communist movies, the industry would be less fortunate. In 1941, Harry Warner defended his studio against Nye's accusations; in 1947, his brother Jack would not defend his screenwriters who were accused of Communist subversion. Yet Harry probably would have agreed with Jack. Both of them considered Nazism evil; but so was Communism, which was Nazism, Soviet style. During the war, Nazism eclipsed Communism; when the eclipse was over, the evil was still there, but it had a different name. It all came down to the dichotomy between fascism and Communism, which the brothers refused to accept because they regarded them as synonymous. To the brothers there may not have been a difference between fascism and Communism, but there was one between antifascism and anti-Communism: the one revealed the industry's strength, the other its weakness.

However, in 1941, no son of Ben and Pearl Warner would be intimidated by a couple of foolish isolationists. Harry Warner proudly admitted that he was "unequivocally in favor of giving England and her allies all the supplies which our country can spare" (p. 339). And he laid to rest the groundless charge that Hollywood supported Britain because it was dependent on the British market: "No one with any business judgment could possibly have acted on the assumption that the policy of this country toward England would be influenced by the relatively small investment of our industries in England" (p. 347).

On 8 September Wendell Wilkie, whom the industry had hired as its counsel, sent a strongly worded letter to D. Worth Clark, stating, among other things, that between 1 September 1939 and 8 September 1941 "only some 50 [movies] have had anything to do with the issues involved in the war or with the ideological beliefs of the participants."[28] Wilkie's figure was even higher than Nye's, which was a conservative twenty. Yet Wilkie's fifty is frequently mentioned[29] as if it were the equivalent of the seven types of ambiguity in literary criticism or the seven kings of Rome in ancient history. At least William Empson's seven types of ambiguity can be listed, and the seven mythical kings can be named; enumerating Wilkie's fifty is another matter.

While there were some fifty movies directly or indirectly inspired by events in Europe, few of them would fit Wilkie's description. In an attempt to give an ideological basis to the Hollywood war film, Wilkie misrepresented the industry. As Nicholas Schenck informed Senator Nye, those films were designed to "enlighten" as well as "entertain." They could hardly carry out their dual function if they were encumbered by ideology. Hollywood's "ideology" was simply that Nazism was wrong and democracy right. Wilkie, however, was correct when he said that, of the fifty, some "portray Nazism for what it is—a cruel, lustful, ruthless, and cynical force," the "some" totalling about a dozen.

To get a clearer picture of the industry's contribution to the European war effort, one should begin not with 1 September 1939 but with the first indications of Hollywood's awareness of Nazism, which manifested itself in the same allusive way its awareness of fascism did in the early thirties. One should begin, therefore, with 1937, the year of *Range Defenders*; the year Fitzgerald completed his screenplay of *Three Comrades* (which, presumably because of

Joseph L. Mankiewicz, became a mildly anti-Nazi film without mentioning Nazism). If the terminus ad quem is extended to December 1941, a subgenre emerges: the pre-Pearl Harbor American World War II film, of which there are eight types:

I. Films Unequivocally Anti-Nazi

Confessions of a Nazi Spy. 1939, Warner Bros. Authentic Nazi espionage; newsreel footage of German war machine augmented in 1940 rerelease

Beasts of Berlin (aka *Goose Step, Hell's Devils*). 1939, PDC (PRC). Anti-Nazi resistance comprising Christians (particularly Catholics) and Jews: scenes of concentration camps and torture of inmates; newsreel footage of invasion of Poland

The Mortal Storm. 1940, MGM. Effect of Nazism on German family; internment of Jews in concentration camps; "good German" renounces Nazism

Escape. 1940, mgm. Son's attempt to rescue mother from concentration camp vies in significance with subplot about Nazi colonel and Bavarian countess

The Great Dictator. 1940, UA. Undisguised satire on German and Italian fascism set within the period from Versailles to Anschluss

Foreign Correspondent. 1940, UA. An American's gradual awakening to fascism and reality of war; unashamed tribute to America with "the only lights left in the world"

Four Sons. 1940, Fox. Plight of Sudetenland family; one son the "good German"

The Man I Married. 1940, Fox. Most vocal denunciation yet of Nazism; "Jew" (in German) used for first time in Nazi context

Three Faces West. 1940, Republic. Austrian refugees in America; Nazism called "worse than cancer"

Arise, My Love. 1940, Paramount. The end of the Spanish civil war to the fall of France within the framework of a romantic comedy functioning as an interventionist appeal

So Ends Our Night. 1941, UA. Political exile and Jewish refugee; Christian hero sacrificing life for Jewish lovers; "Jew" (in English) finally spoken

They Dare Not Love. 1941, Columbia. Austrian prince and bride rescued from tyranny when their boat is captured by the British

Man Hunt. 1941, Fox. Big game hunter hesitates over killing Hitler; loses chance but hounded by ruthless member of Gestapo

Underground. 1941, Warner Bros. Interesting switch on polarized family theme with Nazi brother taking patriot brother's place in resistance

II. Military Preparedness Films

In Old Monterey. 1939, Republic. Ranchers persuaded to sell property to army for war games

Ski Patrol. 1940, Universal. Only film about Russo-Finnish war with no side taken[30] mocks "war is a thing of the past" myth by tracing the past (Ethiopia, China, Austria, Czechoslovakia, Poland) on a map that ends with Finland, whose invasion is not distinguished from that of other countries

Flight Command. 1940, MGM. Tribute to navy Hellcats whose peacetime maneuvers are uncannily warlike

Dive Bomber. 1941, Warner Bros. Navy flight surgeons prepare for "the main event."

Parachute Battalion. 1941, RKO. Pitch for paratroopers made with cooperation of Fifty-first Parachute Battalion

I Wanted Wings. 1941, Paramount. Air preparedness as a sign of an America on the alert

III. Anglo-American Alliances

Women in War. 1940, Republic. British nurses braving the bombs

A Yank in the RAF. 1941, Fox. American flier joins RAF and sees action over Germany and at Dunkirk

International Lady. 1941, UA. Scotland Yard cooperates with FBI, and title character changes over from Axis to Allies

One Night in Lisbon. 1941, Paramount. Unalloyed Anglophilia epitomized by line, "Into the life of every English girl a little American should fall" and by the fervent singing of "There'll Always Be An England"

Confirm or Deny. 1941, Fox. American news hound learns integrity from the British

Paris Calling. 1941, Universal. Triple homage to the democracies; a Yank in the RAF, the French underground, and a British rescue mission

International Squadron. 1941, Warner Bros. Ronald Reagan joins the RAF and dies

Sundown. 1941, UA. Native girl works with British to stop Nazis in East Africa; she turns out to have a British father so she can marry an Englishman (thus upholding good taste requirement of interracial romance)

IV. Films Set in the First World War with a Philosophy More Applicable to the Second[31]

The Fighting 69th. 1940, Warner Bros. Sheer jingoism anticipating the flagwaving of the war years

Sergeant York. 1941, Warner Bros. Alvin York's rifle, bent by lightning, is put straight along with his pacifism

V. U-Boat Adventures

Mystery Sea Raider. 1940, Paramount. U-boats raid passenger and merchant ships

Escape to Glory (aka *Submarine Zone*). 1940, Columbia. Nazis torpedo British ship with Americans aboard

VI. Spy Thrillers

Pals of the Saddle. 1938, Republic. Foreign agents after poison gas found in the West

Cipher Bureau. 1938, Warner–Fine Arts. Spies with German accents from unidentified country

Panama Patrol. 1939, Warner–Fine Arts. Sequel to *Cipher Bureau*

South of the Border. 1939, Republic. Gene Autry foils attempt to set up submarine base in Mexico

Espionage Agent. 1939, Warner Bros. Two-way argument for counterespionage—to maintain American neutrality or despite it

The Lone Wolf Spy Hunt. 1939, Columbia. Rita Hayworth as enemy spy

They Made Her a Spy. 1939, RKO. Female undercover agent exposes spy ring headed by doctor with German accent; climax in Washington Monument

Television Spy. 1939, Paramount. Unidentified spy ring after plan for transmitter

Charlie Chan in City of Darkness. 1939, Fox. Spies in Paris from unnamed country; critical of Munich pact

Mr. Moto's Last Warning. 1939, Fox. Prophetic title for one of last films in short-lived (1937–39) series terminated because of worsening Japanese-American relations; here the Japanese sleuth prevents unnamed country from setting Britain and France at odds with each other at Suez

Enemy Agent. 1940, Universal. Unidentified spies after aircraft blueprints

Charlie Chan in Panama. 1940, Fox. Unnamed but obviously German spy ring plotting sabotage in Canal Zone

Murder in the Air. 1940, Warner Bros. Ronald Reagan masquerades as enemy spy and leaps from burning dirigible

Phantom Submarine. 1940, Columbia. Search for sunken gold reveals underwater submarine base and plot to prevent American aid from reaching the Philippines

Sky Murder. 1940, MGM. Nick Carter melodrama; fifth columnists in Washington

Burma Convoy. 1941, Universal. Eurasian spies on Burma Road

Dangerously They Live. 1941, Warner Bros. Eminent psychiatrist revealed as Nazi; spies in Yorkville

Devil Pays Off. 1941, Republic. Shipboard espionage en route to Havana without reference to Germany

Man at Large. 1941, Fox. Villain is blind mystery writer, transmitting convoy sailing information to Berlin

Mystery Ship. 1941, Columbia. Spies and saboteurs' odyssey

Scotland Yard. 1941, Fox. British Nazis, called such, planning to ship gold to South America

World Premiere. 1941, Paramount. Three Axis agents (two German, one Italian) sabotage premiere of antifascist movie

VII. Patriotic Comedies

Buck Privates; In the Navy; Keep 'Em Flying. 1941, Universal. Abbott and Costello promoting the army, navy, and air force in three films

Caught in the Draft. 1941, Paramount. Bob Hope learns respect for the Selective Service Act

VIII. Films Suggesting Nazism through Association or Metaphor

Range Defenders. 1937, Republic. Black-shirted bullies with ss-style insignia intimidate citizens

Three Comrades. 1938, MGM. Violence and bookburning by un-
identified hooligans
Conspiracy. 1939, RKO. Revolution in banana republic suggesting
Nazi Germany
The Sun Never Sets. 1939, Universal. African Gold Coast dictator
by name of Hugo Zurof foiled by British
Chip of the Flying U. 1940, Universal. Munitions runners with for-
eign accents out west

That one-third of the pre-Pearl Harbor films deal with espionage
is not surprising. The industry repeated what it had done in the First
World War and launched an espionage cycle. In World War I films,
spies are everywhere—plotting shipyard and aircraft sabotage, stealing secret plans, dabbling in germ warfare. There are male and female spies, German and German-American spies; male spy catchers
and female spy catchers. The preponderance of spy films in wartime
is due, in part, to the association of war with espionage, and to the
assumption that where there are spies, there are saboteurs. Also, and
more important to a filmmaker, spy movies have a perennial fascination and are easy to write. All that is needed is a MacGuffin,
which, as Hitchcock told Truffaut, is "the device, the gimmick . . .
or [what] the spies are after."[32] What the spies are after can be anything from a blueprint to a timetable, from the brooch a woman is
wearing to the plans written on her back (in invisible ink).

A writer can also take a fact or a current event and turn it into
pop history. The conventions of the espionage tale are easily grafted
onto a headline, producing a hypothesis that results in a plot. This
is the method Howard Estabrook used for *International Lady*, the
most stylish of the pre-7 December spy films, with Ilona Massey of
the provocative beauty mark as a Norwegian Mata Hari who per-
forms folk songs containing encoded messages over the radio. Estabrook's screenplay is a literate blending of spy lore (carrier pigeons,
the melody with the message à la Hitchcock's *The Lady Vanishes*),
fact (Lisbon as spy center and embarkation point for Europeans
seeking refuge in America, German agents on Long Island), and un-
canny speculation (Long Island as the natural landing site for a German submarine, which indeed landed there in 1942).

If, as Turrou revealed, there were spies in upstate New York, Estabrook could have them in Yonkers and Utica. According to the
rules of the genre, the ringleader should be a model citizen in an
innocuous profession; a Long Island candy manufacturer would fit
the type. Spies work out of places too nondescript to arouse suspicion—a Yonkers shack, a Utica granary. Through an alchemy

known to the best spywriters, Estabrook melted down the incredible to the probable, doing the same to the heroine, who, unlike the original Mata Hari, repents and proves her sincerity by intercepting a bullet meant for a G-man. And while she must stand trial for espionage, no jury is going to convict a Norwegian who has risked her life for an American.

Sometimes a writer will fantasize about an event and produce wonderfully inventive variations on a theme. Headline: GERMAN ESCAPES FROM CANADIAN INTERNMENT CAMP. Suppose the German is shot while escaping; suppose further that a British agent must take his place, working with a G-man who is posing as a photographer. Pull a type off the character rack: the female news hound who, thinking the photographer/G-man has killed the German, pursues him to New York, encounters a blind mystery writer who is a Nazi agent, and becomes entangled in a spy ring specializing in encoded radio ads. The result is John Larkin's honeycombed script of *Man at Large* (1941).

In comic espionage like Paramount's *The Lady Has Plans* (1942) (the script of which was completed in September 1941), the conventions of the spy story are combined with those of comedy. *The Lady Has Plans* reduces recognition by signs (e.g., moles, scars), one of the oldest ways of establishing a character's identity, to the absurd. Instead of a birthmark on her back, the lady, as the title says, has plans—plans for a torpedo written on her back in invisible ink. This kind of comedy is based on the "up the ante" principle: the writer adds as many devices as the plot can accommodate—mistaken identity, as the heroine is mistaken for the lady with the plans; bedroom farce, as foreign agents struggle to get a glimpse of the heroine's bare back; topical references such as the RAF's bombing of German cities; and the contemporary windup as the audience hears again that Lisbon is Europe's center of espionage and the rendezvous point for Germans flying to Dakar.

Although not all pre-Pearl Harbor spy films were so clever, they still did their job, which was the same as that of the posters in municipal buildings showing Uncle Sam with a finger pressed to his lips or a torpedoed ship with the caption "Someone Talked." If one saw enough movies, the warnings on the posters were superfluous. Spy films had already taught audiences to trust no one, especially benign types and pillars of the community. If a blind man can be an enemy agent, so can the retired teacher next door.

Espionage films alone did not anticipate the war; the entire pre-Pearl Harbor cycle did. Yet it was more than just a preparation for war; it was a declaration of war—first against fascism, then against

Paulette Goddard and Ray Milland in The Lady Has Plans *(1942), espionage comedy marked by a touch of class—the white telephone. Courtesy* MCA

any country spying on America, and finally against Nazi Germany. Americans who went to the movies regularly would not have been surprised that their country was at war at the end of 1941. The only surprise was that the enemy was Japan. While America declared war first on Japan, then on Germany, Hollywood did it in reverse. But it would soon make up for the mistake.

It was probably better that Hollywood refrained from tackling Japan until 1941; otherwise, the results could have proved embarrassing. While Roosevelt, Hull, and Stimson suspected in the summer of 1941 that a Japanese attack was imminent, they were sure it would be on the Philippines; Marshall thought it might be on the Panama Canal. If there had been a movie in release at the time of Pearl Harbor either about a Japanese raid on the Philippines or about a thwarted attempt to destroy the Pacific Fleet, the film would have had to be recalled and recut with a different ending.

Warner Bros. might have made such a film if it had purchased the rights to Robert Carson's story, "Aloha Means Good-By," before it was published, whipped up a screenplay, and rushed it into production for a late 1941 release. In Carson's story, which was serialized in *The Saturday Evening Post* in five installments beginning 28 June 1941, a government agent, posing as an army deserter, foils an attempt by Japanese terrorists to blow up two American warships at Pearl Harbor.

On 15 December 1941, screenwriter Richard Macaulay urged Hal Wallis to buy the screen rights to "Aloha Means Good-By" since he was eager to write the screenplay. Wallis did so, and "Aloha Means Good-By" became *Across the Pacific* (1942). Macaulay retained the pre-Pearl Harbor setting, but just barely; the film ends on 6 December, as a close up of a desk calendar is careful to emphasize, with the Panama Canal replacing Pearl Harbor as the target of attack.[33]

Yet Carson's story is uncannily accurate. "Big trouble in Hawaii," a character notes: "hell is going to pop very shortly,"[34] which it did within four months of the last installment.

5. Hollywood Mobilizes

Until 1941, Japanese aggression in Asia was material for a *March of Time* or a newsreel, but not for a feature film. The reason was certainly not fear of losing the Japanese market, which as of 1937 was "virtually lost."[1] There were several reasons. The Far East afforded less drama than Europe. Even if some drama could be extracted from the war in China, casting would pose a problem. Since the studios never groomed Orientals for stardom, the leads would have to be played by such veterans of racial transformation as Paul Muni, Luise Rainer, and Sylvia Sidney, although there were just so many times they could be dressed in pajamas by Edith Head and have their eyes slanted by one of the Westmore brothers. The alternative was the "Yank in China" film, but this, too, would create difficulties; any love interest would be interracial. While the Production Code did not forbid miscegenation, it placed it in the category of Special Subjects, to be "treated within the careful limits of good taste"—the implication being that interracial marriage was in poor taste.

Yet Hollywood could not ignore the rise of Japan any more than it could the rise of Germany. To deal with the subject it needed an event—not just the sinking of an American gunboat or the bombing of a Chinese city—that would put Japan on a par with Germany, which Hollywood had declared the world's number one enemy. Finally, Hollywood found what it wanted in September 1940 when Japan joined the Axis; now the Japanese could be as villainous as the Nazis. Another incident occurred a month later to suggest there might be an additional source of drama in the Far East: the reopening of the Burma Road, the seven hundred–mile supply route over which war matériel was transported to China. Anything might happen on a mountain road, especially if the Japanese wanted to prevent the supplies from reaching their destination.

Even before Pearl Harbor, MGM and Fox were planning movies about the Burma Road—*A Yank on the Burma Road* and *China Girl*, respectively; Fox also had a property about Japanese espionage in Shanghai, *Secret Agent of Japan*. *A Yank on the Burma Road* was completed three weeks before Pearl Harbor; the others were then in the script stage. Still, with only the slightest modifications, all three were able to incorporate Pearl Harbor into the action. Although it was extrinsic to the plot, Pearl Harbor provided a second climax, giving each film an emotional value it would otherwise not have had. If these films had been made just a few months earlier, they would have been only a tribute to China and an indictment of Japan. After Pearl Harbor, the charge carried considerably more weight.

MGM thought there was a movie in the story of Daniel Arnstein, the former Chicago cab driver who became the United States Commissioner to the Burma Road in 1941 and broke the Burma Road bottleneck, so Lend-Lease material could reach China. The Arnstein story was reworked as the familiar tale of the uncommitted American who burgeons into a patriot once he witnesses the bravery of, in this case, the Chinese.

A Yank on the Burma Road began production on 22 October 1941; it was completed in a scant three weeks and scheduled for release in February 1942.[2] With the attack on Pearl Harbor, MGM lost no time in making six changes that resulted in *A Yank on the Burma Road*'s being the first Pearl Harbor movie, even though Pearl Harbor had nothing to do with the plot.

The changes were easily made. First, a new opening title: "On December 7th 1941 Japan attacked the United States of America and engaged it in war. This is the story of one American who tackled Japan a little before the rest of us—and what he started the rest of the Yanks will finish."

Originally, the heroine was married to a mercenary who was flying for Japan and who had previously flown for Franco and Mussolini—which said something about his politics. After Pearl Harbor he was changed into a German mercenary, and with two lines of dialogue—"his allegiance is with Germany and her allies," making him "an enemy of England and China"—he was made the villain as well. With America at war with both Germany and Japan, it was patriotic, as well as economical, to create villains with dual affiliations, thereby suggesting complicity between Germany and Japan—a notion many films exploited to the point of implying that German agents knew about Pearl Harbor before 7 December.[3]

After Pearl Harbor, it was not only possible for screenwriters to heap opprobrium on the Japanese with varying degrees of grossness; it was also obligatory. Thus the next addition is a racial pejorative, although a relatively tame one. Still, if the screenwriters had thought about it, they would have realized they were mixing metaphors as well as cuisine: "Get the men off the road before those Jap butchers make chop suey out of us."

Since the most important addition involved Pearl Harbor, the simplest way to work it into the plot was to have someone announce that "Japanese planes have attacked the Americans at Pearl Harbor, and Japan has declared war on the United States." The remaining new dialogue was given to the hero: "We're partners, now, allies!" he cries to one of the Chinese soldiers; "That's for Pearl Harbor!" he shouts as Japanese soldiers fall to his machine gun; and finally, "We're headin' for Tokyo, Yokohama, and points East." With these additions, a film that would have been anti-Japanese because of Japan's treatment of China became even more so because of Japan's attack on Pearl Harbor.

A week after *Yank* was finished, Jack Andrews and Steve Fisher completed their screenplay, *Burma Road*, for Fox, which had acquired the rights to the Daniel Arnstein story, planning to use it as a springboard for a "Yank in the Far East" movie.[4] The Andrews-Fisher script might have been entitled *Two Yanks on the Burma Road* since it involved an American freight lines owner and his dispatcher, sent to China "to keep the open door from swinging shut." For the love interest, there was the damsel in distress, a dancer stranded when her show folded—apparently the usual plight of American chorus girls in the Far East. Although Andrews and Fisher worked independently of the team that authored *A Yank on the Burma Road* (Gordon Kahn, Hugo Butler, and David Lang), they used two of the same themes: the importance of the Burma Road as an artery to China, and the uncommitted hero who develops a conscience after witnessing Chinese heroism. And since the hero had an inamorata, Niki, she became as engagée as he, even driving one of the supply trucks.

Pearl Harbor intervened between the first (21 November 1941) and second (13 January 1942) drafts. The title became *Over the Burma Road*, with the action starting on 7 December and the hero still uncommitted but now a photographer. Zanuck raised his usual objections; having just produced *A Yank in the* RAF, he wanted a similar plot, one that would not open on the day of infamy but a month earlier so the photographer could evolve into a patriot. A week later, Andrews and Fisher gave Zanuck a new treatment and a new title,

A Yank in China; Zanuck was still dissatisfied. He had now decided the photographer should have a romance with a Chinese girl, even imagining Gene Tierney in the role (which she did ultimately play) because the actress was "actually . . . oriental looking."[5]

Zanuck believed he could satisfy the good taste requirement for an interracial romance and score a hit with our Chinese allies at the same time: "There is no need for the Hays office to become alarmed. . . . I am positive the Chinese will be delighted by the idea of a romance between a modern Chinese girl and a young American. The old chestnut barriers are on the way out."[6] Actually, there were never any barriers; Zanuck had already decided that the romance would not culminate in marriage: "At the end of our story, nothing has culminated romantically."[7] It rarely did in films where the lovers belonged to different races; usually one or the other, or both, died (as happens in *Northwest Mounted Police*, 1940, and *The Story of Dr. Wassell*, 1944 respectively).

Like any producer's motives, Zanuck's were mixed; they were an amalgam of discretion, exploitation, love of topicality, patriotism, and concession—the last being particularly important in view of the prevailing bias against miscegenation. Having determined at the outset that white and yellow would not mingle, Zanuck had to find a way to separate them at the end.

In March 1942 Zanuck called in Ben Hecht, who experimented with various ways in which boy would not get girl: the boy would fly off to fight the Japanese while the girl either looked up longingly at the sky or else stayed behind to tend the wounded. When neither ending seemed to work, Hecht decided she should die and the boy would avenge her death by blasting Japanese planes out of the sky.

Since all Hecht did was carry out Zanuck's instructions better than Andrews and Fisher had, it was natural that he should receive screenplay credit for *China Girl* (Hecht's choice of title) and that Zanuck should receive story credit—not under his own name, of course, but under his familiar pseudonym, Melville Crossman. The film had evolved into something quite different from the Andrews and Fisher script: it had evolved into a Darryl F. Zanuck production. Everything Zanuck wanted—Gene Tierney in the title role, a November 1941 opening so the climax would be Pearl Harbor, a detached hero who developed convictions, and an interracial love affair, doomed as movie interracial romances generally are—he got, except a major film.

While Andrews and Fisher were trying to satisfy Zanuck with *Burma Road*, John Larkin was busy completing an original screen story about an American fugitive from justice who fled to Shanghai, opened a bar, and became involved in an espionage caper.[8] It would out-Hitchcock Hitchcock, with a female British agent posing as a jade dealer, German sea raiders torpedoing American supply ships, musically encoded messages, and the conversion of the hero from a neutral to a fighter.

Although Larkin completed the story by 4 December 1941, he might well have written it after Pearl Harbor: the shadow of war was everywhere. But it was not the war that history decreed. Larkin's war, which was averted, would have been between the United States and Germany as the result of a U-boat's sinking an American refugee ship. Larkin also envisioned a Shanghai teeming with Nazis in league with Japan, thus corroborating the suspicion that Axis nations worked together.

By 10 December, Larkin's screen story was the screenplay for *Secret Agent of Japan*, with Pearl Harbor as climax. By the time the final screenplay was finished (30 December 1941), every contingency had been covered. The national origins of the characters— American, British, German, Japanese, Chinese—automatically categorized them as Allies or Axis. The characters themselves were familiar types (or soon would be): the female spy; the hero with the criminal past who, when war comes, has to fight for one of the Allies (as Rick does in *Casablanca*) because he cannot return to the States; the Japanese villain so reminiscent of an American racketeer that he can be said to be "out gunning" for the hero; venal exporters lamenting the oil embargo and praising their Japanese customers as "wonderful people"; romance as moral confrontation, in which the heroine is so successful at getting the hero to shape up that he goes off to fight for China.

Common to *A Yank on the Burma Road*, *China Girl*, and *Secret Agent of Japan* is the detached hero politicized by the war. In two of the films, *China Girl* and *Secret Agent of Japan*, a woman is instrumental in effecting the hero's transformation. All three intimate that the Tripartite Pact resulted in a Nazi-Japanese coalition. *China Girl* and *Secret Agent* go even further, maintaining that German fifth columnists knew in advance about Pearl Harbor—a belief similar to the one circulated on 8 December that Germany was behind the Pearl Harbor attack. In *China Girl*, the photographer discovers a code message reading "Pearl" and "7" and realizes its significance only after 7 December. *Secret Agent* posits the existence of a "list of Japanese agents at work in Honolulu, names of trusted men and women prepared to direct Japanese air raiders by short wave transmitters, who will cut arrows in fields of sugar cane, pointing way to Pearl Harbor secrets." Since arrows in the cane fields was a common rumor at the time, it was only natural that Larkin should succumb to it. However, some knowledge of geography might have prevented this "singularly illogical" blunder: "Missing Pearl Harbor from the air over Oahu would be like overlooking a brass drum in a telephone booth."[9]

Yet the rumor persisted. The following year, *Air Force* (1943) repeated the charge of "local Japs" in Hawaii, thus perpetuating the myth of a Japanese fifth column in Honolulu that had been discounted in 1942. After *Air Force* was released, Warner Bros. received letters protesting the allegation of sabotage by fifth columnists at Pearl Harbor and Hickam Field. The studio replied that the information came from the War Department: "We must take their word on the events that occurred rather than accept statements that we are unable to check as to their accuracy."[10]

When Norman Thomas also accused Warners of misrepresenting the facts in *Air Force*, Elmer Davis, head of the Office of War Information (OWI), agreed but lamented the office's lack of success in making the studios realize their obligation to be accurate.[11] Davis's admission was ironic since the Bureau of Motion Pictures in OWI was especially created to assist Hollywood in furthering the war effort by enhancing the audience's understanding of the facts.[12] But Hollywood had become the vox populi, and the voice of the people was not going to be muffled.

The public wanted to believe the worst about a nation "nurtured at the breasts of hate and destruction," as Republic's *Remember Pearl Harbor* (1942) expressed it. Since Republic's films did not attract discriminating audiences, shown as they were in side-street movie houses or at Saturday matinees, nobody protested such lines as "If you see any Japs, don't shoot until you see the yellow of their eyes." Nor did anyone challenge the accuracy of a plot set in the Philippines on the eve of the war and featuring an assortment of stock characters, including the army playboy who pulls himself together in time to fly a plane, kamikaze style, into a Japanese machine gun nest, crying "Remember Pearl Harbor, you yellow rats!"; the ubiquitous Nazi agent; the Japanese bartender who heads the espionage ring; and the token good Filipino. Since the Philippines was bombed about ten hours after Pearl Harbor, the film assumes that there was accompanying fifth column activity, analogous to the nonexistent sabotage that accompanied the attack on Pearl Harbor.

It seemed that America was so obsessed with spies and saboteurs that it could not distinguish between them.

I Spy / We Spy / They Sabotage

By the end of 1941, Blayney F. Matthews's *The Specter of Sabotage* had arrived in the bookstores. The book itself has gone into oblivion along with the author, a former FBI agent who became director of plant protection and superintendent of personnel at Warner Bros. Appropriately, the book is dedicated to the brothers Warner, "courageous and far-seeing Americans, who were among the country's first industrialists to recognize the menace of the Fifth Column, and to engage in a relentless fight against subversive elements."

The dedication is, at least, accurate, reflecting the studio's refusal to be intimidated by Bundist threats during the filming of *Confessions of a Nazi Spy* and its willingness to take a public stand against Nazism (and Communism), as Harry Warner did in his June 1940 address. The rest of the book reads like a mediocre spy story: millions of Nazis are "massed for an invisible invasion of the United States," which is already honeycombed with Japanese, Italian, and German agents working in concert and targeting industrial plants, mines, military bases, and forests for sabotage—the most bizarre form of which is crop dusting with arsenic by Japanese truck gardeners.

All were rumors that "the FBI, military intelligence and local law enforcement officers tracked down . . . and found . . . false."[13] However, rumor has rarely deterred a screenwriter. While it is impossible to determine how many screenwriters read *The Specter of Sabotage*, it seems that a good number thought along the same lines as the author. A headline or an incident (verified or otherwise) often became the nucleus of the narrative. A screenwriter might read about the uncovering of a spy ring or a fire in a munitions plant; the rest was screenplay. Although it is true that where there is espionage there is the possibility of sabotage, the probable—not the possible—is the stuff of drama; and to a writer with an imagination, the probable can easily become the actual.

In Hitchcock's *Saboteur* (1942), the hero (Robert Cummings) charges a fifth columnist with serving the country that "killed my friend and is killing thousands like him." The friend was an aircraft worker who died in a fire set by a saboteur. Movie dialogue often tends to be hyperbolic, but in this instance, the truth was not exaggerated: it was absent. In 1941, the FBI found a negligible amount of espionage but no organized sabotage; in 1942, although 218 persons were convicted of sabotage, not one case could be attributed to a foreign power.[14] In 1943, there were 90 convictions, none involving the enemy. In 1944, the number of convictions decreased to 51, again, with no evidence of complicity with the enemy. Thus, when *The House on 92nd St.* was released in the fall of 1945, the epilogue could boast that "after the United States went to war December 7, 1941, 16,440 enemy agents, saboteurs and dangerous enemy aliens were arrested. . . . Not one single act of enemy-directed sabotage was perpetrated within the United States, nor was one major war secret stolen."

However, 1945 was not 1941, and Hollywood could not wait for the FBI to reveal that industrial damage was often accidental and that the motives for sabotage ranged from a disgruntled employee's desire for satisfaction to an urge to make mischief. A far more realistic case of wartime sabotage occurs in Republic's *Man from Frisco* (1944), in which a disappointed lover's refusal to deliver a vital message results in the collapse of a ship's superstructure and a young boy's death. In *Man from Frisco*, reason has not been exiled to the backwater of the mind. Other films are less rational, equating an act of espionage not with the threat of sabotage, but, through a leap of illogic, with sabotage itself, so that every spy is a potential saboteur and every saboteur an actual spy.

These saboteur/spies—or spy/saboteurs, depending on their major field of concentration—could be lethal or ludicrous. They could resemble Prohibition gangsters, their faces glowing menacingly in the low-key darkness, their hat brims pulled down so severely that part of their faces seemed to be missing. They could also be bumblers, unworthy of such iconography.

In comic espionage, the spies cannot be so inept that they turn into zanies; they must be a menace, but a cartoon menace. The zany is the comic hero or heroine—Bob Hope, Judy Canova, Abbott and Costello—whose simplemindedness reaches such heights that it becomes a shield of simplicity, able to deflect the most sophisticated weapons.

In *They Got Me Covered* (1942), a Bob Hope comedy, the saboteur-spies work out of a Washington, D.C., beauty parlor. The film begins as farce; even Germany's invasion of the Soviet Union is played for laughs. After reassuring his newspaper that Hitler would abide by his pact with Stalin, Hope learns of the invasion, flees Moscow in disguise, and returns to Washington. En route, he tells another reporter, "You can't trust Hitler; he'd doublecross his best friend." "You're telling me," replies a Mussolini look-alike.

There is often an undercurrent of seriousness in comedy, even in a Bob Hope comedy. In *They Got Me Covered*, a burlesque queen tries to extricate herself from the clutches of the "swastickers" for whom she has been working, only to stagger off stage with a dagger in her breast. "Swastickers" is a misnomer; the saboteur-spies are a mix of Italians, Germans, and Japanese plotting to paralyze Washington by disrupting public services. Oddly enough, as a postmark (May 1941) indicates, the time of the film is pre-Pearl Harbor; yet at the end, as the villains are being carted off, Hope kicks a Japanese agent in the rear, saying "That's to save face"—a line that has meaning only in a post-Pearl Harbor context.

When Arch Obler was about to adapt Claire Booth Luce's play, *Margin for Error*, he began, as usual, with a treatment on which he wrote, "The Nazi murderers aren't funny. Not any more. I started to work on the treatment with that attitude which led me directly to the conclusion that I wanted to make a picture funny in itself and the devil with propaganda."[15] The treatment was dated 13 September 1941, but it was over a year before the final script was ready, and by then Obler was no longer associated with the project.

By the fall of 1942, the Nazis could be whatever one wished, but rarely human. If the Third Reich was ludicrous, anything it represented, even anti-Semitism, was ludicrous; and, if ludicrous, then comic. *Margin for Error*'s point of departure is the hiring of three Jewish policemen to guard the German consulate (the hub of espionage, as it is also portrayed in *Watch on the Rhine* and *The House on 92nd St.*). Whenever the film threatens to be serious, the outrageous intervenes: a parrot called Mr. Churchill dies of poisoned grapes; the grandmother of the consul's secretary is revealed to be Jewish; four Nazi longshoremen arrive to blow up a pier; and the consul himself inadvertently drinks the poisoned brandy he has prepared for another.

Most series protagonists had a chance to tangle with the enemy at least once during the war, for a series is unlike a serial in that the characters are not subject to the same laws of consistency required by an ongoing plot. They can be in uniform in one film; in mufti in the next. Laurel and Hardy, past their prime, had to settle for being air raid wardens (*Air Raid Wardens*, 1943), but Ellery Queen could battle secret agents, Charlie Chan could join the secret service, and the Dead End Kids could foil a Nazi spy ring (*Keep 'Em Slugging*, 1943) by using the same street tactics they had demonstrated in *Dead End*.

Saboteurs even lurk in the sagebrush. A Japanese agent masquerades as a Filipino cook (*Texas to Bataan*, 1942); cattle rustlers work with spies (*Texas Man Hunt*, 1942); the Nazis infiltrate Montana (*Valley of Hunted Men*, 1942); a barmaid extols the new order (*Cowboy Commandos*, 1943); saboteurs disrupt tent shows in Texas (*King of the Cowboys*, 1943).

Tarzan (Johnny Weissmuller) temporarily restrained from fighting Nazism in Tarzan Triumphs (1943). Courtesy RKO *Radio Pictures*

Having served their country on land, sea, and in the air, Abbott and Costello were allowed to defend the homefront in *Rio Rita* (1942), MGM's updating of the Broadway musical, now set on a Texas ranch where Nazi agents make radios in the form of artificial apples so fifth columnists can get their instructions through encoded commercials. Typical of the film's humor (though not of Abbott and Costello) is a dog's swallowing an apple and becoming a transmitter.

In 1943, Tarzan had two chances to match wits, or lack of them, with the enemy. When the State Department decided that Tarzan was "an important propaganda weapon," producer Sol Lesser set out to make a film that would illustrate the triumph of democracy in "Tarzan's quarter of the world."[16] *Tarzan Triumphs* (1943) takes its cue from Germany's intended conquest of Africa, from the southwest to the Sahara; it is set in mythical Polandria, a name that may elicit a smile from etymologists. Polandria is a jungle utopia soon to lose its utopian status when a contingent of Nazis arrives to implement the new order.

At first, Tarzan is indifferent to the Polandrians' plight: "Jungle people fight to live; civilized people live to fight," he mutters in one of the better examples of that rare trope, antimetabole (a worthy challenger of Molière's "One should eat to live, not live to eat"). It is only when one of the Nazis abducts Boy that Tarzan stops sulking: "Now Tarzan make war," he shouts, brandishing a knife. Nazis fall to its blade (when they are not being tossed over parapets). Even Boy shoots a Nazi, much to Tarzan's grinning approval.

The ending is pure Tarzaniana: The Nazis in Berlin, trying to make telephone contact with Polandrian fifth columnists, hear Cheeta chomping away at the other end. Assuming it is their Führer, they salute his picture, and the film ends with a close up of the chimp—the Führer reduced to simian status.

The mentality behind *Tarzan Triumphs* is more interesting than the film, which is one of the worst in the series. Tarzan has become the familiar politicized neutral, illustrating the principle that neutrality ends with the first taste of totalitarianism. Then, anything is justifiable—luring Nazis into lion traps and even nodding approvingly when a boy kills his first human. (But then, Nazis are not human.)

Ten months after *Tarzan Triumphs*, RKO released *Tarzan's Desert Mystery*, in which the ape man leaves his escarpment for the sands of the Sahara. There he meets the familiar stranded lady who has been entertaining the troops in North Africa with her magic act. If their meeting sounds improbable, the magician's mission seems incredible: she must deliver a secret message from a Yale-educated sheik to one of his former classmates. On the other hand, if prehistoric monsters from *King Kong* (1933) can be matted into the frame, and a "foreign agent" can be arming border tribes after El Alamein, there is no reason why a Yale graduate cannot be in an African village or why the magician cannot belt out "Boola Boola" in the market place to attract his attention.

The most logical candidate for confrontation with Nazis saboteur-spies was Sherlock Holmes. The series had just been reactivated at Universal when Lynn Riggs and John Bright refashioned Conan Doyle's "His Last Bow" into *Sherlock Holmes and the Voice of Terror* (1942), a film far more interesting than its source. The action is set in wartime London, where a mysterious voice broadcasts sabotage activity over the radio at the exact moment that it is occurring.

As far as authenticity is concerned, the espionage film has always been hit or miss. Since it is a genre where invention takes precedence over factual accuracy, ingenious plotting can compensate for historical errors, which is the case in both *Saboteur* and *Sherlock Holmes and the Voice of Terror*. Although Abwehr agents were operating in Britain in 1939–40, they were never as successful as they are in *Sherlock Holmes and the Voice of Terror*; many, in fact, were downright inept and showed it by their inability to master British currency, paying in pounds when shillings were required. However, Riggs and Bright were correct in having Holmes say at the end that all the agents had been rounded up, for those who were not executed or imprisoned became double agents.

The "voice of terror" is another matter; it is one of those minor inspirations, so easily overlooked in B movies. The voice was inspired by the broadcasts of Lord Haw-Haw, *né* William Joyce, an American-born Englishman. Formerly a member of Oswald Mosely's British Union of Fascists and later its propaganda director, Joyce was accused of embezzling party funds and finally left for Germany, where Goebbels hired him to demoralize the British over the radio, starting on 10 April 1939.[17] As Lord Haw-Haw, he tried to instill fear into the minds of his listeners by using the vocabulary of intimidation ("panic," "German avalanche," "annihilation"). However, his broadcasts had the opposite effect. At first, they were popular because they lampooned British traditions; they lost their appeal when they started attacking Churchill. In the film, however, the voice of terror is irony raised to the level of menace—omniscient, confident, and articulate.

While the premise of *Sherlock Holmes and the Voice of Terror* is Holmesian, the morality is not. It is wartime morality, the morality of expediency, which even Holmes espouses. To unmask the voice, Holmes persuades Kitty (Evelyn Ankers), a Cockney prostitute, to galvanize the rabble of Limehouse, who have been accused of being saboteurs. Playing on her patriotism and her lack of self-esteem, Holmes paints a picture few hookers with a conscience could resist: "Your friends will become an army, and you will be at their head." Limehouse, then, is the disaffected society that rallies when branded as Nazi—a designation even criminals resent. Kitty is not only converted; she also turns her assignment into a crusade in which the crusaders are equals: "There's only one side: England. It doesn't make any difference how high or low we are." If Kitty seems a bit to the left, it may have been because her creators, Lynn Riggs and John Bright, were a liberal and a Communist, respectively.

Holmes's manipulation of Kitty is in keeping with a principle that had been expressed earlier in *Paris Calling* and would be reiterated in *Notorious* (1946): the female agent's obligation to sleep with or marry her quarry if necessary. Kitty is the precursor of Alicia Huberman in *Notorious*, the loose woman turned patriot. One never loses sight of what Kitty is; the decolletage, blowsy manner, curled eyelashes, and lipstick-layered mouth serve as constant reminders. The Nazi whom Kitty must seduce is an Englishman, and it is Holmes who arranges the seduction. Kitty's task is made even more unpleasant by the Englishman's character. He is a Nietzschean superman who, at one point, recounts a childhood dream in which, armor clad, he tramples over the bodies of his inferiors. "What if this was no dream? What if it is prophecy?" he muses, glassy eyed.

The ending is tentative, as it must be in 1942. Kitty is shot, yet she "merits our deepest gratitude" as Holmes notes in one of the shortest eulogies on record. The rhetoric is reserved for the peroration, which is the parable of the east wind taken straight out of "His Last Bow"—the only time the screenwriters indicate any indebtedness to their source.

By promoting the myth of the ubiquitous spy, espionage melodrama complemented the propaganda posters that warned of agents who could eavesdrop on any conversation. Certainly one would not want to incur the wrath of the Uncle Sam who peered down from the post office wall, a finger pressed to his lips as he surveyed the line at the stamp window. Thus one was loath to speak even when there was nothing to divulge.

In its way, espionage melodrama helped maintain the unity that was indispensable to America's winning the war. Espionage had been divested of its glamour; no longer was it as romantic as it had been in *Mata Hari* (1932) and *The Spy in Black* (1939). Now it was the bane of the home front, ugly and sordid. With aircraft factories as likely targets of sabotage, films like *Saboteur* and *Joe Smith, American* (1942) suggested what might happen if the enemy infiltrated defense plants. In the latter, the title character (Robert Young) is an aircraft worker captured by agents of that notorious unnamed country. Even when he is tortured and pliers applied to his fingers, Smith refuses to reveal the bombsight information his captors want.

Joe Smith, American is relatively short, and since there is just so much one can take of Robert Young with one eye bulging and the other shuttered, much of the movie is flashback. Between beatings, Smith tries to think happy thoughts, which is not especially easy. Yet he succeeds in conjuring up memories of wife and child, so that love of country and family and the need to endure torture, if necessary, to preserve both become inseparable. One who does not talk is a true patriot, a Nathan Hale. The comparison is suggested at the beginning of the film when Smith junior mentions Hale, much to the embarrassment of his father who has never heard of him; it is confirmed at the end when Smith senior is feted by family and friends as the modern Nathan Hale.

If there are Nathan Hales, there are also Benedict Arnolds. In *Saboteur*, there is a gallery of traitors arranged hierarchically from ranch hands, sheriffs, ranch owners, and fifth columnists on Fifth Avenue to the title character himself. (There is even a prissy father who refuses to cut his son's hair because he always wanted a daughter—Hitchcock's equation of subversion with inversion).

Hitchcock deliberately wanted American types for the spies in *Saboteur*. For the role of Tobin, his first choice was Harry Carey, whose face belonged, if not on Mount Rushmore, then on a commemorative stamp. Mrs. Carey was outraged. "After all," she exclaimed, "since Will Rogers' death the youth of America have looked up to my husband."[18] But that is exactly why Hitchcock wanted Carey. By casting a beloved character actor as a fifth columnist, Hitchcock would be reminding audiences that even the most American of faces could belong to a Nazi. Hitchcock had to settle for Otto Kruger; the choice was obvious, but the lesson less effective. Still, Hitchcock showed how easily American society could be subverted and, indirectly, how the Hollywood western could help. *Saboteur* may be the only film in which the escaping hero is lassoed by Nazi cowboys on horseback.

Saboteur reaches its climax atop the Statue of Liberty where hero and villain confront each other. Hitchcock always excelled at defamiliarizing the familiar, making a shower bath a blood bath, Radio City Music Hall and the United Nations scenes of murder, and a carousel a merry-go-round of death. The statue in *Saboteur* is not the familiar lady with the torch; it looks like the Greek Ananke, Necessity—austere, forbidding. The first time the statue is seen, it looks as if it is about to topple over, as if liberty and all it represents are on the verge of tottering. When the saboteur falls over the railing surrounding the torch, he clings to the cleft between the thumb and index finger of the statue's hand. He is literally in the hand of liberty, yet his fate also depends upon another hand, a human hand—the hero's, extended in an offer of help. Hitchcock cuts from the hand of the statue to the hands of the two men trying to make contact; then to the hero's hand grasping the sleeve of the saboteur's jacket, which slowly begins to rip. There is a cold, rigid morality about the sequence. Somehow the Statue of Liberty stands for more than just freedom; it also stands for retribution. Liberty cannot tolerate the impious, much less hold him in her hand. Thus she lets the saboteur fall to the place of judgment below.

Hollywood did not miss the opportunity to explore the moral implications of espionage. If women were expected to sell themselves for their country, men might be expected to kill their brothers; it was even better if the brothers were German: one could be the "good German," and an act of fratricide would be a mark of patriotism.

MGM's *Nazi Agent*, completed a week after Pearl Harbor and released in early 1942, opens with a montage of trains being derailed, planes crashing, and bridges being dynamited as an offscreen voice demands that "America . . . stand guard and relentlessly ferret out this hidden enemy." The enemy is quite visible, however; it is none other than Conrad Veidt playing twins, one of whom is the good German, a naturalized American; the other, a Nazi. Even as children, they were different: one carried a book, the other a sword; as adults, one drinks milk, the other brandy. At least audiences can tell them apart. Since the Nazi twin is also a saboteur, the good German kills him; and since the murdered twin is a high-ranking Nazi, the good German assumes his identity and, to satisfy the Production Code, atones for his brother's ways.

Another—and better—dark *Menaechmi* is Republic's *Secrets of Scotland Yard* (1944), which despite its confessional title is first-rate espionage and one of the studio's classier efforts (indicated by the bell tower logo instead of the usual eagle in the clouds). Furthermore, it featured the venerable C. Aubrey Smith as head of Room 40, the legendary cryptoanalysis section of Scotland Yard. Since the twins are British, it is not a question of the good brother versus the bad one, but of the live brother versus the dead one. When the cryptologist brother is murdered, his twin, a Scotland Yard detective, takes his place in Room 40 and exposes the Nazi agent who has been planted there.

Secrets of Scotland Yard is another instance of a minor film that shows considerably more intelligence than many major ones. It is the only film of the period to explain the techniques of cryptoanalysis, particularly how page numbers of a book can provide the key to a code. In the film, the book is Hans Fallada's *Little Man, What Now?* (1933), a logical choice since many Germans would have read it. Books were indeed used in this way. It is known, for example, that a Hamburg radio station sent messages in a transposition cipher keyed to Rachel Field's novel *All This, and Heaven Too* (1938).[19]

When William Seebold, a naturalized American citizen, returned to his native Germany in the summer of 1939, his passport was stolen. It was all part of a scheme hatched by the Gestapo to recruit him as a spy—the gambit being that his Jewish grandfather's life would be endangered if he refused. Seebold salved his conscience by informing the FBI and working as a double agent. He was so successful that by June 1941 the FBI had rounded up thirty-three enemy agents. The

William Eythe, gun in hand, as the Seebold figure in The House on 92nd St. *(1945). Courtesy Twentieth Century-Fox Film Corporation*

Seebold case became the basis of two Fox films: *They Came to Blow Up America* (1943) and, to a great but unacknowledged extent, *The House on 92nd St.* (1945). In both films details of the case were blended with material from others, on the assumption that the Seebold case was not sufficiently interesting in itself to carry an entire film.

They Came to Blow Up America incorporated material from the case of the eight saboteurs whom Hitler dispatched to America in June 1942 in retaliation for the Seebold doublecross. Four of them landed on Long Island, the rest on the Florida coast; but before they had the opportunity to use their T.N.T., they were all apprehended. Six were electrocuted; one was sentenced to life imprisonment; and the last, George Dasch, who informed on his fellows, insisting he was really anti-Nazi, was given thirty years.[20] In the film Seebold is merged with Dasch to form Carl Steelman. At first, Steelman is a committed Nazi who returns to Milwaukee after three years in South America and starts preaching Third Reich propaganda to his father. Papa Steelman knows how to cure advanced fascism; he whips off his belt and before director Edward Ludwig can yell 'Cut!"

Carl is working for the FBI. Dispatched as a double agent to Abwehr school, he ends up as one of the eight saboteurs. At this point, history yields to fiction; Carl is told he must stand trial to make the conviction of the other seven more meaningful. While George Dasch received thirty years, one has to assume that Carl Steelman reverted to William Seebold before sentence was passed.

Perhaps the best known espionage film of the war years is *The House on 92nd St.*, "adapted from cases in the espionage files of the Federal Bureau of Investigation," as the opening title attests. "And from various films," it might have added, since the plot includes a *Gedaechtniskuenstler* or memory expert, not unlike Mr. Memory in Hitchock's *The Thirty-nine Steps*; a sleeper spy who was a former hairdresser on a German liner, as was the Johanna Hoffmann character in *Confessions of a Nazi Spy*; and a sex revelation as denouement in which the enigmatic master spy, Mr. Christopher, turns out to be a woman—the reverse of Hitchcock's *Murder* (1930) in which the killer is a male transvestite.

While *The House on 92nd St.* has never lacked admirers, it is hard to regard it as the landmark film it purports to be. One must take on faith the claim made by the opening title that the "story . . . could not be made public until the first atom bomb was dropped on Japan." But which story? There are two. The first, already made public both in the press and in Fox's earlier film, *They Came to Blow Up America*,[21] was nothing other than the Seebold case. Although the double agent is now called Bill Dietrich, the details are basically the same: the visit to Germany, the attempted recruitment for espionage, the disclosure to the FBI, the double agent's establishment of credibility as an engineering consultant.

It was the second story, the one with which the Seebold case was combined, that had to wait for the bombing of Hiroshima: the story of the plot to obtain Process 97, "the secret ingredient of the atomic bomb." Fox obviously wanted to be the first studio to usher in the atomic age. And screenwriters Barre Lyndon, Charles G. Booth, and John Monks, Jr., wanted a subplot for *The House on 92nd St.* The Seebold story needed a MacGuffin. But where to find one? In the files of the FBI, of course.

On 18 March 1941, Julio Lopez Lido was fatally injured in a New York traffic accident.[22] Lido was a Nazi agent; his real name was Ulrich von der Osten, code-named "Phil." On his body was found enough evidence to track down another agent, Kurt Friedrick Ludwig, code-named "Joe K."

The traffic accident would make a good opener; but since the war was over, the information found on the dead man should have nothing to do with anything as dated as supplies being sent to England, but with something far more relevant: the A-bomb. Thus, in *The House on 92nd St.*, when the Nazi agent, now called Ruiz, is killed in the accident, he is carrying a message in cypher: "Mr. Christopher will concentrate on Process 97." The writers had their MacGuffin, what the spies were after: Process 97.

Since Process 97 is identified early in the film as a component of the atomic bomb, there can be no suspense, only surprise; and the surprise is not that the spies fail to obtain it but that their leader, Mr. Christopher, is a woman. In film, discrepancies and inconsistencies are more easily overlooked than in literature where they can be checked by rereading. Thus it is easy to forget that, apart from the prologue and epilogue, which are contemporary (i.e., 1945), the main action of *The House on 92nd St.* is set in 1940–41. Process 97, which is never explained except as "the secret ingredient of the atomic bomb," must be something discovered after 1938, the year German scientists split a uranium atom. It cannot refer to the epochal nuclear chain reaction discovered by Enrico Fermi's group in December 1942. Process 97 would appear to be plutonium (atomic number 94, which may have suggested Process 97), discovered in 1940. However, the screenwriters were not thinking of plutonium, but of uranium 235, which in 1945 was such a taboo word that even a casual reference to it could result in surveillance, reproach, or firing;[23] hence the revised shooting script (16 April 1945) includes a parenthesis after the first reference to Process 97 "(Name withheld until release from proper authority can be obtained)." In *The House on 92nd St.*, as frequently happens in historical fiction, a present attitude was applied to the past; the atmosphere of secrecy that prevailed in 1945 was imposed on 1940–41.

When *The House on 92nd St.* opened six weeks after Hiroshima, the name was still withheld; the "proper authority" had not yet sanctioned the use of the forbidden word (which was uttered a year later in *Notorious*). It really does not matter that Process 97 is never identified. As the MacGuffin, it is an anticlimax, historically as well as dramatically. In the period covered in *The House on 92nd St.*, the main threat of atomic espionage was more likely to come from the Soviet Union than from Germany.[24] Fear of Germany's nuclear capabilities ultimately proved groundless; by 1944, the United States and Britain knew Germany had abandoned the idea of manufacturing an atomic bomb—a decision Hitler, never very interested in the bomb anyway, may have reached in November 1943 after the raid on the Norsk Hydro Plant in Norway, which, while it did not cut off

Germany's supply of heavy water, certainly hampered its atomic efforts.

The only parts of *The House on 92nd St.* that are genuinely historical are the prologue and epilogue—the documentary parts—which explains why the film never achieves the seamless blend of fact and fiction that later Fox semi-documentaries, especially *Call Northside 777*, do. The epilogue, in fact, is so accurate that it reduces the saboteur to the bogeyman of myth by asserting that during the war there was not a single act of enemy-directed sabotage. For all its realism, there is nothing in *The House on 92nd St.*—not even the scene in which Signe Hasso kicks off her pumps, pulls off her wig, and slips into a suit to become Mr. Christopher—to compare with Frye's fall from the Statue of Liberty in *Saboteur*, his arms extended as if to make contact but embracing only the void.

Although the Office of Strategic Services (o.s.s.) was not created until June 1942, for security reasons Hollywood was unable to dramatize its activities until after the war; even then, it was highly selective. Once the war was over, Paramount, Fox, and Warner Bros. lost no time in acquainting moviegoers with America's first intelligence agency. In 1946, each studio had a film about the o.s.s. in release: *o.s.s.* (Paramount), *13 Rue Madeleine* (Fox), and *Cloak and Dagger* (Warner Bros.).

In 1946 the studios had no difficulty finding former o.s.s. agents to act as technical advisers. For *o.s.s.*, Paramount secured the services of Commander John M. Shaheen, a former Chicago press agent who later became president of several international oil companies. For *Cloak and Dagger*, Warner Bros. hired Lieutenant Michael Burke, an ex-football player who went on to become president of the New York Yankees. The February 1947 *Movie Story* spotlighted Major Peter Ortiz as the technical adviser of *13 Rue Madeleine*. That same issue contained a synopsis of the film that began, "On June 13, 1942, a tired man in a wheelchair picked up a pen and signed a paper. . . . For with the signing of that historic document was born the Office of Strategic Services—o.s.s.—America's first real espionage service. To Washington as director came Colonel William J. (Wild Bill) Donovan, hero of World War I, and after him came thousands upon thousands of men and women of strange and varied talents."

Even as late as 13 May 1946, the script of *13 Rue Madeleine* called for the film to open with a homage to the o.s.s., followed by an extended prologue describing o.s.s. activities and methods of recruitment. The main character, Bob Sharkey (James Cagney), was a lawyer like "Wild Bill" Donovan. But when *13 Rue Madeleine* was released in 1946, too late for *Movie Story* to revise its synopsis and strike the profile on Major Ortiz, Sharkey had been demoted to an ex-serviceman, and the o.s.s. had become an embryonic army intelligence unit, code-named 077. All references to Donovan and his organization had been expunged. Apparently, Donovan had found some of the scenes objectionable, and "Fox promptly seized on this excuse to delete all references to o.s.s. and thus reduce competition from other o.s.s. pictures."[25] One can only speculate on which scenes offended Donovan, but it would seem more likely that he objected to the entire subplot, in which an o.s.s. trainee is really a German spy. Implying that the o.s.s. was susceptible to Nazi infiltration would undermine the credibility of the prologue, which stressed the security precautions taken in recruiting agents.

Actually, the subplot had more to do with expediency than truth. Fox planned *13 Rue Madeleine* as the companion piece to *The House on 92nd St.* with the same producer and director, Louis de Rochemont and Henry Hathaway, and one of the same screenwriters, John Monks, Jr. Monks and coscreenwriter Sy Barlett used the reverse of the situation in *The House on 92nd St.*, so that instead of an American agent's posing as a Nazi, a Nazi agent would pose as an American. Audiences had grown too accustomed to enemy agents infiltrating Allied intelligence to be deprived of a familiar convention, especially one that screenwriters found so easy to use.

However, *13 Rue Madeleine*'s real problems began even before Donovan raised his objections; they began when Joe Breen read the script. One might expect Breen to veto allusions to the L-tablets, the suicide pills that every o.s.s. agent was expected to take if captured and that Donovan himself had claimed he would swallow if necessary. But it was the denouement that bothered Breen.

Fearing that Sharkey, who has been captured by the Germans, will break under torture, Colonel Gibson (Walter Abel) authorizes a bombing raid on 13 Rue Madeleine, the Abwehr headquarters in Le Havre where Sharkey is being held. Gibson believes that as long as Sharkey can bear the pain, he will not talk, but that he probably cannot bear it. Breen, who had studied Thomistic philosophy, realized that Gibson was equivocating; he therefore insisted on the principle of double effect: if 13 Rue Madeleine was to be bombed, the reason had to be the destruction of the building, not the killing of Sharkey: "The general flavor of the revised lines, which we understand you will send on, should be that the fact that the American must die is unfortunate but that a job has to be done."[26]

Breen got his revision, but it was a Pyrrhic victory. He must have been satisfied with Gibson's saying that the building housed the Gestapo and "that's an important reason for destroying it." But Gibson goes on: "It's not the only reason. There's an American agent in that house, and if he talks, it may cost the lives of a great many American soldiers. Right now he's suffering the cruellest tortures the Germans can devise; but he won't talk. Not as long as he can stand the punishment; and no human body can stand it too long. . . ." And so, bomb the building and kill Sharkey—in that order, except that both will occur simultaneously.

o.s.s. does not equivocate; except for its dramatization of *o.s.s.* activity in France prior to the Normandy Invasion, it has little in common with *13 Rue Madeleine*. While the latter demythologizes intelligence work, stripping off the cloaks to reveal the daggers, *o.s.s.*, while not romanticizing it, portrays it within the context of boy meets/dislikes/loves/loses girl—boy and girl being *o.s.s.* operatives. Although Donovan's foreword gives *o.s.s.* the seal of approval, the film really marks the completion of Alan Ladd's wartime education; having advanced from apathy to commitment in *Lucky Jordan* and *China*, he now progresses from male chauvinism to a moderate feminism, to the extent of accepting women in intelligence work. Again, the instrument of his conversion is a woman who, the film would have us believe, is an average American, as it would have us believe of the typical *o.s.s.* agent. There was nothing average about Donovan's elite, however; many came from the whitest of the white collar professions: law, banking, college teaching, university administration, and the arts. Elaine (Geraldine Fitzgerald), a sculptress, educated in France, is hardly average.

Avoiding a documentary approach, *o.s.s.* illustrates the training of the operatives in an introductory montage of fast-moving scenes with rapidly delivered dialogue. The unorthodox methods of warfare mentioned in the foreword are also shown: explosives inserted in modelling clay and tubes of paint, revolvers shaped like pipes and so on. While both *13 Rue Madeleine* and *o.s.s.* stress the overriding importance of the mission, each does it in its own way, the former demanding stoic resignation from an agent hearing of a spouse's death; the latter allowing an agent to shed tears for a woman more valiant than himself. In *o.s.s.*, after Elaine is captured, Ladd returns to the deserted farmhouse from which she has been taken; in a display of emotion rare for Alan Ladd, he weeps for her, head in hand.

o.s.s. is a highly suspenseful film with some memorable scenes: an agent blanching with fear when he realizes a French waiter has seen him holding his fork in his right hand—American style, an escape that is almost thwarted when a car horn becomes stuck in traffic, a Nazi scrutinizing a hat in which a roll of microfilm has been concealed. *Cloak and Dagger*, on the other hand, has one memorable scene: Gary Cooper's fight with a Fascist, which illustrates a rule the recruits are taught in o.s.s.: "Forget everything you've ever been told about fair play and sportsmanship." Cooper does, and rather effectively from the point of view of the unit manager, who noted in a nasty memo (4 May 1946) that the fight was the only thing Cooper did well because it did not require his memorizing lines.[27] Cooper's difficulty with the dialogue was only one of several reasons for the film's being eighteen days behind schedule. The others were Cooper's digestive tract, which reacted negatively to the apples he had to eat for a particular scene; director Fritz Lang's bladder; and a script in need of shortening. In fact, the script needed more than shortening; it needed a different ending, as the studio realized after the film was previewed.

Consequently, those who saw *Cloak and Dagger* prior to its release saw one reel more than the general public would. And when some critics alluded to Cooper's "God have mercy on us" peroration, they were referring to a speech only they and a few others had heard.

The premise behind *Cloak and Dagger* is atomic espionage, which Hollywood rightly assumed would be an important postwar theme, with the atomic spies coming from whatever country happened to be America's arch foe. In *Cloak and Dagger*, the arch foe is still Nazi Germany. In the discarded last reel Nazi atomic production plants were shown housed in caves, on the order of the underground rocket research center at Peenemünde. Three of the plants were located and destroyed, the fourth transferred piecemeal to either Argentina or Spain—a strange choice, although it may suggest what the screenwriters, Ring Lardner, Jr., and Albert Maltz, thought of Peron and Franco. The closing scene was a prayer delivered by Cooper as an atomic physicist recruited into the o.s.s.: "God have mercy on us if we ever thought we could really keep science a secret—or even wanted to. God have mercy on us if we think we can wage other wars without destroying ourselves. And God have mercy on us if we haven't the sense to keep the world at peace."

An early Warner Bros. publicity release referred to the four plants and quoted the final line of the prayer. The revised publicity release of 29 August 1946, issued about five weeks before the film was scheduled to open, neither mentioned the plants nor quoted the line.

Fritz Lang did not know why the last reel was cut, although he suspected that Warners had decided not to darken the already low-

·ering mushroom cloud.[28] The studio must have realized that the final speech was not only critical of the bombing of Hiroshima but was also skeptical of America's ability to use atomic energy for peacetime purposes. (MGM did not have such problems with its A-bomb movie, *The Beginning or the End* (1947), which concludes with a speech from the grave delivered by a former scientist who is confident, as only a spirit can be, that "men will learn to use this [atomic] knowledge well.")

Warners was right in removing the final reel if it meant removing Cooper's Kyrie eleison. The peroration makes sense only in a post-Hiroshima context. In *Cloak and Dagger*, however, the Germans are still in Italy, so the time of the action would have to be 1943. The script had already experienced the kind of transmogrification found in mediocre à clef fiction where characters are patterned after historical figures but with such indifference to detail that they barely have anything in common with their counterparts. Alvah Jasper (Gary Cooper) is supposed to evoke J. Robert Oppenheimer, but only in that Jasper is a nuclear physicist. Likewise, Katerin Lodor, the female scientist in the film, might encourage one to think of Lise Meitner; but Lodor's murder rules out any further similarities. The best and most authentic part of the film, the cooperation between the O.S.S. and the Italian Communist underground, shows the screenwriters at their most knowledgeable. Since they were more interested in the Italian resistance than in the A-bomb, the scenes with the underground are the only ones that ring true.

Of the three O.S.S. films, only *O.S.S.* seems at all credible, perhaps because it is the only one to which Donovan lent his name as well as his support.[29] At least one believes Alan Ladd and Geraldine Fitzgerald can manage in French. Accepting James Cagney as an O.S.S. operative posing as a Vichy official or Gary Cooper as an atomic physicist working with the Italian resistance requires an act of faith.

6. Plotting the War

War itself is not dramatic; the real drama lies in the people caught up in it or in the events that lead to it. A battle is even less dramatic because it is plotless; its prelude is a battle plan, which, whether it is explained at a briefing session or diagrammed on a blackboard, is only talk. Even when the talk becomes action, it is still just sound and fury. When the sound and fury signify something, however, there is the possibility of drama; when they signify something human, there is the start of characterization; when the characters interact, there is the basis of a plot.

A combat script would seem relatively easy to write: battle action converted into dramatic action, an event decked out in narrative trappings. But screenwriters often had nothing more than an event to work from. When Paramount decided to make the first World War II combat movie, for instance, Will Burnett had only a title to go by: *Wake Island*. He had to work from the outside in, from the event to the plot. The battle dictated the title for which Burnett had to provide the story.

A greater challenge was the training film, but it was a challenge Hollywood failed to meet. The training film was a descendant of the military preparedness film—a promotional pitch for one of the services with a story line that sometimes consisted of training for a battle followed by the battle itself (e.g., *Gung Ho!*, 1943). One cannot say that nothing was learned from such movies; only that what was learned was not worth knowing. For example, in *Crash Dive* (1943), the hero, in one of the longest closing speeches on record, enumerates every vessel in the United States Navy from tender to cruiser, although the film is supposedly about the importance of the PT-boat. "The PT-boats are swell," the audience is told, but their significance is never dramatized (as it is in *They Were Expendable*

(1945), in which the PT-boat is the means of MacArthur's departure from Corregidor).

Zanuck knew that some training scenes were necessary in a film that focussed on a single branch of the service, merely to acquaint the audience with what happened after the recruits were sworn in. But when Fox decided to film Moss Hart's play, *Winged Victory* (1944), Zanuck wanted a minimum of training scenes. After a 15 May 1944 story conference, he wanted even less: "I realize the various tests were authentic, but I didn't want to see any more of them."[1] At one point, John Larkin had been called in to revise Moss Hart's screenplay, and increased Hart's two pages of tests (blood pressure, depth perception, psychiatric, etc.) to five. A compromise was finally reached, but it did not save a film that was virtually plotless.

Whether a war movie is a combat or a training film, it needs a plot. There are any number of plots, each with its own permutations, that are suited to war. Romance—two servicemen in love with the same woman (*Crash Dive, They Were Expendable*); one woman in love with two men (*Flying Tigers*, 1942); two service-women in love with the same man (*Cry Havoc*, 1943). Clash of wills—over strategy (*Bombardier*, 1943; *Fighter Squadron*, 1948) or personality differences (*Bataan*, 1943; *Sands of Iwo Jima*, 1949). Conversion—from agnostic to believer (*Destination Tokyo*, 1943; *God Is My Co-Pilot*, 1945); from wisecracker to fighter (*Air Force*), from playboy to hero (*Flying Tigers, Wing and a Prayer*, 1944). Odyssey—by air (*Air Force*); by sea (*Destination Tokyo, Action in the North Atlantic*, 1943); by land (*Objective, Burma!*, 1945). "And Then There Were None"—*Bataan, Manila Calling* (1942).

In a combat film, everything builds up to the climax, the battle whose outcome is often the denouement. In many cases, the real writing is done prior to the battle, which in itself is primarily visual and aural. Thus, if one closes one's eyes and just listens to a typical war movie, the conclusion consists largely of noise. It is the same principle behind any action film, especially the western, where the cavalry charge, the Indian attack, and the shoot-out are an avalanche of sound, little of it verbal.

Combat in the Pacific

Since *Wake Island* is the first World War II combat film and its production file is fairly complete, its genesis is worth tracing.[2]

Even before Wake Island fell on 23 December 1941, Paramount was planning a movie about it; the very act of holding out against

*Major Catton (Brian Donlevy) officiating at Lieutenant Cameron's burial in
Wake Island (1942), the first American World War II combat film. Eddie
Brandt's Saturday Matinee, courtesy MCA*

the enemy was enough to justify a film, whatever the outcome of
the battle. Thus it was neither ironic nor accidental that Will Burnett had completed an outline for a Wake Island movie on 23 December.

Burnett did not have an ending for his story since history was just
deciding one. But he did have a plot—the familiar "two men in love
with the same girl," the men being a major and a lieutenant whose
arrival at Wake Island was the means of introducing the other characters, all of whom were in a state of pre-Pearl Harbor somnolence.
It would be an "at dawn we slept" movie in which the characters,
as Burnett described them, would "stand for millions of Americans
. . . not disloyal—merely going their own ways, selfishly pursuing
their own aims, none of them actually giving a thought to the welfare or the probable fate of their country."

By 23 December, Burnett had gotten as far as the girl's death in
the Pearl Harbor attack, which was one way of eliminating rivalry
and awakening the somnolent. Three days later, he had an ending:

the major would die while radioing to Pearl Harbor that the Japanese had landed on Wake Island.

Over the next few months, Burnett acquired a coauthor, Frank Butler, and the film acquired five technical advisers from the Marine Corps plus a technical director and a wealth of information so confidential that the 24 March 1942 script carried a warning: "It is essential, that you exercise especial care in handling this script. Make certain that it is not read by unauthorized persons; and, except when absolutely necessary, do not take it out of the studio. Please do not discuss the script with anyone not connected with the picture."

One can only conjecture what "the extremely confidential information supplied by the U.S. Marine Corps" was. It may have been the fact that Japan's special envoy, Saburo Kurusu, had stopped off at Wake en route to Washington; that friction existed between the civilian construction workers and the military, particularly between Nathan Dan Teters, superintendent of construction for Contractors Pacific Naval Air Bases, and the Marine Corps. According to an eyewitness, Teters was "jealous of his position and determined that no one should get the idea that he was subject to military discipline of a routine nature."[3] Yet when the bombs started falling on 8 December Teters's first question was, "What can I do?"

In the film, Kurusu's clipper stops at Wake where the envoy expresses his "yearning for peace" before departing for Washington. Although the hub of the plot is still a clash between two men, one of them has been made a construction engineer; thus the major locks horns with a civilian, McCloskey, who is also a former college football star like "Big Dan" Teters. And when the attack on Wake begins, Major Catton and McCloskey patch up their differences and die as friends.

Screenwriters are notoriously tenacious of their material, discarding only what cannot be recycled. Rather than eliminate the lieutenant and the girl in the treatment, Burnett made them husband and wife, with the girl's death at Pearl Harbor becoming the wife's fate. Catton comes to regard the lieutenant as a surrogate son, a widower like himself, a man with memories: "From the time a man can remember, his main memories are those given to him by women. . . . Even those women he might like to forget—even they give him memories that might help sometimes. . . . You're like me, now—a man with a memory."

Although *Wake Island* appears to be a wartime quickie, its construction is by no means slapdash. There is no Yellow Peril propaganda, no resorting to the sound of battle as a substitute for dialogue. It is a film in which characters are paired and contrasted:

first, the major and the lieutenant; then, with the lieutenant's death, the major and the contractor. For contrast, there are the clowns, Doyle and Smacksie, who furnish comic relief but share the fate of their superiors. Thus, when the attack comes, it ends the lives of friends—men who found each other in battle.

Film historians tend to prefer *Guadalcanal Diary* (1943) to *Wake Island*, perhaps because the title sounds more literary or because the source was Richard Tregaskis's best seller of the same name. However, even aside from its low humor and lack of characterization, *Guadalcanal Diary* is just a series of vignettes, the only dramatic moment being William Bendix's improvised prayer to the unknown God that concludes with an "Amen" from the chaplain. Yet even that cannot compare with the scene in *Wake Island* in which the major is so overcome by grief that he is unable to finish the eulogy for the lieutenant. The men in *Wake Island* are human, all too human; those in *Guadalcanal Diary* are government issue.

The significance of Doolittle's Raid on Tokyo of 18 April 1942 was not lost on Hollywood: it was the first time in the war that Japan had been bombed, an event worthy of a film—or several films. It was a morale booster for Americans despite the fact that the bombs did little damage. The raid was filmworthy for another reason: eight fliers, forced to crash land in China, were tried as war criminals and sentenced to death, and three were actually executed. Reconstructing the trial would be a challenge to a filmmaker's imagination.

RKO came out with the first "raid on Tokyo" film, *Bombardier* (1943), which contains references neither to the raid nor to Lieutenant Colonel James Doolittle, although it is clear that the climactic bombing was America's first strike at Japan. The plot involves two friends at loggerheads over strategy: dive-bombing (Randolph Scott) versus high-altitude precision bombing (Pat O'Brien). The twist is that the method O'Brien advocates indirectly causes his friend's death. But duty comes before friendship, and all O'Brien can do is bid a tearful "Goodbye, Mr. Chips" to his buddy. (The twist would really have been ironic if Doolittle's Raid had been an example of high-altitude bombing, but it was not; it was an example of low-level flying—fifteen hundred feet, as opposed to bombing from twenty thousand feet, which is what O'Brien argues for.)

Although no one in *Bombardier* seems to know the difference between a B-17 and a B-25, the film at least has some kind of structure. *Thirty Seconds over Tokyo* (1944), on the other hand, does not have even the loose episodic form of *Guadalcanal Diary*. It consists of three related but disunited plots, each of which could inspire a separate film: the husband's departure for war, his crash landing in China and rescue by the Chinese, and his return to civilian life as a maimed veteran. The appearance of Doolittle (played with patriarchal sternness by Spencer Tracy) at the beginning and the end indicates that the raid is merely a framing device.

Yet a raid, or any military expedition, is no different from a battle in that it cannot sustain interest by itself; the screenwriter must search for something that will. Delmer Daves and Albert Maltz had such a problem with *Destination Tokyo*, which involves a preliminary expedition to the coast of Japan to obtain information that is transmitted by radio to Admiral Halsey's *Hornet*, the carrier from which the raid is launched. But even the landing is not enough to carry the film. Since no one episode can command attention for very long, the plot keeps bifurcating. Daves and Maltz try to make the captain (Cary Grant) the unifying force by giving him a sacerdotal aura, so that he becomes a skipper-priest with a sailor-flock. As a result, the whole crew of the *Copperfin* seems to be Christian: everyone knows the Lord's Prayer and can sing "It Came Upon a Midnight Clear." And since apparently only Christians die at sea, the skipper beseeches "Christ Jesus, Our Lord" to grant the departed eternal rest.

Such moments, while edifying, are pietistic filler. Fortunately, one of the writers read a news item in the *Chicago Daily News* or *Reader's Digest* about a pharmacist's mate who performed an appendectomy in a submarine by following instructions in an anatomy text. Or perhaps one or both of them heard Ranald MacDougall's radio play, based on the appendectomy story, in "The Man Behind the Gun" series. Whatever the source, the scene in which William Prince takes out Robert Hutton's appendix while Hutton dozes off saying the Lord's Prayer, slipping into unconsciousness with "Thy will be done" and and awakening with "And lead us not into temptation," is the only memorable one in the film.

Although it is better than *Thirty Seconds over Tokyo*, *Destination Tokyo* is still a formula film. There is nothing wrong with formulae as such; epic poets have used them as literary means to a narrative end. But the end in *Destination Tokyo* is not so much narrative as didactic. One expects didacticism in a closing title or a voice-over epilogue predicting an Allied victory or the coming of others to replace those who have been killed. That is old-fashioned, shoulders back, eyes front, pledge of allegiance patriotism. But now the posture is crooked; the shoulders sag, the eyes bulge, and the pledge is a catechism recitation. The drama the appendectomy has generated dissipates into a digression on agnosticism, and then on miracles, as the pharmacist's mate becomes a believer when he sees what his unskilled hands have wrought.

Agnosticism is also the theme of *God Is My Co-Pilot*, which, again, is only peripherally connected with the raid: it is the big event the hero misses when a B-17 bombing raid, to have coincided with Doolittle's, is cancelled. Still, he gets his chance to go "upstairs" with the Flying Tigers in China where, among other things, he learns to pray. Released in the spring of 1945, *God Is My Co-Pilot* seemed an excuse for a homily on perseverance, as if Warner Bros. were asking Americans to hang on for a few more months. The message was heard because *God Is My Co-Pilot* was a huge hit, even though it contains one of the worst anticlimaxes in film. It might have ended prosaically, but honorably, with the missionary's saying "more things have been brought about by prayer than the world dreams of." Instead, he goes on to recite a poem of faith, Don Blanding's "They Speak of God," which he had quoted earlier. However, no one seemed to mind: Warner Bros. was flooded with requests for copies, and ministers based their Sunday sermons on it.

God Is My Co-Pilot is at least based on fact—Colonel Robert Lee Scott's book of the same name; it also presents an accurate picture of the Flying Tigers, portraying them as mercenaries and depicting General Chennault, who organized the Flying Tigers, as an unorthodox commander with little use for "textbook pilots."

The Purple Heart, on the other hand, uses Doolittle's Raid as a springboard for fiction, but fiction of a special kind: embellished fact. The embellisher was Darryl F. Zanuck himself, under his Melville Crossman pseudonym, as author of the original story on which Jerome Cady based the screenplay. An author's note in the published screenplay states that *The Purple Heart* is "the author's conception of what may well have happened" to the eight fliers who were captured by the Japanese and put on trial.[4]

"What may well have happened" is phantasmagoric. The imaginary trial reconstructed in the film set jurisprudence back centuries. The Japanese do not observe the terms of the Geneva Convention; they do not even observe courtroom etiquette. When the fall of Corregidor is announced, the soldiers break into a ritual sword dance, disrupting the trial.

The Purple Heart leaves only memories of violence. Farley Granger (who lost his sight in *The North Star*, 1943) loses his speech in *The Purple Heart*. When it is his turn to be taken from the cell for interrogation, one wonders how he will return; his buddy has come back unable to use his hands. When Granger rejoins the others, he cannot speak, though he is able to open his mouth wide enough to show his tongue. One can only guess what was done to him. But that is the point of the film: it is an exercise in "what may well have happened." What may have happened to a pilot unable to talk is anybody's guess.

While there was more drama in the Philippines than in Doolittle's Raid, it all centered on one person: Douglas MacArthur, whose story, even when it reached the screen (*MacArthur*, 1977), was told with almost the same reverence the mere mention of his name received in the forties.

Hollywood regarded MacArthur as a deity, occupying a place in the same pantheon with Jesus Christ and President Roosevelt, and treated him with the same delicacy on the screen. Christ was a presence, a silhouette (*The Last Days of Pompeii*, 1935). Only once did President Roosevelt allow himself to be impersonated on the screen—by Captain Jack Young in *Mission to Moscow* (1943). Otherwise, moviegoers had to be satisfied with a look-alike (e.g., the character in *Yankee Doodle Dandy* known only as "The President") or a trademark (e.g., the Scottish terrier resembling Fala in *Princess O'Rourke*, 1943). The only film of the forties in which MacArthur appears as a character is *They Were Expendable*. Not only is MacArthur's aura maintained by an unidentified actor's impersonating him, it is enhanced by the way the general is photographed—in extreme long shot, striding toward the PT-boat that will take him from Corregidor to Mindanao, "The Battle Hymn of the Republic" accompanying each step he takes. The mood is so solemn, the departure so processional, that an awestruck sailor asks the deity to autograph his hat, probably hoping it will take on the same numinosity as the general's gold-braided cap.

By 1950 long shot had contracted to medium shot, the lighting had become brighter, and "The Battle Hymn of the Republic" had yielded to "The Stars and Stripes Forever." But the reverence lingered on. At the end of *An American Guerrilla in the Philippines* (1950), MacArthur, played by Robert Barrat (who, unlike his anonymous predecessor, received billing), returns—not wading ashore at Leyte, as the newsreels showed him, but waving from a jeep to throngs of cheering Filipinos.

Even in 1950, there was no criticism of "Dugout Doug"; no mention of MacArthur's being a victim of Roosevelt's "Europe first" policy, which resulted in his being ordered to Australia in March 1942 and in the abandoning of the Philippines. In *An American Guerrilla in the Philippines*, when Tyrone Power finds a pack of cigarettes with MacArthur's "I shall return" stamped on it, he bitterly repeats the celebrated promise; but Micheline Presle immediately replies that he will return "and when he does, it'll be all right again."

That kind of dialogue about MacArthur is typical: skepticism countered by faith, criticism answered by defense. Even prisoners of war defend MacArthur. In *The Purple Heart*, when a Japanese officer tries to undermine an American's faith in MacArthur, the American gives the party line: "General MacArthur undoubtedly received orders to leave. . . . I imagine he found his orders as difficult to obey as we find ours." Perhaps the most pathetic defense of MacArthur comes from the doomed hero in *Manila Calling* (1942): "General MacArthur promised that he'd be back. Be ready for him because he will be back. He never made a date yet that he didn't keep. If you don't believe me, ask Mrs. MacArthur. Yeah, and ask little Arthur MacArthur, too."

If MacArthur's troops knew they were being sacrificed for a policy that called for Germany's defeat before Japan's, they were not to show it—in the movies, that is. Instead, they must say that "General MacArthur needs time to reorganize" (*Bataan*); or that "he's needed more there [in Australia] than he is here [in the Philippines]" (*So Proudly We Hail*, 1943). They can be allowed a moment of self-pity, but anything more is grounds for a brawl. In *Bataan*, the cynical Todd (Lloyd Nolan) mocks a Moro who still believes reinforcements will arrive. Todd asks Sergeant Dana (Robert Taylor) to bury him and the others face down to spare them from searching the skies for B-17s that will never come. To Dana, these are fighting words.

Todd was behaving like a real "battling bastard of Bataan," the sort that called MacArthur "Dugout Doug" and made up crude verses about him sung to the tune of "The Battle Hymn of the Republic," which makes the use of that hymn in *They Were Expendable* so ironic. But in the movies, the abandoned of Bataan rationalize their desertion by calling it a holding action: by buying time for their country, they are winning the war. It is the kind of rationalization, however, that results in hyperbole and contradiction: "the men who died here [on Bataan] may have done more than we'll ever know to save this whole world" (*Bataan*); "we haven't a chance, but we're winning the war . . . that's why this little peninsula is so important" (*Cry Havoc*).

Historically, the abandoned of Bataan were not so accepting; when they dubbed themselves "the battling bastards of Bataan" with "no mama, no papa, no Uncle Sam," they were admitting that they were the losers in a trade-off. But "bastard" is a vulgarism, forbidden by the Code. Thus the Red Cross nurses in *So Proudly We Hail* are more genteel: they call themselves "the battling orphans of Ba-

Robert Taylor firing away at the end of Bataan *(1943). Courtesy* MGM/UA

taan"—the difference being that an orphan can be adopted, but there is no salvation for a bastard.

The fall of Bataan was a problem for Hollywood: how could defeat, much less the largest single capitulation in America's history, be ennobled? The answer was to make the same distinction between defeat and destruction that Hemingway would in *The Old Man and the Sea* (1952): "A man can be destroyed but not defeated." A Bataan or a Corregidor film must end on a heroic note—certainly not with the ignominious death march. The march cannot be shown but only suggested; and then it must look like a recessional, as it does in *They Were Expendable* when the men left behind walk along the beach in the moonlight to an unspecified but easily inferred fate.

The heroes of Bataan must die with dignity. At the end of *Bataan*, Dana, having dug a grave for each of his men, now digs his own. Until he dies, his grave serves as his foxhole. As the enemy approaches, the camera tracks in for a close-up of the muzzle of his machine gun; a superimposed title rolls up the screen, justifying the death it refuses to show: "So fought the heroes of Bataan. Their sacrifice made possible our victories in the Coral Sea, at Midway, on

New Guinea and Guadalcanal. Their spirit will lead us back to Bataan."

With MacArthur reduced to a presence, and Bataan to a holding action that led to the miracle at Midway, plots became scarce. The inspiration for *So Proudly We Hail* came from a news story about eight American nurses who were evacuated from Corregidor to Australia in May 1942. MGM was able to release two Bataan films in 1943, *Bataan* and *Cry Havoc*, because the latter was an adaptation of a play, Allan R. Kenward's *Proof Thro' the Night* (1942),[5] which had failed on Broadway but which MGM believed would make a good movie because the all-female cast it required would be a diversion from male-dominated combat films.

While *Cry Havoc* originated as a play, *Bataan* was an original script, but not one that was especially difficult to write. The plot is the "cross section of humanity" kind—thirteen men from different branches of the service, different religions, and different races—with an "and then were were none" resolution as the death of the last brings the film to its close.

Bataan's epilogue promised a return—"back to Bataan." RKO fulfilled that promise two years later in a film with exactly that title. The year before, MacArthur had also fulfilled his promise when, on 20 October 1944, he waded ashore at Leyte and shortly thereafter proclaimed, "I have returned." *Back to Bataan* (1945) does not celebrate that historic return; it is simply RKO's attempt to wring a film out of the Battle of Leyte Gulf, the first stage in the liberation of the Philippines. Since the victory at Leyte cannot sustain an entire film, it is tacked on at the end, completing a retrospective of the war in the Philippines that begins with the tragedy of Bataan. In between is the story line: pages from the Philippines resistance interleaved with a romance between a guerrilla and a patriot posing as a Filipino "Tokyo Rose."

Leyte occurred in October 1944; *Back to Bataan* was scheduled for a late May 1945 release. Thus the script needed something contemporary—circa 1945. Since the papers were filled with news about the Philippines, it was easy to find something pertinent; and since the plot was so general, whatever the screenwriters came up with would fit. The writers decided on the liberation of the Japanese prison camp at Cabanatuan on 30 January 1945, with newsreel shots of the liberated men for prologue and epilogue, and voice-over narration that slights neither the Americans who worked with the guerrillas nor the U.S. Rangers who joined the guerrillas to raid the camp.

While MGM had the honor of making the first film to bear the name of Bataan, it was PRC that laid claim to "Corregidor." The OWI was especially proud of the assistance it gave PRC with *Corregidor* (1943); yet if the result is indicative of what the OWI had to offer Hollywood, it would seem that Hollywood could have managed by itself.

Corregidor, advertised as "Twenty-eight Days of Epic Heroism That Shook the World," recalls *Wake Island* with Frank Jenks and Rick Vallin standing in for William Bendix and Robert Preston— always arguing, bragging about their conquests, but dying bravely when the chips are down. The friendship in *Wake Island* between the major and the contractor appears as a love triangle (husband/ wife/wife's lover) with an interesting variation: the principals are all doctors, including the wife (Elissa Landi in her last film role). Before the husband is conveniently killed, he tells the lovers they belong together, comparing the "blood red rock" (had the screenwriters, Doris Malloy and Edgar G. Ulmer, been reading T.S. Eliot?) of Corregidor with Mount Sinai. The biblical parallel is reinforced at the end when the recently evacuated Landi stands against a tree by a river, with a shot of Mount Sinai superimposed over her face.

The War in Europe

The Longest Day (1959), Cornelius Ryan's epic account of the Normandy invasion, was fifteen years away from being published, and the film version sixteen years away from being made, when Hollywood started taking an interest in Normandy. The interest developed slowly: an allusion, a denouement, a setting for a love story, and finally a reenactment. Before Zanuck recreated the first twenty-four hours of 6 June 1944, Normandy was the climax of the war in Europe (*The Master Race*, 1944), the event for which the O.S.S. prepared the French resistance (*O.S.S.*, *13 Rue Madeleine*). Then, when Warner Bros. was making *Fighter Squadron* (1948), Jack Warner decided it should end with the Normandy offensive.

Although *Fighter Squadron* is memorable only for Rock Hudson's film debut, it is an interesting example of the way an event that could not even have been simulated in 1948, when the industry was retrenching, could be incorporated into a movie without affecting the budget.[6] Since *Fighter Squadron* was designed as a paean to the Air Force (which was so pleased with the result that it used the movie for instructional purposes), Warners was given access to the Central Film Depository at Wright-Patterson Air Force Base to select whatever stock color footage it wanted. Although the navy also loaned the studio footage and the Coast Guard supplied a print of its *Normandy Invasion*, it was the Air Force that approved the script, supplied the technical advisers, counselled screenwriter Seton I. Miller on how fighter squadrons were designated, and made Oscoa (Michigan) Air Base available for exteriors.

Once the Normandy footage was obtained, it had to be integrated with the plot as the logical culmination, not as an afterthought. Since it had already been determined that the hero would die, he might as well perish on D-Day, plummeting into the Channel in his flaming Thunderbolt. However, he has to live long enough to see the plot through to its climax. The hero, Major Hardin (Edmond O'Brien), gets to Normandy in a circuitous way. First he battles with the wing commander to make fighters better covers for bombers. Here Miller was on the right track. Fighter escorts were always running out of fuel, but if they were equipped with fuel containers ("belly tanks") that could be dropped when empty, the fighters could escort the bombers to their target. Once that problem was solved, the fighters could participate in the bombing of Germany.

To get the hero from the skies of Berlin to the clouds above Normandy, Miller implies that the experience the fighters gained in low-level flying over Germany enabled them to provide target cover on D-Day. As a result, those knowing nothing about D-Day might think Normandy was an aerial offensive. But a movie celebrating the Air Force, whose role in the Normandy campaign was unquestionably significant, is not going to show a beachhead; especially not a movie dedicated to "those who streaked across the skies to make possible the victory below"—a claim that anyone who was part of the greatest armada in history would consider something of an exaggeration.

In *D-Day the Sixth of June* (1956), Normandy has shrunk to a pre-invasion maneuver and a means of sending a potentially adulterous husband back to his wife. Although it is a Fox film, it is not one that Zanuck had nurtured. Zanuck was eager to make a Normandy movie, but the year *D-Day the Sixth of June* was released, Zanuck left his position at Fox as head of production to form his own company.

Zanuck never stopped fighting World War II. It was his war; it made him Lieutenant Colonel Zanuck; it won him the Legion of Merit; it gave him the friendship of Eisenhower, Mark Clark, Mountbatten, and Montgomery. Even when the political climate in America changed and the Communists replaced the Nazis and Japanese as arch villains, Zanuck still assumed audiences wanted movies about World War II. The truth was that he still wanted to make movies about World War II because he wanted to rethink and re-live it.

Although America had not grown politically wiser, Zanuck had. He would never make another *Purple Heart*. Between 1949 and 1952, Fox's World War II films became less monolinear and more psychological. They showed what war could do to men: it could give them breakdowns (*Twelve O'Clock High*, 1949) or migraines (*Halls of Montezuma*, 1950). But if the war that made men crack up or pop pills was World War II, that was all right because it was a war worth fighting.

At the end of *Halls of Montezuma*, Anderson (Richard Widmark) smashes his bottle of pain-killers after he hears what a pharmacist's mate had written before he died: "If any part suffers, all suffer; if any part loses freedom, all will lose it." Afterward, Anderson no longer needs the pills; the pain, bred of doubt and despair, is bearable because he understands his place, and that of World War II, in the scheme of things.

In his mildly revisionist way, Zanuck presented an alternative picture of the Axis. War may mean that wives in British North Borneo must be separated from their husbands, that they must be interned and even assaulted by their Japanese captors; but with Sessue Hayakawa in charge, as he is in *Three Came Home* (1950), who can be critical? How often does a Japanese officer ask a writer for her autograph or win the writer's sympathy when his family is killed at Hiroshima?

At Fox even the Nazis and their agents changed. In the forties, selling information to the Third Reich was traitorous. When James Mason does it in *Five Fingers* (1952), one cheers; Mason is so urbane, so eager to retire to Rio de Janeiro, that he is irreproachable. The previous year, Mason played a sympathetic Rommel in *The Desert Fox* (1951); after *Five Fingers*, he was loaned to MGM for Brutus in *Julius Caesar* (1953). The tragic Nazi, the upwardly mobile spy, the Roman idealist are all the same. Joining a plot to assassinate Caesar is no different from supporting one to kill Hitler. Even before Mason played Brutus, he played Rommel as Brutus, presumably with Zanuck's approval.

It was inevitable, then, that when Zanuck finally made his Normandy film, *The Longest Day* (1962), the Germans would not be the usual menacing clods; the film was as accurate a reconstruction of the Normandy invasion as eight million dollars could buy; and six screenwriters (Cornelius Ryan for the basic screenplay, with contributions from James Jones, Romain Gary, David Pursall, and Jack Seddon—and, of course, Zanuck) could write; and five directors

(Ken Annakin, Elmo Williams, Andrew Marton, Bernard Wicki—and, of course, Zanuck) could film.[7]

The production was so monumental that it discouraged emotion; thus it is impossible to gloat when Rommel, convinced the weather precludes a 6 June invasion, decides to return to Germany for his wife's birthday; or when Field Marshall von Rundstedt dismisses a report that the BBC has broadcast the second line from a Verlaine poem, the signal to the French resistance that the invasion is on. For the Germans, Normandy was tragic inevitability without real tragedy—only irony. Yet it was an irony Americans could appreciate, since it was the same irony they knew when the Pearl Harbor attack, anticipated during the last weekend of November, occurred during the first weekend of December.

Although *The Longest Day* cries out to be liked, it can only be respected. It is a throwback to Fox's postwar semi-documentaries—dispassionate, objective, reportorial. Only now there are time and place titles ("Omaha Beach 0.644 hours") and tripartite cutting between the Allies, the Axis, and the resistance. But there is no plot: Normandy is its own plot, proving again that battles, even epic ones, are only events, without genuine characters to lend them dramatic significance. In *The Longest Day*, the characters are the cast—an international one featuring the best of the United States (John Wayne, Robert Mitchum, Henry Fonda, Robert Ryan, Robert Wagner, Rod Steiger), Britain (Richard Burton, Richard Todd, Sean Connery, Leo Genn, Kenneth More), France (Bouvril, Jean-Louis Barrault, Arletty, Madeleine Renaud), and Germany (Curt Jurgens, Werner Hinz, Gerd Froebe, Peter Van Eyck).

For Zanuck, *The Longest Day* had to be a blockbuster; it was his comeback film. Darryl F. Zanuck Productions had not had a single hit since it was formed in 1956. To come up with a winner, Zanuck gave audiences not stars but a pantheon: "I wanted the audience to have a kick. . . . Everytime a door opened, it would be a well-known personality."[8] But the door opened too often, revealing personalities, not persons. While Zanuck thought World War II scenarios that mingled love and war or love and friendship were passé, a painstaking re-creation was not the answer; what was gained in authenticity was lost in humanity. Yet Zanuck would not abandon the academic approach, and would elevate it to the level of a revisionist dissertation in *Tora! Tora! Tora!* (1970).

The only human moment in *The Longest Day* comes at the end when a young GI asks a wounded RAF pilot, "I wonder who won." The line is a good commentary on the confusion that existed during the invasion (planes off course; lost paratroopers, including the one who landed on the steeple of the church at Sainte-Mère-Eglise); but it also explains indirectly why Normandy could never be filmed as it happened: it is a battle with too many winners—over one hundred eighty thousand. *The Longest Day* exemplifies the mistake Horace warned against in the *Ars Poetica* when he cautioned writers against tackling an unmanageable subject like the Trojan War, suggesting instead that they select one aspect of it, like the wrath of Achilles, as Homer had done in the *Iliad*. Normandy was too vast even for Darryl F. Zanuck.

Italians were impossible to dislike even when they belonged to the Axis. Thus, Hollywood never treated Italy as an enemy, preferring to regard Italian Fascism as a temporary aberration that would cease with the ouster of another temporary aberration, Mussolini. That six Italian divisions fought with the Afrika Corps did not seem to matter; the Italians in the desert war were either harmless *buffi*, like the general in *Five Graves to Cairo* (1943) who always complains about getting the "end of the stick that stinks," or penitents, like Giuseppe in *Sahara* (1943) who begs not to be judged by his insignia: "Only the body wears the uniform."

When Italy declared war on Germany on 13 October 1943, she became, if not an ally, a cobelligerent; she also qualified for a movie—for three, in fact, all 1945 releases: *A Bell for Adano*, *The Story of G.I. Joe*, and *A Walk in the Sun* (which did not officially premiere until January 1946).

All three were adaptations, *The Story of G.I. Joe* being the most difficult to adapt since it was based on Ernie Pyle's war vignettes. *A Walk in the Sun* and *A Bell for Adano* derived from novels by Harry Brown and John Hersey, respectively.

The only real Italians appear in *The Story of G.I. Joe*. In *A Bell for Adano*, they are simple but depthless; fascism has made them so acquiescent that Major Joppolo must reeducate them to think democratically. However, his theory that the government is the servant and the people are the master would result in anarchy if put into practice. Yet Joppolo is so successful that the people of Adano hang his portrait where Mussolini's once was. One can respect *A Bell for Adano* for exposing military bureaucracy; on the other hand, military bureaucracy is easy to expose.

There are no Italians in *A Walk in the Sun*, only a couple Italian-Americans, part of a platoon that has landed at Salerno with the objective of blowing up a bridge and taking a farmhouse. In fact,

Italians come in for some harsh criticism. Fascism is "their own fault" because "they let themselves be sold a bill of goods that they were going to boss the world."

Although screenwriter Robert Rossen could not divest himself of his antifascism, he could still have written the kind of unpretentious and forthright script for which he was known. Instead, he tried to out-Hemingway Hemingway with dialogue of lyrical toughness and tortured repetition: "Maybe too many soldiers have been walking on it [the soil]. They have been walking on it for a long time. That's what always happens to a country when soldiers walk on it."

One of the characters, appropriately named Windy (John Ireland), is writing a letter to his sister, but he really seems to be writing the script; Windy is the film's implied narrator, the collective consciousness through which everything is filtered, even the interior monologues of the other men.

Conceived as a gritty prose poem, *A Walk in the Sun* is really a gritty tone poem double framed, first, by a book cover that opens at the beginning and closes at the end; then, by a ballad sung as prologue and epilogue. Lewis Milestone's direction matches the arty framing. Milestone, who proved he knew how to shoot war films with *All Quiet on the Western Front* and *Edge of Darkness*, abandoned tracking for montage and realism for pictorialism; faces loom out of the darkness as if they had broken through the veil of night; bullets are fed through a machine gun at a rate only a lover of Eisensteinian montage can appreciate. If "nobody dies," as everyone in the film keeps saying, the reason is that montage makes death a euphemism; "nobody dies" because everybody expires.

At the end, Windy writes his sister, "We just blew up a bridge and took a farm house. It was so easy—so terribly easy." He might have been summing up *A Walk in the Sun*.

Since the best often comes last, it should be no surprise that the best World War II combat films arrived at the end of the war and at the end of the decade: *The Story of G.I. Joe* and *Battleground* (1949), both directed by William Wellman. Neither film is the standard case of a plot fitted on to a battle; neither is fictionalized history. Each portrays the war in microcosm—the Italian Campaign, the Battle of the Bulge. Each shows that war is not all combat; it is also what transpires between the combatants as well as between the combatants and the victims of combat—the people in the towns and villages that the G.I.s enter.

The Story of G.I. Joe is quietly atypical. There is no antifascist dialogue and relatively little tracking; just straight cutting and close-ups. Panning occurs only when the situation requires it: when the men listen to Axis Sally singing a sentimental song or when they gaze enviously at a truck that has been converted into a bridal suite for two newlyweds. Otherwise the camera is unobtrusive; it wants to record the responses of people, real people—an endangered species in most combat films.

Howard Hawks claimed some of his films were male love stories; William Wellman could have said the same of *The Story of G.I. Joe*. Initially, he was unsympathetic to the subject. As a former member of the Lafayette Flying Corps during World War I and as the director of *Wings* (1928), one of the greatest aviation films ever made, Wellman was put off by a script that glorified the infantry.[9] Yet, after reading Pyle's *Brave Men* and meeting the author, he went ahead with it, even though in the film Pyle (Burgess Meredith) bitterly contrasts the way infantrymen and fliers die—the former "miserably dressed," the latter "clean shaven." These miserably dressed men look anything but heroic. They are actors in a drama they have not written and often do not understand. Their bewilderment is not of the "I wonder who won" kind; they are not that ingenuous. Instead, they vow to buy a map when they return to the States to find out where they have been. Even the Lothario is not the moronic macho that Dane Clark usually had to play; in *G.I. Joe*, he at least has a sense of subtlety: "I dream in technicolor," he sighs, digging his feet into the earth.

G.I. Joe is a religious film, but its religion is unforced. The men pray because they want to, not because a screenwriter thinks they should. War does not respect the privacy of prayer. A G.I. kneels at the altar while a sniper is shot down from the belfry. A wedding takes place in a gutted church; the chaplain has no sooner pronounced the couple man and wife than he shouts "Hit the dirt," as the bombs start falling.

The couple spend their wedding night in the back of a truck, their feet sticking out of an opening in the canvas. This may have been the first time since 1934 that a man and a woman slept alongside each other and not in the mandated twin beds. Perhaps Joe Breen consented because a truck could not accommodate twin beds; or perhaps the visibility of the couple's toes implied they were sleeping on their backs.

The only disturbing note in the film is the justification of the Allied bombing of Monte Cassino, one of the most controversial acts of the war. The Benedictine monastery is not mentioned by name, but it is clear that the "monastery" referred to is Monte Cassino. The voice-over narration that has been so assured now grows cautious. The voice justifies the bombing on the grounds that human life is more important than a building, but it declines to give the reason for the bombing, which, historically, was that the Allies believed the Germans were using the monastery as an observation point—an assumption that was later disproved. Although the bombing scene is brief, it is the only time the film falters, as if it wants to say more; perhaps to question what it has shown, perhaps to apologize.

The Story of G.I. Joe does not make the usual distinction between conqueror and conquered. The mutual devotion the Americans and Italians feel for each other creates a different distinction: that between liberator and liberated. But the distinction soon fades as a reciprocal relationship develops. What the liberators give the liberated is matched by what they receive from them—a lesson in survival, in life continuing amid death.

At the end, when Walker is killed, Dondaro kneels by his side, holding his hand and on the verge of bending over to kiss him; but the hands about to cup Walker's face only straighten his collar. The ritual completed, Dondaro rises and joins the others as they march against a sky that whitens to contrast with their silhouettes. The final image is one of stark monochrome; its beauty, that of an ink sketch of black figures so completely assimilated with a white background that there is not even the illusion of depth.

It is hard to say how many years should elapse between an event and its fictional recreation. Some would say fifty, citing *War and Peace* as an example. But the best American World War II novels appeared a few years after its close: Mailer's *The Naked and the Dead* (1948), John Horne Burns's *The Gallery* (1948), James Jones's *From Here to Eternity* (1951). It was even earlier with the American combat film: *G.I. Joe* a month after V-E Day, *Battleground* four years later.

Before it could achieve any artistic importance, the combat film had to evolve into something beyond battles and beachheads; but it could only do that when the war was winding down or over, when the war could be understood as a conflict that, for all its horrors, was able to reveal something about the combatants that would never have come out in peacetime. In *G.I. Joe* and *Battleground*, movie males had finally reached their higher form. Previously they had appeared, for the most part, in their lower form—as stereotypes: the smarmy womanizer, the sergeant whose skin was hide, the hayseed who only needed hay in his hair to complete the image, the dreamer.

Jarvess (John Hodiak) and "Abner" (Jerome Courtland) in Battleground
(1949), one of the finest American World War II films. Courtesy MGM/UA

whose eyes were pools of introspection but nothing else. Now males
had become men; they had gone from creatures of gender to beings
with sex; they had finally turned human.

Like *G.I. Joe, Battleground* also grew out of an event: the Battle of
the Bulge, in which screenwriter Robert Pirosh had fought. Remembering the brutal winter of December 1944, he was able to integrate
it with the plot. The weather made warmth, in both the physical
and emotional sense, vital to the men of the Third Platoon. The
desire for warmth pervades the film, starting as the need for physical
proximity and progressing to the desire for spiritual union. The men
sleep close together, each drawing heat from the other; but the other
is the opposite, and warmth comes from the attraction of opposites.

Jarvess (John Hodiak) is the college man of the platoon; his buddy
is not someone even moderately intelligent like Layton (Marshall
Thompson) or "Pop" (George Murphy), but a rube, "Abner" (Jerome
Courtland), who speaks like his comic strip counterpart: "That's for
sure, that's for dang sure"—an expression that infuriates the trilin-
gual Jarvess. Yet when "Abner" is killed, Jarvess starts using his sig-

nature phrase. The two naifs, Layton and Hooper (Scotty Beckett), are separated soon after joining the platoon. Hooper dies, and Layton, once a babe in the wood, becomes a man of the world, smoking a cigarette rakishly as he marches into Bastogne. Layton becomes Wolowicz's buddy; when Wolowicz is wounded, he bequeathes Layton to Holley (Van Johnson), noting, by way of endorsement, that "he sleeps warm and quiet."

The men in the platoon speak with an openness that is neither masculine nor feminine and certainly not androgynous. Yet it is an openness that probably would not have been seen in civilian life, because it reveals traits that men are trained to conceal, like resentment over a friend preferring another's company. Jarvess's refusal to spend his leave with anyone from the platoon makes the others feel inferior because none of them is his "speed." They can speak of one man's being another's speed because they have become a group with its own mores and idioms, although some idioms, in civilian life, would be more suited to women.

Battleground is one of the few war films to make terrain and weather integral to the action, with nature supplying the imagery and symbolism. "Abner's" death precludes his ever kicking off his shoes again, but they are still present, lying in the snow as nature's artifacts. Rodriguez (Ricardo Montalban), who as a Californian revels in his first sight of snow, is buried in a grave of snow by his surrogate father, "Pop."

While many films come full circle, *Battleground* first reverses, then repeats, its beginning. Although it opens and closes with the singing of "Sound Off," there is a difference. Initially, the men had spirit because they were untested. At the end, they sit by the side of a road, weary and bedraggled, as reinforcements arrive. Their work is over; in their own way, they have achieved a small triumph. And since victors do not sit on the sidelines looking dog-faced, their tobacco-chewing sergeant (James Whitmore) rouses them to their feet, orders an "about face," and moves them from the side to the center of the road where they belong, flanked on either side by columns of reinforcements.

Battleground is a film of small moments and small triumphs that take on greatness because they represent something great: the American fighting spirit. Hollywood had been heading toward this type of film since *Wake Island*; but always before propaganda had taken precedence over plot, relevance over character, or panorama over view. It was not necessary for the platoon's chaplain to tell the men: "Don't ever let anyone say you were a sucker to fight in the war against fascism." They might not have known where they were, or even that they were in Belgium; but they knew why they were there. And that knowledge, never articulated but expressed through action, would make anyone understand why the United States won a war it was so ill prepared to fight.

7. The People's War

The politicians who called this a "people's war" were right, probably more right than they knew at the time.
—Edward R. Murrow, 10 September 1940

This is not only a war of soldiers in uniform; it is a war of the people—of all the people—and it must be fought, not only on the battlefield, but in all the cities and in the villages, in the factories and on the farms, in the home and in the heart of every man, woman, and child who loves freedom.
—*Mrs. Miniver* (1942)

The Resistants

Throughout the 1940s, World War II was called a "people's war," and Hollywood interpreted "people" as everyone not in uniform. If the war was fought as much on the home front as on the battlefield, then "the people" also included the antifascist underground; in occupied countries, the home front was the battleground where, to complete the paradox, the soldiers were civilians. Like the American home-fronters, resistants were of no one type. Being one required three qualities, two of which loyal Americans already possessed: love of country and hatred of fascism. But there was a third that Americans never had to cultivate because America was never invaded: a refusal to remain passive when a country's honor was at stake and human rights were being violated.

Hollywood realized the resistance would have great popular appeal. Since resistants were "just people," as Paul Henreid described them in *The Conspirators* (1944), audiences could identify with them, marvelling at the way the mere presence of Nazis in a French village would release wells of courage previously untapped and send it forth in such bold but simple ways as slowdowns on the job, defacing Wehrmacht posters, or wearing the Cross of Lorraine in public. Moviegoers who took their action neat could delight in the way resistants derailed trains, dynamited bridges, and engineered assassinations.

The resistance afforded a change from the usual Allies-hero, Axis-villain movie; the resistants were the heroes, but the villains were often their collaborationist countrymen and women. Hollywood never glossed over the existence of collaboration, especially in France and Norway. *Paris Calling* (1941), the first film about the French resistance, set the precedent for including collaborationists in the plot. In *Paris Calling*, the collaborationist is a domestic fascist, modelled after Pierre Laval, who wants to replace the Third Republic with the Third Reich. Naturally, the heroine kills him. Resistants can be ruthless. In *Hotel Berlin* (1945), Helmut Dantine, looking like an executioner, shoots collaborationist Andrea King in cold blood while she is professing her love for him. The Quisling in *Hangmen Also Die* (1943), who purports not to know German, gives himself away by laughing at an anti-Hitler joke while the camera chillingly pans the unsmiling faces of the underground.

The resistance offered something for everyone, particularly screenwriters. The clandestine nature of the resistance made it difficult to know much about its operations. Hence, a resistance script required little research. Invention was all, or at least three-quarters. Furthermore, astute screenwriters arrived at some of the same conclusions that historians reached later: resistants came from all walks of life; women played a major role in the movement; the working class provided the best saboteurs; the principle of succession required the new to replace the old, and children to replace parents; and, especially, most resistants were not affiliated with any particular organization ("Many resisters, perhaps the majority . . . belonged to no groups"[1]).

The movie resistants, therefore, represent a cross section of society: children (*The Cross of Lorraine*, 1943), teenagers (*The North Star*, 1943), teachers (*This Land Is Mine*, 1943; *Hangmen Also Die*), peasants (*O.S.S.*), clergy (*Till We Meet Again*, 1944; *Edge of Darkness*, 1943), newspapermen (*Hostages*, 1943), doctors (*Hangmen Also Die*), workers (*The Seventh Cross*, 1944).

Often a film dramatizes a citizen's transformation into a resistant.

Unable to remain a moderate any longer, a minister leaves his pulpit to man a machine gun (*Edge of Darkness*); a timid school teacher finds his courage when the Nazis burn his favorite books (*This Land Is Mine*); peasants choose to scorch the earth rather than to see it in the hands of the Boche (*The Cross of Lorraine, In Our Time*, 1944). There is drama even in the principle of succession, with a freedom fighter's sons following in their father's footsteps (*Watch on the Rhine*).

A shadow war meant shadowy love. The male resistant endangered his life; the female, her virtue as well. "Make love to him if he expects it," the heroine is told in *Paris Calling*. When a woman's virtue isn't being imperilled, her reputation is. She may have to risk ostracism by posing as a collaborationist (*Tonight We Raid Calais*, 1943) or by marrying a Nazi (*First Comes Courage*, 1943). For a woman willing to sacrifice her life, the condemnation of the public is a mere inconvenience.

To its credit, Hollywood has never portrayed life in the resistance as easy. Since the resistance was "the anthill of a nation,"[2] it needed people willing to adopt the habits of ants and endure the drudgery such work entails. What matters was the goal, not the tedious and often grubby means to achieve it. In *The Seventh Cross*, a delicatessen owner explains the resistance in the form of a parable about a colony of ants that invades a sugar bowl and, by the end of the day, has succeeded in moving the sugar from one end of the store to the other.

In the American World War II film, a resistant's politics are simply antifascist; no party label is necessary (especially if the resistants are Communists as, historically, many were. The Chinese guerrillas in *Thirty Seconds over Tokyo* are Communists, as Dalton Trumbo knew but did not, and could not, mention). There are films, however, in which the resistants appear to have the same politics as well as the same goal, so that one seems to be in the presence of a left-wing, if not Communist, cadre. When the resistance leader in *Paris after Dark* (1943) announces that "there are no more Royalists, Democrats or Communists" and that "today either a man is for the Nazis or against them," he is echoing the philosophy of the communist-controlled Front National, which tried to achieve the widest possible representation by downplaying allegiances and appealing to national sentiment. Similarly, a line like "It's better to fight here than die like slaves and hostages in Germany" (*Paris after Dark*) is a variation on La Pasionaria's famous "It is better to die on your feet than live on your knees!"

If the resistants in *Paris after Dark* seem to be left-wing, Harold

Buchman, the screenwriter, may have intended it; Buchman was a radical and may well have been a Communist. Left-wing screenwriters—Robert Rossen (*Edge of Darkness*), Vladimir Pozner (*The Conspirators*), Maltz and Lardner, Jr. (*Cloak and Dagger*)—tended to create the best undergrounds: organized, disciplined, and ruthlessly efficient.

The same qualities characterize the underground in *Hostages*, which Lester Cole adapted from Stefan Heym's 1942 novel. Although Heym may never have belonged to the Party, he was as much a Communist as Lester Cole, who later became one of the Hollywood Ten. Heym called the main character in his novel Paul Breda, a name Cole repeated in the screenplay. Although Heym believes he was not consciously thinking of Rudolf Breda (*né* Otto Katz), the Czech Communist famous in American antifascist circles as a fund raiser, he has admitted that the choice of name was not coincidental in a novel about the Czech underground, especially since he had known Breda.[3] Again, these were touches too subtle even for the critics, who dismissed *Hostages* as just another "underground flick," not realizing that such details as the hero's name and a female's being a resistance leader gave the film a basis in reality.

Since "resistance" evoked France more than any other country, the French resistance was one of the most commonly featured in the American World War II movie. The first French resistance film, however, was not made by a major studio, any more than the first film set in Nazi Germany was; it was made by Universal. The film is *Paris Calling*, written by Benjamin Glazer and John S. Toldy, the same team that coauthored the original screen story that became *Arise, My Love*. As might be expected, therefore, the script has some foundation in fact. Although the facts were sparse, their imaginative use makes *Paris Calling* more than a historical curiosity.

Glazer and Toldy took their cue from two events: de Gaulle's 18 June 1940 appeal over Radio London to keep "the flame of French Resistance" burning, and his 8 July broadcast in which he linked the destinies of "two great peoples," France and England.[4] It did not matter that the 18 June appeal was largely unheeded because it was largely unheard. What mattered was that the French resistance was born and that England had witnessed the birth. To dramatize the event, England should be shown coming to the aid of the French. What could be more dramatic than a rescue operation, a flotilla à la Dunkirk, to ferry the resistants across the Channel where they could join the Free French? Thus *Paris Calling* ends with the arrival of the British and the singing of "La Marseillaise." While there was no historical analogue for the evacuation, the inspiration came from the voyage made by fishermen from the Ile de Sein who, on 25 June 1940, spurred on by their community, crossed the Channel in their fishing boats to join de Gaulle in London.

Anglo-French cooperation was constantly emphasized in Free French and French resistance films. In *Tonight We Raid Calais* (a misnomer if there ever was one, since Calais is not raided), a British agent mobilizes the French, even asking them to burn their fields before the RAF bombs a German munitions factory. In *Assignment in Brittany* (1943), the British parachute a Free Frenchman into a Breton village to impersonate a look-alike. The real saboteur in *Uncertain Glory* (1944) is a Free French operative based in England. *Passage to Marseilles* (1944), a rousing tribute to the Free French, opens in England, with the plot unfolding in the form of flashbacks within a flashback. Of all the Free French films, *Passage to Marseilles* is the most vehemently anti-Vichy (but without the subtlety of *Casablanca*, which reduces Vichy to a bottle of Vichy water discarded in a trash can).

Paris Underground (1945) is really a triple alliance: England, France, and the United States. Best remembered for Gracie Fields's performance as an Englishwoman who, with the aid of an American (Constance Bennett), forms an escape circuit in Paris for RAF fliers, *Paris Underground* proves de Gaulle was right when he claimed in his 18 June broadcast that "behind [France] is a vast empire . . . the British Empire." Though he did not know it, behind both of them was Hollywood.

Hollywood's Francophilia during the war even surpassed its prewar Anglophilia. France, more than England, which had not been occupied, became a symbol of freedom in chains. At RKO, Joan of Arc became the patron saint of the resistance with *Joan of Paris* (1942), which implies that any *jeune fille* can be another Joan of Lorraine. In 1943, the same studio made the best allegory of the war, *Mademoiselle Fifi* (1944). While other films (e.g., *Sergeant York*, *Wilson*) have drawn analogies between the present and the past, none has ever made such an analogy the basis of an entire movie.[5]

It is unfortunate that *Mademoiselle Fifi*, which was favorably reviewed and even called "noble,"[6] has been so ignored. The director, Robert Wise, went on to become an important filmmaker; the producer, Val Lewton, who at the time headed RKO's horror unit, was such a master of terror by suggestion that Hitchcock paid him homage in *The Birds* (1963) by quoting a scene from *Cat People* (1942), Lewton's first production. Had *Mademoiselle Fifi* been released in 1942 and by a bigger studio, instead of in 1944 by RKO, its impact might have been stronger and its reputation greater. But then, a big-

The laundress (Simone Simon) and the Prussian (Kurt Kreuger) in the World War II allegory Mademoiselle Fifi *(1944). Courtesy* RKO *Pictures*

ger studio might have obscured the theme and smothered the story; Lewton's budget did not allow for excess, but only for a modest but tasteful production.

Mademoiselle Fifi is based on two Maupassant stories, both of which are set during the Franco-Prussian war—a good analogue with World War II and a better one with France, as the prologue notes: "1870. The Franco-Prussian War. Then as in our time there was occupied and unoccupied territory."

Eight French people, including a "little laundress" (Simone Simon), are travelling by coach from Rouen to Dieppe. The coach is a metaphor for occupied France; the collaborationists are the affluent passengers, who consort with the Germans but complain of their manners; the sole patriot is the laundress, who regards the Germans as "great pigs with spiked helmets." The dialogue has an undisguisedly World War II flavor, with its allusions to spies, traitors, guerrillas, and identity card checks; its references to "many kinds of Frenchmen"; and its criticism of those who have welcomed the Germans as friends.

While the other passengers snub the laundress, they are not reluctant to eat her food, not having brought any of their own. When the laundress offers to share hers with them, she becomes the celebrant and the coach the scene of a communion ritual, complete with wine, which they drink from chalicelike goblets. There are two other meals in the film: in the second, the laundress is scapegoat; in the third, avenger. The perversion of the ritual meal is an important theme in *Mademoiselle Fifi*. At Tôtes, the laundress is propositioned by a Prussian soldier who will not allow the coach to proceed until she dines with him. The Prussian acts like a Nazi, making the meal an occasion for debasement by blowing cigar smoke in the laundress's face. By an intricate plot twist, she dines with him again, but this time the meal culminates in his murder—not because the Prussian degrades her or draws blood when he kisses her, but because he insults France. At the end of the film, the church bell that was silent in protest now rings triumphantly. High up in the church tower is what appears to be a statue: it is the laundress elevated to the stature she deserves, looking down on the funeral of the man she had killed.

In a typical Resistance film, the people suffer nobly under the yoke of Nazism. The collaborationists are unprincipled, but patriots are above reproach. Hostages go to their death with a raised fist and a cry of long life to their country (*Hostages*). If four hundred of them must die, "then so be it. What are four hundred lives? This is a war of millions" (*Hangmen Also Die*).

Uncertain Glory is atypical. The patriots are treacherous; they do not think in terms of millions, but hundreds—one hundred, to be exact. If they can save a hundred hostages by framing an innocent man, then so be it. It is clear that *Crime and Punishment* provided the screenwriters, Laslow Varaday and Max Brand, with the motif of the police inspector and the criminal who grow to respect each other because, like Porfiry and Raskolnikov, they are doubles. And like Raskolnikov, the criminal, Jean Piccard (Errol Flynn), makes a totally free choice: he confesses to being the saboteur the Nazis are seeking in order to save the lives of a hundred French hostages.

While Piccard is preparing to save the village, the villagers are preparing to frame Piccard by reporting him to the Gestapo, not knowing he has willingly assumed the role of scapegoat without their forcing it on him. The villagers are worse than collaborationists; they are guilty of the ultimate Dantean sin—treachery; in this case, treachery against guests, since Piccard is really a visitor. Finally, Piccard succeeds in winning his own martyrdom, with the glory accruing to himself alone. The words of the title, then, form a strange trope in which "uncertain" and "glory" are united as cause and effect. The glory produces feelings of uncertainty in Piccard, who cannot articulate his reasons for performing an act that is literally self-effacing. What he cannot say, "La Marseillaise" can; as he gropes for the right word, the right music is heard on the soundtrack, making it absolutely clear that the reason is France. At the end, when a village girl asks the inspector (Paul Lukas) what kind of man Piccard was, the camera tracks in for a close-up of Lukas's face as he delivers one of those climactic lines for which Warner Bros. is famous: "He was a Frenchman."

Between September 1942 and September 1943, five films were released about the occupation of Norway: PRC's *They Raid by Night*, Columbia's *Commandos Strike at Dawn*, Fox's *The Moon Is Down*, Warner Bros'. *Edge of Darkness*, and Columbia's *First Comes Courage*. The five vary in quality from the inconsequential *They Raid by Night*, with the claustrophobic look and postcard sets that are PRC's trademark, to *Edge of Darkness*, with Lewis Milestone's sweeping tracking shots and the periodic eruption of "A Mighty Fortress Is Our God" from the soundtrack.

The Norwegian resistance had much to offer Hollywood. Since its invasion in April 1940, Norway had been constantly in the news. Its leading collaborationist and short-lived prime minister, Vidkun Quisling, gave his surname to the world as a synonym for traitor. Churchill's 1941 prediction that Norway "shall be cleansed, not only from the invader but from the filthy quislings who were his tools" (a prediction perhaps occasioned by Britain's embarrassment at being unable to save Norway from Hitler) perpetuated the highly exaggerated impression of a Norway betrayed from within by a fifth column; and wherever there is a fifth column, there is a potential movie.

To filmmakers Norway offered diversity: British commandos and SOE (Special Operations Executive) officers. And if that were not enough, there was the speech that President Roosevelt gave on 16 September 1942 at the Washington Navy Yard when he presented the Royal Norwegian Navy with a submarine chaser "as a token of the admiration and friendship of the American people." Although Roosevelt probably did not know it, his speech contained one of the most effective devices in oratory—epistrophe, repetition at the end of clauses. Apart from producing a definite rhythm, epistrophe creates a natural emphasis. It is not at all inappropriate, then, that Roosevelt's words, spoken in a Rooseveltian voice, ring out at the end of *Edge of Darkness*: "If there is anyone who still wonders why this war is being fought, let him look to Norway. If there is anyone who has any delusions that this war could have been averted, let him look to Norway; and if there is anyone who doubts of the democratic will to win, again, I say, let him look to Norway."

Commandos Strike at Dawn, which anticipated Roosevelt's exhortation, was almost finished by the time the president was determining the direction in which the world should look. Since the SOE was extremely active in Norway, Columbia was able to obtain the cooperation of the British government for the film as well as the services of two of Britain's leading actors, Cedric Hardwicke and Robert Coote. That cooperation may explain the curious climax—a commando raid on a Norwegian airstrip that does not seem to grow out of the plot.[7] While any one of several actual commando raids could have inspired the climax, there was none on an airstrip. Yet there could have been if Operation Jupiter, a plan Churchill conceived in early 1942, had been put into action.[8] Operation Jupiter would have used Canadians to bomb Norwegian airfields to prevent the Luftwaffe from launching attacks on convoys bound for the Soviet Union. In the film, then, a plan is executed that, historically, never materialized. If Operation Jupiter had occurred, *Commandos Strike at Dawn* would be a prophetic film; instead, it is just prefigurative.

Near the end of the film, five Norwegians are on a boat bound for England; when the quisling with them reveals himself, he is tied up and thrown overboard. The following year Hitchcock made *Lifeboat* (1944), in which five survivors, upon realizing that the Nazi U-boat captain they rescued has killed one of their number, pummel him and throw him overboard. Coincidence or influence?

In March 1943, Warners' *Edge of Darkness* and Fox's *The Moon Is Down* were released within two weeks of each other. Fox purchased *The Moon Is Down*, John Steinbeck's 1942 play-novella, for $200,000, even though the play survived on Broadway for only eight performances.[9] Fox had high hopes for the film version, having done well by Steinbeck with *The Grapes of Wrath* (1940). The OWI too had high hopes for the film; planes dropped 16 mm prints of it over Norway to bolster the people's spirits. But *The Moon Is Down* failed to bolster anyone's spirits, finding favor with neither audiences nor critics.

Beginning on a blatantly melodramatic note, with Hitler's hands moving greedily over a map of Norway, the film soon settles into a dialectic that is provocative but nondramatic. Steinbeck's distinction is not the usual one between the occupier and the occupied, but between free people and "herd" people, each category having its own subdivisions. Thus the herd class comprises both Nazis and

Nazi reprisals in The Moon Is Down *(1943). Courtesy Twentieth Century-Fox Film Corporation*

quislings, all of whom are different. The Nazi colonel is civilized; the quisling is not the standard collaborationist. Although the quisling is amoral, he does not understand why, after paving the way for the occupation, he is of no further use to the occupiers. The resistants are equally complex, ranging from the usual patriots to Molly Morden, who lures a German to her bedroom and kills him. The German's murder is disquieting because he is sympathetic character; drawn to Molly out of loneliness, he courts her with Heine's poetry. Steinbeck refused to take the easy way out and paint his characters in monochrome; his colors, however, were not the ones a wartime audience wanted to see. That the Germans prove to be ineffectual does not matter; they are ineffectual not because they are stupid but because they are not part of the group, or to use a favorite Steinbeck word, part of the "people."

Steinbeck's ideas are stimulating but they remain on the level of abstraction. The ending contradicts one of the film's most important points: "Free men can't start a war, but once it's started, they can still fight on in defeat." The noble paradox is not borne out by the conclusion, in which the hostages die, singing their love for Norway; that may not be defeat but it is also not fighting on.

Perhaps the Norwegian resistance, like the French, needed a couple of left-wingers at the helm: a radical director (Lewis Milestone) and a (then) Communist screenwriter (Robert Rossen), whose collaboration resulted in *Edge of Darkness*, the best of the Norway movies. Although the setting, Trollness, is fictitious (it suggests Trondheim and should be imagined as being somewhere between Bergen and Trondheim), the details are not.[10] The periodical, *News of Norway*, and the Norwegian Embassy's pamphlet, *Norway Fights*, were used to authenticate locales and resistance activity, including the work of the SOE.

Unlike most World War II movies, *Edge of Darkness* does not have a conventional prologue. Instead, Rossen uses a framing device: the arrival of a German flight patrol at Trollness, where the square is strewn with corpses. The film then flashes back to the events preceding the massacre that occurred when the Norwegians rose up against the invader.

William Woods's novel, *The Edge of Darkness* (1942), was not difficult for Rossen to adapt since it was in the tradition of his screenplays, notably *Marked Woman*, with its call for involvement and its attack on apathy. In *Marked Woman*, there are the law and the syndicate, with the "hostesses" in the middle: in *Edge of Darkness*, there are the resistants and the invaders, with neutrals and collaborationists in the middle. The hostesses of *Marked Woman* are silent until a girl's death impels her sister to speak out; what galvanizes the neutrals of *Edge of Darkness* are two acts of Nazi brutality: a schoolteacher's degradation and a woman's rape. After the Nazis toss the teacher in the air, they tie him to a cart and parade him into the square where his books are burned. Although the villagers are not passive, they are still not ready for armed resistance. They can only march alongside the cart until they reach the square where they confront the Nazis, Norwegians and Nazis at opposite ends of the frame, with pointed bayonets occupying the space between them. (Milestone would repeat this confrontation composition in *The North Star*.) The scene reaches its dramatic conclusion when the minister begins singing the national anthem, which the others take up, one by one, turning it into a chorale.

The teacher's degradation is an affront to the mind: "We have no use for philosophers," the Nazis boast. The rape of Karen (Ann Sheridan) is an affront to morality. A teacher's humiliation can stir up feelings of revulsion; rape can incite rebellion. Like any scene of sexual violence during the studio years, the rape is photographed

connotatively and is therefore more horrifying than if it were dramatized.

Karen is abducted while leaving church. The abduction, like the
subsequent rape, is elliptical: a knees-to-feet shot as she is dragged
away. Tracking back to the street, the camera complements the shot
of Karen's feet with one of marching boots—a juxtaposition pointing to gang rape. When Karen finally appears at the resistance meeting, she is framed in the doorway, her hair stringy from the rain. "Let
them hear!" she cries. It is not they who hear, but we who see; and
what we see is not the rape but the lodge the Nazis have converted
into a brothel. It is just one shot, a shot of soldiers laughing rau-
cously; but it is enough to make anything further seem superfluous.
It is also enough to galvanize the group. As "A Mighty Fortress Is
Our God" peals forth, the camera pans the faces. The surging righ-
teousness of the music precludes the need of dialogue: the group
knows what it must do.

In Rossen's screenplays dealing with human degradation, loss of
self-respect is often equated with moral apathy. In *Edge of Darkness*,
a Polish actress is ensconced in the lodge to service the Nazis, loathing herself for it. The character recalls the hostesses in *Marked
Woman* and anticipates Sarah in *The Hustler* (1961). Rossen also
equates sudden moral awakening with extreme action, with a stand
that is the complete reverse of neutrality—a stand that might ordinarily seem extreme, but under the circumstances is not only justifiable but even noble. In *Edge of Darkness*, the minister is at first
neutral; then, like Luther, he takes his stand—behind a machine
gun in the church tower, firing away at the Nazis below.

One thing film can do better than any other art form is to use one
event to evoke another. There is a moment in *Edge of Darkness* that
accomplishes this, a scene that evokes the Holocaust. When the resistants are forced to dig a mass grave, the setting is no longer Norway but the forests of Poland and the Ukraine where mass graves
were the mode of burial for countless numbers of executed Jews. In
fact, the entire film encourages associations that go beyond the plot:
guilt, acquiescence, self-deprecation, and especially resistance as a
form of religion, as seen in the way "A Mighty Fortress Is Our God"
evolves into a battle hymn.

Late in the summer of 1943, the last of the Norway films appeared: *First Comes Courage*, whose claim to fame is its director,
one of the few women filmmakers in the industry—Dorothy Arzner.[11] This time, the SOE is blowing up oil dumps on the Norwegian
coast. The obligatory quisling (Merle Oberon) turns out to be a
member of the underground who only marries a Nazi to obtain in-

formation for the resistance. The wedding ceremony is the film's highlight: the couple walks up the aisle toward an altar on which is a leatherbound edition of *Mein Kampf.*

Once Russia became synonymous with Communism, the folly of Communism became a standard theme, especially in the films of the thirties. Communism was a trap for the unwary rich, particularly rich women, which left no doubt as to which sex Hollywood considered the weaker. College girls (*Fighting Youth*, 1935; *Red Salute*, 1936), socialites (*Public Deb No. 1*, 1940), and daughters at odds with their wealthy fathers (*Soak the Rich*, 1935) were most vulnerable. In thirties' argot, they were dizzy dames whose boredom with affluence and yearning for a different life led them to embrace an ideology promising the end of ennui. But they soon learned that capitalism, even when practiced by rednecks (*Public Deb No. 1*) and jingoists (*Red Salute*) is preferable to Communism, which is so fraudulent that a pair of silk stockings (*Ninotchka*, 1939) or the appearance of Clark Gable (*Comrade X*, 1940) could convert the daughters of Marx into the nieces of Uncle Sam.

Even in 1940, the Soviet Union was "full of stuffed shirts double-crossing the masses" (*Comrade X*); but not for long. The following year that kind of talk was out, and "We're going to cement Russian relations" (*Background to Danger*, 1943) was in.

When Hitler invaded the Soviet Union in June 1941, Russia joined the Allies. The following December, *Mission to Moscow* by Joseph E. Davies, the American ambassador to the Soviet Union in 1936–38, was published. If it seems odd that a former ambassador would write such a book four years later, and not immediately after he had returned, the reason was that President Roosevelt, or Roosevelt and Davies together, decided it would be a good way to convert Americans from Russophobia to temporary Russophilia, now that there was a new and unexpected ally.

In less than a year the movie version of *Mission to Moscow* was underway at Warner Bros., again at the request of Roosevelt, who, knowing that film is a more effective means of propaganda than print, was able to persuade Jack Warner to sacrifice his anti-Communism to the war effort.[12] Thus, audiences managing to endure two hours of Stalinist apologetics learned that the purge trials were an attempt to rid the Soviet Union of Trotskyites; and that the Russo-Finnish war of 1939–40 began when the Soviet Union, knowing it would be invaded (although how it knew after signing a non-aggression pact with Germany is never explained), politely asked Finland to occupy some strategic positions there, and, when the ungracious Finns refused, attacked. About the only truth spoken in the film occurs when a heckler asks Davies (Walter Huston) what Russia has ever done for the United States and is told, "Russia has given us time."

Whatever one's feelings about Stalin, the Russians were something else; their suffering, especially during the siege of Stalingrad, made them (as Steinbeck would say) "people." It was as people that Hollywood decided they should appear—not as ordinary people but as resistants in a country of resistance. Only two films deviate from the national resistance image of the Soviet Union: *Background to Danger* and PRC's *Miss V. from Moscow* (1942), which have Russian agents in Turkey and Germany, respectively; the latter film mocks history by showing a Russian spy ring in Germany passing on intelligence secrets to the United States and England.

Most screenwriters were so eager to make the Russians into people that they created a race of puppets in babushkas and cossack shirts. In almost every case, the reason was the screenwriter's politics—radical in Lillian Hellman's case (*The North Star*), Communist in Paul Jarrico and Richard Collins's (*Song of Russia*, 1943). *Song of Russia* does not even try to conceal its pro-Soviet bias. When a symphonic conductor (Robert Taylor) on a tour of the Soviet Union visits a nightclub with a young Soviet pianist (Susan Peters), he is surprised that "everyone seems to be having such a good time." "Is that wrong?" the pianist asks. "No," he replies, "except that I always thought Russians were sad, melancholy people. You know, sitting around brooding about their souls. This is such a surprise." Indeed it is, but there is more, including a Jerome Kern–E.Y. Harburg song in a Moscow nightclub. Russia is so much like the United States, in fact, that the date of its entry into World War II is given the Pearl Harbor treatment: the calendar page close-up, not of 7 December but of 21 June.

Once the war starts, the pianist, instead of teaching music, instructs her pupils in the art of making Molotov cocktails, first giving a brief history of the makeshift incendiary: "It was first used by the people of Spain in fighting the invasion of their country." In fact it was the Finns who perfected the Molotov cocktail during the 1939–40 war with Russia and hurled some 70,000 of them at the invaders. However, no one would dare make this point in a pro-Soviet film.

While Lillian Hellman's *The North Star* is an improvement over *Song of Russia*, it still suffers from the same defensive posture, as if she too believed that the Russians needed idealization to appear human. Hitler's view of the Slavs as subhuman was certainly not corrected by screenplays depicting them as superhuman. *The North*

Robert Taylor and Susan Peters, the capitalist and the Communist, in Song of Russia *(1943). Margaret Herrick Library, courtesy* MGM/UA

Star was supposed to have been a documentary; when it became a fiction film, Samuel Goldwyn gave it a production that was so at odds with Hellman's conception that she bought out the rest of her contract from Goldwyn, ending an eight-year association with the producer.[13] Goldwyn turned Hellman's script into an unrealistic film; however, Hellman's choice of setting, which Goldwyn retained, did not help. The North Star is a collective farm in the Ukraine where collectivism is extolled as people's farming. The characters live in Edenic bliss until the Nazis invade their fairy-tale kingdom, at which point the men became guerrillas and the women and children resistants.

Hellman's view of Russia as a country of resistance was valid, but setting the origin of the resistance in the Ukraine, where Communism was largely unpopular, was inaccurate, especially since photographs exist showing the Ukrainians welcoming the Germans as their liberators. Hellman's historical faux pas was compounded by Goldwyn's hiring Aaron Copland and Ira Gershwin to write the music and lyrics for eight songs that were incorporated into the script, making it a libretto; and David Lachine to choreograph the ethnic dances, doing for the Ukrainians what he had done for the Muscovites in *Song of Russia*.

Goldwyn's additions were not able to stifle Hellman's voice, which resounds in the speech Walter Huston gives before he kills Erich von Stroheim: "To me you are the real filth. Men who do the work of fascists and pretend to themselves they are better than those for whom they work." This is the old Hellman, the Hellman of the Popular Front; the giveaway is "fascist," a word so hated by the old left that it dominated its vocabulary. Huston's speech would have been perfect in *Watch on the Rhine*; on a Ukrainian collective it is out of place. But then, so is Huston.

The best Russian resistance film is the least known—RKO's *Days of Glory* (1944). It is really a love story, though not in the way in which it was advertised. Casey Robinson wrote the screenplay primarily as a vehicle for his wife, Tamara Toumanova, and secondarily for Gregory Peck's film debut. Since Toumanova was Russian and Robinson wanted to star her in a film that would show her to advantage, he decided to adapt an original screen story about Russia under seige. Since Robinson was "if anything . . . politically conservative,"[14] *Days of Glory* was a labor of conjugal love rather than a labor of politics, which might explain why it is the best of the "Russian allies" films.

Although the voice-over prologue claims that *Days of Glory* could have taken place anywhere, there is no attempt to conceal that the setting is Russia and that the partisans are mostly Communists who, happily, are not as self-righteous as those in *The North Star*. No one castigates "Comrade Professor" Semyon for reading decadent authors like Pushkin; when the partisans want to kill a Nazi captive, Semyon reminds them that the Nazi is a prisoner of war, which in most films makes little difference. While the obligatory "fascist" is used, no one delivers an antifascist harrangue. *Days of Glory* is a love story in the Casey Robinson tradition; Robinson excelled at transforming women from a lower to a higher form—from hedonist to saint (*Dark Victory*, 1939), from dominated to liberated (*Now, Voyager*, 1942); and in *Days of Glory*, from dégagée to engagée, as the prima ballerina of the Moscow Ballet, who can neither cook nor sew, learns to kill for her country.

Days of Glory has some wonderfully subtle touches. The guerrillas retreat to the ruins of a monastery, where they lead a communal existence not unlike that of the original occupants. While most of the guerrillas are Communists, Nina (Toumanova), the ballerina, is

Tamara Toumanova as the Russian ballerina turned partisan (but not Communist, as evidenced by her cross) in Days of Glory *(1944). Courtesy* RKO *Radio Pictures*

not. She wears a cross around her neck. When her rival is killed, a funeral service is conducted inside a monk's cell. Nina joins in the prayers while Vladimir (Gregory Peck), the guerrilla leader, remains outside the cell until the service is over.

When Nina joins the guerrillas, she does not remove her cross, even when Vladimir administers the guerrilla oath requiring her to swear allegiance to the Soviet Union. At that point politics do not matter, however, because a German tank is moving toward them. Thus, Communists in the audience could say that Nina died as one of theirs; Christians would be pleased that she kept her cross; and Gregory Peck became an overnight star.

American Russophilia was short lived. As the war in Europe drew to a close, Russophobia staged a comeback, and the Hollywood Russian reverted to prewar caricature (Eve Arden in *The Doughgirls*, 1944) before emerging as the Red Menace. Nothing, therefore, could save Columbia's *Counterattack* (1945), which opened shortly after VE Day. *Counterattack* had originated as a play, running for eighty-five performances on Broadway in 1943. Everything about the film reveals its origins, especially the setting—a cellar, in which a Soviet paratrooper (Morris Carnovsky in the play, Paul Muni in the film) holds a group of Nazis at bay with the partial assistance of a female partisan. John Howard Lawson's unshakable devotion to the Soviet Union made him the ideal adapter of *Counterattack*. But in the spring of 1945, it would not have made any difference who adapted it. America's love affair with the Russian people was over.

Hollywood managed to cover most of the European resistance movements, directly or indirectly. *To Be or Not To Be* (1942) acknowledges the existence of a Polish resistance, and one seems to be forming at the conclusion of *In Our Time*, which ends with the siege of Warsaw. Since Italy was part of the Axis, the Italian underground was not depicted until after the war, when it seemed to be dominated by Communists (*Cloak and Dagger*). While Portugal was neutral, Lisbon was the last stop on the refugee trail and the embarkation point for flights to the United States. Lisbon was also Europe's espionage capital: o.s.s. operatives and British intelligence agents worked out of Lisbon, and it was from Lisbon that the Abwehr sent its spies to Britain.[15] If there were Nazis in Lisbon, there had to be antifascists; their activities are dramatized in *The Conspirators*, which also pays tribute to the Dutch resistance in the person of the Dutch resistant-hero.

Greece was a notable omission; *Chetniks* (1943) vaguely alludes to Greek guerrillas, but it was not until *The Angry Hills* (1959) and *The Guns of Navarone* (1961) that Americans saw them in action.

The Greek resistance was uncommonly complex. The two leading guerrilla organizations were politically bipolar: the Communist-dominated ELAS and the republican EDES. Their coalescence, achieved through British efforts, was purely temporary; when it ended, civil war erupted (although it was nowhere as bloody as the internecine massacres in Yugoslavia). If screenwriters had difficulty with the Spanish civil war, they would have been equally uncomfortable with the Greek resistance and its Communist and anti-Communist factions.

There was a similar problem with the Yugoslav resistance with its two politically distinct guerrilla bands: the Chetniks led by the royalist Drazha Mihailovich and the Partisans under the Communist Tito. In 1942, Mihailovich was a likely prospect for a film; the British still supported him (though not for long), and he had appeared on the cover of *Time*. Thus Fox went ahead with *Chetniks*, subtitled *The Fighting Guerrillas*, which may well be the greatest embarrassment of the 1940s: it is never revived or shown on television, nor can it be rented. While Britain was able to salvage its film about the Yugoslav resistance, changing the title from *Chetniks* to *Undercover* (1943) and the focus from the Chetniks to the Partisans, Fox was stuck with its paean to Mihailovich; the dedication only attests to the unalterably admiring tone of the film: "This picture is respectfully dedicated to Draja Mikhailovitch and his fighting Chetniks—those fearless guerrillas who have dedicated their lives with a grim determination that no rest shall prevail until the final allied victory and the liberation of their beloved fatherland, Yugoslavia, has been achieved."

On the other hand, a movie about Tito's Partisans would have ended up on the House Committee on Unamerican Activities' list of subversive films and might have been a different sort of embarrassment: a Yugoslav *Song of Russia*. Favoring the right can be as precarious as favoring the left. But in 1942 Fox could not have known that the British would back Tito, or that in 1946 Mihailovich would be sentenced to death on a collaboration charge and executed as a fascist. While *Chetniks* shows Mihailovich (Philip Dorn) killing Nazis, it also shows him ransoming Italians, who were still members of the Axis. It was precisely because of such activity that the British stopped supporting Mihailovich.

Admirers of epigrammatic dialogue should not dismiss *Chetniks*. When a Nazi colonel discovers that Mihailovich has feigned a retreat, he tells one of his generals, "The exodus of the children of Israel has started, and you will have the opportunity of playing the

Red Sea." Surely a movie with such a line warrants at least one airing on the Late Late Show.

Les hommes dégagés

America's emergence from the sleep of isolationism into the reality of world war was reflected in the increasing number of characters who underwent a similar rite of passage. By 1943, the awakening neutral, who started appearing before Pearl Harbor (e.g., the countess who opens her fairy-tale castle to a political prisoner in *Escape*, the wife who heils her heel of a husband in *The Man I Married*, the adventurers who discover their conscience in Chiang Kai-shek's China in *A Yank on the Burma Road* and *China Girl*), had become a stock character.

Neutrals came in all varieties, from the disaffected to the opportunistic, with the disinterested, uncommitted, and apolitical in between. Some were unregenerate; those Hollywood scorned just as Dante did. But the cocky, brash loner was something else; he could change. Since apathy was the underside of involvement, it was merely a matter of reversing a position rather than assuming a new one; it was also easy on the screenwriter, who could make conversion the fulcrum of the plot. The convertible neutrals were those who were not so enmeshed in self or in crime that extrication was impossible. They could be on the wrong—but not the opposite—side of the law; they could be capitalists whose love of money has not yet hardened into avarice.

Alan Ladd had a chance to play both types. As the title character in *Lucky Jordan* (1942), Ladd is not really a crook, just a bit crooked; not a racketeer but in the rackets. Attempting to avoid the draft, he hires an Apple Annie type to pose as his dependent mother. Although the scheme fails, a mother-son relationship develops between Jordan and the woman. There is nothing like the sight of a woman's battered face to get a neutral off the fence. When he sees his "mother" after some Nazi hoods have paid her a visit, his apathy turns to anger. For Jordan, the entire experience is a lesson in synonymy: "Nazi is another way to spell cockroach." (*Lucky Jordan*, incidentally, includes another example of Hollywood speculation gone astray. When Jordan goes AWOL, he becomes involved with Nazi agents, one of whom is a former associate. The agent admits peddling troop movement information and playing a role in the sab-

Loretta Young and Alan Ladd, regenerative woman and uncommitted man, in China (1943). Courtesy MCA

---

otaging of the *Normandie*—which never occurred.) However, truth is not the issue; the making of a patriot is.

The following year, Ladd was seen selling oil to the Japanese in *China* (1943). The Chinese Nationalists despise him for it, but he is indifferent to their contempt (although he is far less odious than the oil exporter in *Secret Agent of Japan*). Again Ladd is radicalized by a woman. Women, as Hollywood had discovered, could bring out the avenging knight in the least chivalric of men. Yet a woman could be *dégagée* also.

One woman in particular stands out in the "disinterested Amerian" movie, the eponymous character of MGM's *The War Against Mrs. Hadley* (1942), which, while not a major film, was considered sufficiently important by Lux Radio Theatre to be turned into a radio play for a 7 December 1942 broadcast marking the first anniversary of America's entry into the war. By 1942, 7 December had become a benchmark date. Thus, the sight of a cake reading "Happy Birthday Mrs. Hadley December 7, 1941" would automatically provoke a hum of recognition. When one character asks another, "How are the peace negotiations coming along with Japan?" one can almost feel the vise of irony clamping down on the plot. And when someone turns on the radio for a concert, as thousands of Americans were doing on the afternoon of 7 December, expecting to hear the New York Philharmonic, one knows it is only a matter of time before the broadcast will be interrupted with an announcement about Pearl Harbor.

Even by Christmas eve, Mrs. Hadley is still indifferent to the war that cast a pall over her birthday party. She is even willing to wangle a draft deferment for her chauffeur so he can remain in her employ. But when her son wins the Distinguished Service Cross, Mrs. Hadley sees the light. "Well, those Japs and Nazis better look out now that Stella's in the war," a friend exclaims at the fadeout.

The most famous reconstructed neutral and the coolest patriot in movie history was Rick Blaine, owner of the world's best known gin joint. While *Casablanca* has become such a part of our national mythology that audiences in revival houses can recite the dialogue if the sound goes awry, it was never intended as a mere divertissement. Of course, *Casablanca* will always be synonymous with entertainment in the best sense of the word: it gave, and will continue to give, pleasure—aesthetic, moral, and personal.

Casablanca is fiction elevated to fable, then translated into myth where the implausible, improbable, and unlikely are no more questioned than the exploits of a deity or the adventures of a hero. Films that evolve into sacred texts are rare, for the sacral is a peculiar kind of art. Its basis is myth conceived of as sacred history. Of course, the history on which *Casablanca* is based is verifiable. History, however, is not really the groundwork; it is only a grid thrown over the real foundation, myth. The evolution of *Casablanca* from an unproduced play to a film classic has been traced.[16] What has not been explained is how an unproduced play became a film classic. Part of the reason lies in the interconnection between the hero and the plot; the plot is the myth, and the transformation of cafe owner into champion of freedom is inseparable from the transformation of melodrama into myth.

At the beginning, however, *Casablanca* seems like any other war movie. For those weak in geography, French Morocco is pinpointed on an animated map, and an unperturbable voice describes the escape route, originating in Paris and ending in Casablanca, from which the fortunate fly to Lisbon and thence to the United States. Casablanca's peculiar situation in 1941, the year in which the plot is set, is explained early in the film when Captain Renault (Claude

Rains), prefect of police, refuses to return the Nazi salute to the visiting Major Strasser. Renault reminds the major that Casablanca is part of "unoccupied France," which is correct. Although the distinction between occupied and unoccupied France had all but vanished by the time *Casablanca* was released, it existed in December 1941, the time of the action. Hence the setting is plausible, although French Morocco was more pro-Vichy than the film cares to admit. Apart from reducing the margin for error, setting the action before Pearl Harbor has another advantage: surefire irony. When Rich says, "If it's December 1941 in Casablanca, what time is it in New York? . . . I bet they're alseep in New York. I bet they're asleep all over America," one can almost hear a 1942–43 audience murmuring assent. Like Marie Browning (Lauren Bacall) in *To Have and Have Not* (1944), some might not have known the difference between Pétain and de Gaulle, but everyone knew the difference between waking and sleeping.

There is another reason, a practical one, for leaving Pearl Harbor out of the plot: it would prevent Rick from practicing his newly found patriotism. He would have to agonize over whether or not to return to the States. For reasons that are "a little vague," as Renault observes, Rick cannot return, presumably because a jail sentence awaits him. If *Casablanca* ends before 7 December, Rick can still do his duty: he can join the Free French, the next best thing to fighting for Uncle Sam.

If *Casablanca* has a sophistication that most wartime melodramas lack, it is partly because its source, *Everybody Comes to Rick's*, the unproduced play by Murray Burnett and Joan Alison, lends itself to the same kind of urbane treatment as the grand hotel/express train/luxury liner film in which the characters find themselves at a crossroads and rise to the level of wit, aphorism, and gesture that the occasion demands. Burnett and Alison provided the basic story line, which a series of screenwriters—acknowledged and otherwise—embellished, each adding something that was lacking in the play. Julius and Irving Epstein contributed humor and wit; Howard Koch gave Rick a radical past.[17]

In the play, Rick is an attorney specializing in lost cases; in the film, he is a champion of lost causes—Ethiopia, Loyalist Spain. Victor Laszlo, who also appears in the play, is a Czech antifascist. In the play, there is no reason why Laszlo has to be Czech, except that "everybody comes to Rick's," including Czechs. The screenwriters provided an excellent reason. They decided that Ilsa should be married to Laszlo when she meets Rick in Paris a few months before the fall of France in June 1940; thus Laszlo must be from a country that fell before the spring of 1940, a country that must also have an active underground. Even if Burnett and Alison had not made Laszlo a Czech, the screenwriters might have, since they were at pains to make each character's background plausible. Czechoslovakia was a logical homeland for Laszlo since it had two resistance movements—one for officers, another for activists and intellectuals, to which a political writer like Laszlo would belong.

The screenwriters pushed the play's metaphor to its logical conclusion, making Casablanca a microcosm of the pre-Pearl Harbor world, a place where Nazis mingle with citizens of the countries they have invaded and where an American-owned cafe buzzes with a polyphony of accents. To achieve the right geographical and political mix, the writers could not leave the national origins of the characters to chance; nor could they leave the characters intact. The play's heroine, Lois Meredith, had to be transformed. Lois is the proverbial lady of easy virtue who goes off with Laszlo (who is unmarried) at the end. Once the screenwriters decided to make Laszlo and the heroine a married couple, the freedom fighter had to have a wife worthy of him; and a sleeparound would not do. And so Lois Meredith became Ilsa Lund.

Like her husband, Ilsa should be from an occupied country. Although Ingrid Bergman was Swedish and had played a Swede in her American debut, *Intermezzo* (1939), she could not appear as one of her countrywomen in *Casablanca*. Sweden was neutral, and the wife of an underground leader should not come from a neutral nation. On the other hand, if Ilsa were Norwegian, she could share in the growing sympathy for occupied Norway that Hollywood kept alive by its 1942–43 Norwegian quintet.

The care taken in establishing the national backgrounds of the characters was not limited to the leads; it also extended to the supporting cast. The screenwriters rounded out the cast with some additions of their own: the "good Germans" are represented by a couple en route to the United States; the Soviet Union by Sascha, the anti-Nazi bartender; Free France by Berger the Norwegian, who has responded to de Gaulle's call and proves it by a ring that opens to reveal the Cross of Lorraine. Annina appears in the play, but the film makes much of her desire to emigrate to America with her husband since their homeland, Bulgaria, had joined the Axis in March 1941.

The film also comes to grips with an important fact about Casablanca: as part of unoccupied France, it is also part of collaborationist France, a point that is not downplayed. Although Renault is not exactly a collaborationist, he is not a Gaullist, either. Thus there is

The climax on the runway in Casablanca *(1942). Courtesy MGM/UA*

hope for him since he dwells in a political no-man's-land. But so does Rick. In a sense, they are doubles—Renault's conversion coincides with Rick's as they go off to enlist in the Free French, thereby adding two more bodies to an organization that was never very large to begin with. However, there is a true collaborationist in the film— Yvonne, a holdover from the play, who begins consorting with the Nazis when Rick rebuffs her. But even she cannot resist the appeal of "La Marseillaise," which is also sung in the play but without Yvonne's rousing "Vive la France!"

In the television documentary *Hollywood: You Must Remember This* (1972), Ingrid Bergman reminisces about *Casablanca*, remarking that no one, not even director Michael Curtiz or producer Hal Wallis, knew how the film should end, whether it should be with Ilsa's going off with Rick or with Laszlo. This was not entirely true; Casey Robinson sketched out the ending in a memo to Wallis, although it was not until forty years later that Robinson's contribution to *Casablanca* was discovered.[18] Even so, given the way the plot is constructed, Ilsa has no other choice but to remain with her husband. Her sympathy with Laszlo's antifascism transcends her infatuation with Rick; when Laszlo leads the singing of "La Marseillaise," drowning out the Germans, who bellow "Die Wacht am Rhein" with beer garden gusto, Ilsa's face is resplendent with the kind of pride front lighting can enhance but never create.

Since Rick's Café Américain is the film's focal point and, like America, an international melting pot, its symbolism would be sullied if an American ran off with another man's wife, especially after the wife had rekindled his political conscience; and the symbolism would be destroyed if the American were killed. Now one can appreciate the screenwriters' wisdom in having all the characters, except Rick, come from countries that are fascist, occupied, or beseiged. Rick is the only representative of the free world. Hence his awakening is all the more vital to the preservation of democracy, whose interests would not be served if he turned adulterer or died on the eve of Pearl Harbor.

There are many reasons why each generation claims *Casablanca* as its own. It is the epitome of American Romanticism, itself a blend of stoicism and surrender, in which women redeem men, men redeem other men, sacrifice is existential gesture, eyes shimmer with tears that never spill, anguish is a clutched whiskey glass, a farewell is a letter read in the rain that washes away the script, love is a revolver whose trigger the lover cannot bring herself to pull.

If these were merely isolated moments, conjured up by the imagination and left to fend for themselves in a makeshift plot, *Casablanca* would never have become a popular classic. It is a classic because it is a people's film that also happens to be about people. No other war movie offers such a gallery of types, as empathetic now as they were then. But the characters are not just World War II types. They are mythic types: the reactivated hero; his double, the regenerated Machiavel; the redemptive woman who plays Beatrice to one man and the Lady to another; the Promethean rebel; the repentant Magdalen; the courageous commoners.

Time goes by, but myth is eternal.

Women and Children

Although MGM's *Journey for Margaret* (1942) would have us believe that "this war isn't being fought for us, it's being fought for the children," the truth is that, as far as Hollywood was concerned, World War II was an adult concern. The plight of children could not be ignored, but the dearth of good child actors, the difficulties involved in fashioning scripts for them, and the paucity of plots into which they could fit limited the number of films about war orphans and refugee children. While the peacetime child tends to be amiable, precocious, or belligerent, the wartime child has to be achingly vulnerable or disarmingly tough. Had Shirley Temple been a child star, and not a teenager, in 1941, there would have been no place for her among the children of war because she was neither a waif nor a scrapper. War children must have something about them, either the look of a wounded bird or the hide of a survivor, something that would make one want to adopt them or bring them to the United States. Correspondent William L. White did just that, telling his story in *Journey for Margaret* (1941), which became a movie a year later.

It is impossible to dislike *Journey for Margaret*, which is a variation on the old plot of the child that brings a man and a woman together (e.g., Shirley Temple in *Our Little Girl*, 1935); the couple in question lose their only child and withdraw into self-pity and drink. Margaret, a war orphan, not only brings the couple out of their cocoon; she also inspires the father to bring another orphan, Peter, back to the United States. Films of this sort rely heavily on human interest to compensate for their lack of drama. The only dramatic moment comes when the father (Robert Young) is searching for a passenger willing to make Peter part of the luggage allowance. Finally, an Englishwoman emigrating to Canada, torn between transporting the boy or her heirlooms, decides that a child's future has priority over material goods.

Journey for Margaret differs from the usual war film only in theme; the purpose is the same; to inspire hate for the enemy. When the father cries "O God, let me stay mad; give me the wisdom, the strength to stay mad," he is not praying so much as offering an anti-prayer that confuses one of the cardinal virtues (wisdom) with one of the seven deadly sins (anger). Yet wartime morality sanctions inversion since war itself is an inversion that allows one to invoke heaven's wrath rather than its blessing and to cultivate a vice rather than a virtue.

While *Journey for Margaret* portrays an American's compassion for the children of war, Fox's *The Pied Piper* (1942) shows that even a stuffy Englishman (Monty Woolley) can be moved by their plight. The Englishman's task, however, is more difficult; he has to shepherd six children through Vichy France. Originally, the script called for one of the children to be a Polish Jew, but that would have darkened the tone. The film includes some comic and even ironic touches, making it far more interesting than *Journey for Margaret*, which has neither.

Screenwriter Nunnally Johnson did not plan *The Pied Piper* as an anti-Nazi film; the plot would not allow it since the group is saved from the Gestapo by a Nazi major who asks that his niece, who is half Jewish, be included among the Englishman's charges in return for safe passage across the Channel. With the suave Otto Preminger as Major Diessen, *The Pied Piper* is in the same category as *The Moon Is Down* (another Nunnally Johnson screenplay, which also features a sympathetic Nazi played by Cedric Hardwicke). New York's *P.M.* (13 August 1942) noted the similarity, wondering whether Preminger's performance might be "grounds for the renewal of the storm raised by . . . *The Moon Is Down* over the question of portraying Nazis in any humane light." Naziphobes—and were there any moviegoers who weren't—needn't have worried; the following year Preminger was back directing, and Cedric Hardwicke had rejoined the Allies in *Cross of Lorraine*.

It often happened in the forties that the better example of a certain kind of film came from a lesser studio. Far superior to *Journey for Margaret* is another war orphan film that had little impact because it was made on Poverty Row and released after V-J Day: Monogram's *China's Little Devils* (1945), starring one of the most likeable child actors to appear on the screen, "Ducky" Louie as Little Butch, a Chinese orphan adopted by the Flying Tigers. Butch organizes a children's guerrilla band, the "Little Devils," that ambushes Japanese patrols. Although the Little Devils speak in argot picked up from the Flying Tigers ("They'd never suspect a dame," one says when they decide to use a girl as decoy), there is nothing cute about their tough talk. Even when director Monta Bell has them die Western style, falling sideways and clutching their midriffs, they do it without the slightest trace of self-consciousness.

Although Bell encourages tears at the death of Little Butch, he does not use a child's execution by the Japanese to gain audience sympathy. Death, in war movies, is often the stage before transfiguration. Butch's dream has always been to be part of a bombing raid on Tokyo. To suggest that death has not robbed him of his dream, Bell dissolves from the boy's body to the sky above Tokyo. It is lucky that Monta Bell was working at Monogram; at MGM, Butch's spirit would have been in the cockpit, hovering over the pilot.

Although World War II was hailed as a people's war, one has the impression, from the movies at least, that the people—or the people who mattered—were women. Women were a special case, but then,

The title characters of China's Little Devils *(1945) plus one adult (Paul Kelly). "Ducky" Louie third from left. Courtesy Eddie Brandt's Saturday Matinee*

women were always special to the industry, even at the beginning when nickelodeon owners, in an effort to win respectabilty, wooed middle-class women into their theaters by offering them free admission to prenoon shows.[19] The industry soon learned that women liked to see themselves on the screen and that men liked to see women on the screen. But women came first. There was no male equivalent of "dish night," that phenomenon of the thirties and forties when women would go to the movies and come home with a free piece of dinnerware. While "woman's picture" is a common term, "man's picture" is not.

By the time World War II came along, the movies had already featured women in a wide variety of professions from aviatrix to surgeon, from lawyer to reporter. Even within the extremes of the virgin and the whore, there was variety as well as hierarchy.[20] The *virgo intacta* with her Victorian curls, corseted waist, and rainwater eyes (Lillian Gish) was superior to the fun-loving *virgo ludens* (Martha Raye, Patsy Kelly; later Betty Hutton). The backstreet mistress (Irene Dunne and Margaret Sullavan, respectively, in the 1935 and

Sister Clothilde (Barbara Britton) and the dying Reverend Mother (Lucile Watson) in Till We Meet Again *(1944). Courtesy* MCA

1941 *Back Street)* was nobler than the floozy (Joan Crawford in *Rain*, 1932; Bette Davis in *Marked Woman*).

Having recruited a battalion of celluloid women, Hollywood had no difficulty in mobilizing it after Pearl Harbor. The types remained the same; only the circumstances were different. The regenerative woman had existed earlier, but in the thirties, she was giving men the will to live even though she might be dying (*Dark Victory*); or she was helping them become better men because, as a woman, she was better than they (*Made for Each Other*, *In Name Only*, both 1939). In the forties, she was helping men become patriotic. In *This Above All* (1942), for instance, a woman's impassioned speech to a deserter sends him back to his regiment. In the space of three films, and all because of women, Alan Ladd went from the rackets to the army (*Lucky Jordan*), from oil exporting to guerrilla warfare (*China*), and from male chauvinism to, if not downright feminism, then an awe of woman that bordered on idolatry (*O.S.S.*).

One of the best woman's films of the period, and one that also hints at male feminism, is *Till We Meet Again* (1944). Its success was the result of a collaboration between a screenwriter, an associate producer, and a producer-director, all of whom were predisposed toward films portraying women in a sympathetic light. The screenwriter was Lenore Coffee, who had written the scripts of *Mother's Cry* (1932) and two Bette Davis vehicles, *The Great Lie* (1941) and *Old Acquaintance* (1943). The associate producer was David Lewis, who had produced *Camille* (1937) at MGM and *Dark Victory* at Warner Bros. While Frank Borzage was not a woman's director in the sense that Edmund Goulding and George Cukor were, his romanticism was spiritual, so that no matter how a relationship between a man and a woman began, by the end "she gives him a new, more spiritual outlook on life."[21] This is certainly the case in *Till We Meet Again*, in which Sister Clothilde (Barbara Britton), a novice in a French convent, accompanies an aviator across enemy lines on a journey resulting in his freedom but her death.

High shots and religious iconography establish the superiority of the nuns, distinguishing them from mere mortals. When the Reverend Mother is killed after refusing the Nazis permission to search her convent, the camera cranes upward, framing her and Clothilde in a pietà; similarly, at Clothilde's death, when her hand opens to reveal a rosary, the camera again ascends, as if to indicate where Clothilde has gone.

Women do more than play a major role in *Till We Meet Again*; they play the only role. Even the aviator (Ray Milland) is a feminist; in a speech better delivered than written, he praises his wife as the paradigm of womanhood, recalling how she would make him feel "masculine, superior" and how, in her absence, he would gaze longingly at her clothes. His panegyric is so eloquent that Clothilde compares it to a litany; the aviator's enumeration of his wife's virtues recalls the Litany of the Virgin recited in the convent garden at the beginning of the film. The Virgin's qualities are shared by all women in *Till We Meet Again*—the Reverend Mother who hides enemies of the Third Reich in her convent, the local resistant whose arrest necessitates Clothilde's taking her place, even the proprietress of the laundry who is brave until the Nazis apply a hot iron to her face.

What keeps *Till We Meet Again* from becoming a lacy valentine to the anima is Borzage's appreciation of the paradoxical nature of the religious life. When a woman takes the veil, she becomes a *sponsa Christi* or bride of Christ. Clothilde lives out the paradox by posing as the aviator's wife, serving the Christ-as-other and enjoying a relationship with him as spiritual and symbolic as the one she would have with Christ when she became a nun. Borzage found something unusual in the relationship between the novice and the aviator—a purity that never descends to naiveté because the individuals are too intelligent for regression and too serious for passion.

Borzage had a talent for repeating visual motifs in such a way that they commented on each other. When Clothilde and the aviator leave the cottage they have shared, Clothilde blows out the candle, its spiralling smoke marking the end of their symbolic marriage. When she looks for the aviator in the dark hall of the boardinghouse, a trail of smoke seems to suggest his presence; but it is not the aviator but the Nazi major who steps out of the darkness. Here the smoke denotes another end—the end of Clothilde's life.

When the aviator sees Clothilde for the first time, he is coming down the stairs as she is scrubbing the floor. At the end of the film, he is again making a descent—down a ladder and into a waiting boat. But once he gets into the boat, Borzage reverses their former positions. The aviator is now in the subordinate posture, looking up at Clothilde as he kisses her hands. Clothilde, who resembles a Madonna at the beginning, becomes a Christ at the end. Shot like the Reverend Mother, she also dies with a prayer on her lips as the camera cranes upward for another Borzage high shot.

War brought out the heroine in the most demure types. A professor's virginal daughter saves the life of a freedom fighter by jumping into bed with him so the Gestapo will think they are lovers (*Hangmen Also Die*). The gentle Jade (Katharine Hepburn with authentic oriental eyes) poisons the food of an entire Japanese regiment in *Dragon Seed* (1944). When a stage director yields to Nazi pressure and deletes lines from the Sermon on the Mount, a Jewish actress restores them and delivers the speech intact (*Address Unknown*, 1944).

There is no single explanation for the preponderance of woman's pictures during the forties. One reason certainly was that Hollywood catered to women because, during the war, women formed the bulk of the moviegoing public. Hollywood was not alone in this regard; the fan magazines lauded women's contributions to the war effort, at times making it seem that theirs were more important than men's. The cover of a June 1944 *Motion Picture* is a pitch for war bonds; it shows a hand holding a one hundred-dollar bond, but the fingernails are painted red. The magazines also show the stars looking less than glamorous—returning exhausted from bond drives, wearing overalls, or donning hard hats to chat with the welders, as if to say that even the goddesses are roughing it for Uncle Sam.

When Bette Davis laments that "they're too young or too old" in

Thank Your Lucky Stars (1943), she might well be singing about the plight of the Hollywood moviemakers. "What's good is in the army" might be an exaggeration, but not much of one. The truth is that there were not many male stars who could carry a film by themselves; James Cagney could when he got the right part, which he did in *Yankee Doodle Dandy*; but he would not get another opportunity until *White Heat*. Bette Davis, on the other hand, had been carrying all of her films since *Dangerous* (1935). Even *"Mr. Skeffington"* (1944) is a misnomer: Davis's character, Mrs. Skeffington, is the dominant one. The actors who looked fit for combat were put into combat films—even Cary Grant, who seemed decidedly ill at ease in *Destination Tokyo*. Fortunately, combat films do not require an iconic presence, just action.

Even in movies without a wartime setting, men often played second fiddle to women. In *The Major and the Minor* (1942), the major (Ray Milland) has little to do but play to the minor—Ginger Rogers in a tour de force, impersonating a twelve-year-old and a middle-aged woman when she is not appearing as the heroine. In *Take a Letter, Darling* (1942), "Darling" is Fred McMurray taking dictation from boss lady, Rosalind Russell.

That there were more—and better—actresses than actors around in the forties only meant that scripts had to be created for them. It does not explain the industry's enshrinement of woman, which reached religious proportions in the forties. For that, one would have to enter the psyches of the men who made the movies—men like Louis B. Mayer, whose love of mother made the canonization of woman and the family the hallmark of his studio; like Irving Thalberg, whose adulation of Norma Shearer resulted in her looking more beautiful in his films than anywhere else; like Darryl F. Zanuck and Harry Cohn, whose obsession was with femininity that was cool and brassy or lush and otherworldly. Perhaps it was a collective epiphany that could only happen in a collaborative medium like film: the realization that movie goddesses would satisfy America's craving for a mythology it had never had (and at the same time enable the mythmakers to pay off their mortgages).

The filmmakers of Hollywood's Golden Age found the anima within themselves and held it up for the rest of the world to see, as if in a transfiguring mirror or a magic glass. That the image was universal was a reflection of film's archetypal nature and the Jungian bent of filmmakers who understood the collective unconscious without ever having read Jung. This kind of naiveté or Apollonianism, similar to the sort that Nietzsche claimed created epic poetry, mythologized women in a way not seen since the Middle Ages. The dark and the fair, the terrible mother and the blessed damsel—all the faces of the anima, in fact—were filtered through that cone of speckled light that filled the screen with moving pictures. That one speaks of celluloid woman rather than celluloid man points to an industry dominated by men who discovered their anima, rather than by women who discovered their animus.

By 1941 America had been predisposed toward the superwoman. Since the beginning of the sound era, moviegoers had been seeing women putting children above themselves, defying the mob, facing firing squads, accepting terminal illness with resignation, enduring ostracism to vacation with their married lovers. Now they would see women lashed, imprisoned, and tortured in ways that were either left to the imagination or graphically shown.

The dark or malefic side of woman was pretty much relegated to the dark of the moon for the duration. When the dark lady was allowed to appear, she had a noirish, low-key look that identified her as a nether force (the Nazi agent Veronica Lake plays in *The Hour before the Dawn*, 1944); or she was wearing something totally incongruous that made her seem mindless (the mink coat that Ellen Drew gads about in while her surgeon husband tends the wounded in *China Sky*, 1945).

Those are not real women; they are female parodies. The real woman is inseparable from her country, so that in defending one, a man is defending both. Some countries seem to embody the spirit of the male (Germany, *das Vaterland*), others the spirit of the female (Mother Russia). America is a motherland; it is hardly coincidental that the first sight greeting immigrants was the Statue of Liberty, the Lady with a Torch, or that the song that became America's second anthem during the war was "God Bless America," forever associated with Kate Smith, which proclaims America's gender without the slightest fear of sexism, asking God to "stand beside her and guide her."

The movies made an even deeper connection between women and war. If America is a woman, her virtue must be defended at all costs. Hence rape, actual or possible, real or threatened, is a recurrent theme in the war movies.

The distinction Hollywood made between the way the Germans and the Japanese raped women was based on the distinction it made between the Germans and the Japanese: Germans were inhuman, Japanese subhuman. Being subhuman is worse; as Cary Grant observes in *Destination Tokyo*, "The Japs don't understand the love we have for our women. They don't even have a word for it in their language." (Of course, he fails to add that English also lacks such a word.)

The Germans stalk women as if they were quarry. Although the Germans occasionally commit rape, they are inclined to degrade women or threaten them with enforced prostitution. A Soviet physician is reminded that if she does not curb her tongue, the Reich "will find some work . . . which does not require a skilled hand" (*Bomber's Moon*, 1943). The major informs Clothilde in *Till We Meet Again* that she will not be killed because he has something else in mind for her; a stray bullet prevents his intentions from being realized.

In *Hitler's Madman* (1943), Douglas Sirk's first American film, several Czech girls are detained after school and lined up for inspection before being shipped off to the Russian front. Heydrich (George Sanders) scrutinizes each girl, his comments ranging from "so-so" to "not bad, except the glasses." The horror of the scene does not derive from his sadistic manner, which recalls that of an urbane cattle inspector, but from the way Sirk frames the shot, so that, off to the side, there is a room where a doctor and a nurse are waiting. When one of the girls realizes it is an examining room, she cries, "Don't go in there. We'll all be examined as if we were cattle; then we'll be sent to the Russian front." Rather than submit to such degradation, she climbs up on the window ledge and is shot when she refuses to come down.

Originally, the Breen Office objected to the examination scene "on the grounds of suggestion of white slavery" in accordance with Article 2.4 of the Code ("White slavery shall not be treated"). However, MGM, which released *Hitler's Madman* (which was produced independently by Seymour Nebenzal), believed that "the scene might be possibly passed as a war measure,"[22] as indeed it was—another instance of the Code's flexible interpretation if the enemy is the white slaver.

The Japanese had no Russian front to which to send women; they raped them on the spot, as they did in Nanking where, within a month of its fall in 1937, there were about 20,000 cases of rape. Hollywood never forgot the rape of Nanking, one of the few times the word was applicable in both the literal and figurative sense. In *So Proudly We Hail*, one of the nurses on Bataan, fearing it will fall to the Japanese, expresses her fear of being a prisoner of war: "I was in Nanking. I saw what happened to the women there." Although another nurse begs her to stop, she continues, "When the Red Cross protested, the Japanese called it the privilege of serving his Imperial Majesty's troops. It's an honor you die from."

This kind of dialogue with its grisly ellipses is fairly standard; it is rape by circumlocution, where everyone understands what is left out. In *Salute to the Marines* (1943), burly Wallace Beery warns American women in the Philippines of their possible fate: "Did you women folks ever hear of Nanking? Jap troops were there, too!" From the looks on their faces, one knows they have heard.

Rape by the Japanese has its own conventions; it is committed with gleeful malevolence, with toothy grins and flashing eyes, as if rape were a form of neither gratification nor violence but of perverseness. Japanese soldiers no sooner see a woman than they ravish her. In *Behind the Rising Sun* (1943), they overpower a Chinese woman as the camera pans up to a notice that reads: "All women will welcome all Japanese soldiers"—"welcome" being the euphemism of the age.

In *China* a Japanese soldier, after killing a Chinese girl's father, turns to the now defenseless girl; the sun's glare turns the lenses of his hornrim glasses into spheres of evil. Although the girl's fate is inevitable, one is not quite prepared for the scene in which Alan Ladd and Loretta Young arrive at the girl's house. Director John Farrow composed the shot so that, as the two of them enter, one can see clear across to the bedroom; the door is ajar, and the girl writhes screaming on the bed. Balancing the entrance of Ladd and Young is the exit from the bedroom of three Japanese soldiers; one of them is the soldier with the glasses. Instinctively, Young strips off her raincoat and rushes into the bedroom to cover the girl (who later dies from the ordeal), while Ladd kills the three soldiers (whom he later terms "flies in a manure heap").

Age does not seem to matter to the Japanese. In *Dragon Seed*, they come upon an elderly Chinese woman, too tired to flee; their coarse laughter is followed by her piercing scream. Later in the film, Orchid meets a similar fate. In the Pearl Buck novel, she is raped on the street. In the film, however, she leaves her children in a bamboo wood, instructing her young son that "a little man does not cry out no matter what he sees." To distract the Japanese, she runs in the direction opposite the children's hiding place. Stumbling, she falls to the ground; looking up, she finds herself encircled by Japanese soldiers.

Rape by suggestion is always more horrifying than rape by portrayal. Suggestion encourages voyeurism and guilt, which become so intertwined as to be inseparable. One wants to see more, although one knows one shouldn't; one feels guilty about wanting to. When full-fledged rape finally reached the screen in Ingmar Bergman's *The Virgin Spring* (1960), it induced revulsion, not dread, because there were no ellipses; Bergman had filled them in.

Not every woman could join the armed services and become a WAC like Lana Turner in *Keep Your Powder Dry* (1944) or a nurse like Claudette Colbert in *So Proudly We Hail*. The mothers and wives who tended the hearth, hung the starred flag in the living room window, and waited until the boys came home (or until the telegram arrived from the War Department) were equally vital to the war effort. Naturally, the homefront received less attention from filmmakers than the battlefield; with husbands and lovers away and adultery banned for the duration, plots were at a premium. Nevertheless, by a gamble that ultimately paid off, a minor British novel became a major American film whose name was that of the best known lady of the home front, played by the screen's best known lady—Greer Garson. The film is *Mrs. Miniver.*[23]

That the Minivers were neither an American family nor a typical middle-class family did not diminish the film's popularity; when *Mrs. Miniver* opened at Radio City Music Hall in the summer of 1942, it broke all previous attendance records and went on to win Academy Awards for best picture, best director (William Wyler), best screenplay, best supporting actress (Teresa Wright), best black-and-white photography (Joseph Ruttenberg), and best actress (Greer Garson, who gave the longest acceptance speech in the Academy's history).

Oddly enough, it was the Minivers' atypicalness that made the film so popular, again proving Hollywood's understanding of the mythic process. Because the Minivers were a privileged family, a holy family, they were a mythic family. Myth is exemplary, and so the Minivers became an exemplary family, a model for Americans. They set an example to which others should aspire. Had the Minivers been American, they could not have been mythic. America was not bombed by the Luftwaffe; England was. Americans did not retreat to a bomb shelter and read *Alice in Wonderland* to their children; the Minivers did. *Mrs. Miniver* is also pre-Pearl Harbor; the crucial date is not 7 December 1941, but 3 September 1939, when England declared war on Germany. Although the film covers only the period from the late summer of 1939 to the late summer of 1940, it is enough time for the Minivers to show their mettle.

Obviously, no woman ever behaved like Kay Miniver; but then, no Christian ever faced the lions as fearlessly as Elissa Landi in *The Sign of the Cross*. The point is that, in wartime, one ought to behave

Kay Miniver (Greer Garson) confronting the enemy in her own home in
Mrs. Miniver *(1942). Courtesy* MGM/UA

like Kay Miniver; during a persecution, one ought to behave like
Elissa Landi. One also ought to be civil to the enemy, as Mrs. Miniver is when she comes upon a German flier who has parachuted on
to her grounds. She offers him food, striking him only when he commits a breach of etiquette by boasting that Germany will destroy
Western Europe.

When a Messerschmitt opens fire on the Minivers' car, leaving

Carol, Kay's daughter-in-law, critically wounded, neither woman reacts melodramatically; there is no panic, no cries, no tears. The camera is equally subdued, its restraint affirming that silent suffering is the purest kind. The soundtrack is still; neither Kay nor Carol needs music to enhance her courage. When Carol dies, Kay does not raise an angry fist to heaven; her eyes burn with grief and anger but not with defiance.

The truly heroic home-fronter will behave the same way during a war as before it. This is the acid test, as Wyler shows at the end of the film with another Sunday service recalling the one interrupted by the declaration of war. Again the choristers enter with the vicar as they did on the morning of 3 September; but the Battle of Britain has taken its toll on the congregation. Carol is not present; the seat usually occupied by the stationmaster is vacant; the acolytes' bench has one more space. The service takes place in a shell of a church. Although bombs have ripped open the roof, an RAF fighter squadron passes overhead and fills the void. *Mrs. Miniver* is one of the most cherished films of the war years because it left audiences feeling better about themselves, realizing that while they might not be the paradigm, they could at least approximate it.

Another popular, if less artistic, tribute to the ladies of the home-front, is David O. Selznick's *Since You Went Away* (1944). Although it was directed by John Cromwell, it is in every sense a Selznick production, starting with the screenplay, which is credited to "The Producer." *Since You Went Away* regards woman in same light as *Mrs. Miniver*: she is an irradiating force imparting an aura to everything she touches. The difference between the films is that while Kay Miniver's power reaches across the Atlantic, Anne Hilton's (Claudette Colbert) is more localized, its radius limited to America.

Yet Anne is still a symbol of the American home, the "unconquerable fortress" to which the film is dedicated. Selznick sees home as a feminine place, permeated by womanly virtue; it is unconquerable because woman is unconquerable, and her invincibility shields the entire household. Selznick's only two wartime films, *Since You Went Away* and *I'll Be Seeing You* (1944) both portray the American home as a cult place or shrine. In *I'll Be Seeing You*, a parolee (Ginger Rogers), returning home for the Christmas holidays, meets a battle-shocked soldier (Joseph Cotten) with no home to return to. That he should come to hers, and that her family should become his, is in keeping with Selznick's conception of the home as a place of wonders worked by a hearth goddess. She makes everyone part of the family, even a crusty boarder (Monty Woolley in *Since You Went Away*).

Claudette Colbert learning to weld in Since You Went Away *(1944).*
Courtesy Eddie Brandt's Saturday Matinee

A hearth goddess can work wonders, but not miracles; those are reserved for the Deity, who ordains at the end of *Since You Went Away* that Anne's husband, missing in action, will return. The final shot of Anne and her two daughters framed in the upstairs window is followed by the closing title: "Be of good courage and He shall strengthen your heart." The sentiments are appropriate, but the pronoun is not. Selznick's God is not a "He."

Since woman is a symbol, she must behave like one. She may faint or be stunned, but not become catatonic; she must observe the decorum of bereavement. Mrs. Sullivan in *The Sullivans* (1944) is an embodiment of this ideal. *The Sullivans* has little to do with the war; like many World War II movies, it begins before Pearl Harbor—1939. It scarcely seems a war film at all—the only battle scene lasts 3½ minutes. It is really a film about a family, an exemplary family capable of practicing the art of nobly wrought grief. It is based on the true story of Mr. and Mrs. Thomas Sullivan of Waterloo, Iowa, all five of whose sons were killed when the *ss Juneau*, on which they were serving, was hit and sunk off Guadalcanal in November 1942.

The five Sullivans together for the last time in The Sullivans *(1944). Courtesy Twentieth Century-Fox Film Corporation*

When Commander Robinson (Ward Bond) arrives at the Sullivan home with the news, Mrs. Sullivan (Selena Royle) senses the reason for his visit. "Which one?" she asks. "Is it Al?" her daughter-in-law inquires. "All five," he answers. "All five," Mrs. Sullivan repeats, shocked but not dazed. Her daughter and daughter-in-law leave the room, crying softly. Mr. Sullivan excuses himself, noting that he has never missed a day's work in thirty-three years. He is not being stoic; he is subordinating sorrow to responsibility.

When Commander Robinson appears, Mrs. Sullivan offers him coffee; at first he declines, thinking to accept would be inappropriate. Yet he knows that Mrs. Sullivan is a woman of the amenities to whom even a bearer of tragic tidings is a guest. Realizing that she will not be indulged, he says, "On second thought, I will have that cup of coffee." The glow that suffuses Selena Royle's face is one of those moments in film when an image becomes a portrait of the soul. Mrs. Sullivan's motherhood has been dealt a blow, but her womanhood is intact. Proudly, she brings him the coffee.

While most war films portray woman as a spiritual force, *The Eve of St. Mark* (1944), the screen version of Maxwell Anderson's play, also portrays woman as an emanative force flowing into men. Quizz (William Eythe) is such a part of the women in his life, his mother and his girl, Janet, that while he sleeps somewhere in the Pacific, their being enters his, and they communicate in a three-part exchange. Quizz's destiny is bound up with women. The title refers to a legend that if a maiden stands in a church doorway on St. Mark's eve and looks inside, she will see those fated to die that year. When one of the soldiers recounts the legend, two others look off to the mouth of a cave where a young girl is standing. Then there is a cut to Quizz. Quizz's death, though not shown, is presaged by the legend and the close-up of his face. His mother and Janet do not have to be told what has happened; they are part of him, and he of them.

It is what woman represents—freedom and peace, which in languages with grammatical gender are usually feminine—that make liberty worth defending, whether liberty is envisioned as Libertas, the Roman goddess of freedom with her temple on the Aventine, or as the Lady on Liberty Island. Women must have sensed their personifying power; certainly actresses did. Thus the stars came down to earth: at the Stage Door Canteen, where Katherine Cornell honored a lonely GI (Lon McCallister) by playing his Juliet in a recitation of the balcony scene from *Romeo and Juliet* (*Stage Door Canteen*, 1943); and at the Hollywood Canteen, where Joan Leslie and Bette Davis dunked donuts with homesick servicemen (*Hollywood Canteen*, 1944).

While the all-star extravaganza is Hollywood's least noteworthy tribute to woman, *Hollywood Canteen* merits a footnote in any biography of the fortieth president of the United States. When one of the hostesses asks Jane Wyman, then married to Ronald Reagan, her opinion of a particular GI, Wyman replies, "Don't ask me. I've been Reaganized." This may be the only time the president's surname has been used as a verb.

8. The Masters of the Race

When Churchill announced that England "will never negotiate with Hitler and his gang," he was using a designation for the Nazis that Hollywood had already appropriated. Where there is a gang, there are gangsters; whether they run a syndicate or a Reich, whether they control the North Side of Chicago or a *Gau* in Germany, they are cut from the same cloth. The fiefdoms that crime czars carved out of American cities had their equivalent in the *Gaue* or geographical regions into which the Reich was divided, with the gauletiers who governed them being no better than ganglords.

Since the Hollywood Nazi and the gangster were kindred spirits, they often appeared in the same film (e.g., *Lucky Jordan, All through the Night*) and were distinguishable only by accent. Some films even went so far as to suggest there was no difference between the crooked politicians at home and the Nazis abroad. At the end of *Pilot No. 5* (1943), an Air Force major discovers that political corruption and Nazism are synonymous: "I see them all now as one enemy—one fascist enemy—our enemy who shall be destroyed."

Keeper of the Flame (1942) goes further, imagining the rise of domestic fascism from a Nazi model. Among the papers of the Great American, whose death is mourned throughout the world, is a "Plan for Revolution and Reconstruction of the United States as Ally of the Axis" based on the Hitlerian method of exploiting racial prejudice and feeding the frustrations of the disaffected and the unemployed.

There was, however, an essential difference between gangsters and Nazis in the movies: their treatment of women. Gangsters might rough them up, cut them, or push a grapefruit in their face; but, as a rule, they did not abuse them sexually. The Nazis did, not so much by rape as by sexual intimidation and slimy innuendo. In *Till We*

Meet Again, Major Krupp encounters some girls playing blind man's bluff. When one of them collides with him, he eyes her lecherously, observing that "there is room in the Reich for healthy young girls." Later, he threatens Sister Clothilde with the brothels, never phrasing it so bluntly but reminding her that "the German Reich has use for such women" as she. The Nazis in *Hostages* look upon women as chattel, speaking of them impersonally ("a carload from Poland has arrived") or using their plight to turn a cruel phrase ("the tears of a young girl make the salt of the earth").

These and other films illustrated the Nazis' pathological attitude toward women, conditioned in part by Hitler's own ambivalence toward the female and encouraged by the homoerotic elitism of the ss, Heinrich Himmler's black-shirted knights, who regarded each other as comrades and women as breeders. In a society in which women who bred the master race were told, after every fourth child they bore the Führer, that they were "only a link in the clan's endless chain,"[1] the female was merely an avatar of Mother Earth, with her womb perpetually open.

It was inevitable that the Third Reich would develop an elaborate propagation program complete with breeding farms and pagan marriage rites; it was natural that Hollywood would show an interest in it. But it was more curiosity than serious interest, the kind of curiosity that prompts respectable citizens to take an occasional peek at pornographic magazines. Two films on the theme of propagating for the Fatherland appeared in 1943: RKO's *Hitler's Children* and Monogram's *Women in Bondage*. While the plots are fictitious, the details are not.

Like any film of the forties, *Hitler's Children* resorts to euphemism to describe the love camps where the elite would meet and breed. But when euphemism is used to camouflage something gross, it degenerates into an antitrope; the effect is that of a smutty joke that has been overly sanitized and therefore seems dirtier because the obscenity that is natural to it has been replaced by slick circumlocution. Sometimes the circumlocution results in hilarious archaism: in the "rest homes" (presumably *Lebensborn* maternity homes) lovers "may meet and decide to share the experience that makes them worthy of the Führer."

At the end of *Hitler's Children*, the recalcitrant heroine is sentenced to receive ten lashes, followed by "special treatment" (sterilization) at the women's clinic. One of the most frequently reproduced shots from any World War II movie is the flogging of Anna (Bonita Granville). It is not the flogging as such that embeds itself in the memory, but the way in which it is done—as ritual humilia-

The lashing of Anna (Bonita Granville) in Hitler's Children *(1943). Courtesy* RKO *Radio Pictures*

tion, the sort that occurs in bad dreams. Girls from the labor force troop into the enclosure to the sound of a drum roll; the ss take their position in front of the wire fence; the flagpole rises like a totem into a sky clouding over with swirls of grey; Anna is forced to kneel, her hands tied to the base of the flagpole; the back of her blouse is ripped open; the whip is uncoiled. After the first few lashes, her lover interrupts the flagellation, an action that brings death to both of them.

It is hard to imagine anything more lurid than *Hitler's Children,* but *Women in Bondage* is. Although it opens with a prologue vouching for its authenticity, it is the kind of movie one wishes were pure fiction. Like *Hitler's Children,* it works on the dream level, but evokes the kind of dream that is more loathsome than frightening, the sort from which one awakens with a pasty mouth and an acid stomach rather than with a blanched and sweating face. While "everything in the film is true," it is the truth of the gothic and the grotesque. Consequently, *Women in Bondage* seems distorted because it reflects what is distorted in human nature. That the vehicle for Nazi depravity is a cheaply made, atrociously acted movie is the perfect reductio ad absurdum—Nazism ground to the pulp of exploitation and given a production whose budget is as low as its subject.

In *Women in Bondage*, Margot Bracken (Gail Patrick), the wife of a paralyzed German officer, arrives in Berlin where she is greeted by a contingent of Hitler's women who laughingly vow to make her one of theirs. It is no laughing matter, however; in record time, Margot becomes "Frau Section Leader" of a group that in its dress (white blouse, black tie, black skirt) looks like the League of German Girls. The members' function is to breed the master race, in or out of wedlock.

Although *Women in Bondage* is schlock, it is an accurate reflection of the Reich's breeding program, as formulated by its Mendel, Heinrich Himmler. In the subplot, Toni (Nancy Kelly in pigtails), who is engaged to an ss officer, is told that "only physically perfect women can marry the cream of German manhood." Himmler was so committed to homogenizing the crème de la crème that he made it impossible for ss members to marry without permission of the Central Office for Race and Settlement, which among its other functions aided ss men in their choice of a wife.[2] The writers of *Women in Bondage* speculated on how women might prove worthy of mating with the elite. Given the film's emphasis on the physical, which is never less than morbidly unhealthy, the answer is simple: a physical exam, or to use the sleazy euphemism, "an examination for motherhood."

At first the examination seems a travesty of a group physical. The girls sit on benches, idly chatting; then they are weighed, fully clothed. In the next scene they are draped in sheets as they line up for an eye exam. Why one must strip for an eye exam is never explained, but what has happened in the ugly interim between stepping on the scale and squinting at an eye chart does not so much tease the imagination as pander to it, making the viewer feel unclean for even speculating.

To pass the examination for motherhood, a woman must have eyes in as good condition as any other organ. Toni is deemed ineligible for marriage, not for reasons that have anything to do with childbearing but because she is nearsighted. Devastated, she rushes into the street, peering into the faces of passersby and protesting "But it's only my eyes!" Another examinee, on the other hand, breezes out of the hospital and into the arms of her betrothed, who anxiously asks whether she passed and is delighted by her ecstatic "yes."

Eventually, Margot must report for her examination, but she is chauffered to it and spared the indignity of wearing a sheet. However, she is not exempt from the duty to breed. Since her husband is paralyzed, she is told to copulate with her brother-in-law. Although this may sound like a parody of the biblical command to "increase and multiply," it is not nonfactual. The more preposterous the film seems, the closer it is to the truth. Himmler wanted any married and single women up to the age of thirty-five who did not have four children to beget that number by cohabiting with Aryan males. He also expected his ss officers to impregnate not only their wives but also childless women thirty or older.[3]

The film's accuracy extends beyond eugenics; having shown how the New Order has made sex and breeding synonymous, it goes on to illustrate how Nazism attempts to reconcile all opposites: marriage and promiscuity, Christian baptism and the ss christening ceremony, propagation and euthanasia. When an old woman denounces a girl for her promiscuity, the woman is promptly declared unfit and marked for euthanasia, while the girl mates indiscriminately and delivers her superior offspring in a *Lebensborn* maternity center. If sex, breeding, state-controlled illegitimacy, and euthanasia are interrelated, they must have religious sanction—not of the Church but of the state. Although Himmler became disenchanted with Catholicism, he never forgot its rituals, which were easily transferable to Nazism. He modelled his elite ss after the Jesuits, the elite of the Catholic Church. He fashioned a catechism out of the traditional series of questions and answers about the faith, with the recruits affirming that believing in God is believing in Germany and believing in Hitler is believing in God. He parodied the baptismal rite by having the infant wrapped in a swastika-embroidered blanket and christened on an altar where, instead of a tabernacle, stood the Führer's picture. In *Women in Bondage*, when the ss officer begins the christening, intoning "in the name of the Führer," a priest rushes in and counters with "in the name of the Father," striking a pose ordinarily used by the Transylvanians when they held up a cross to Dracula.

That a Poverty Row studio made *Women in Bondage* was the perfect commentary on the spiritual impoverishment of the Third Reich. The real irony, however, was that Himmler's theory of racial selectivity was the basis of an exploitation film, the forties' equivalent of soft-core pornography. Stud farms, state-sanctioned promiscuity, women subjected to gynecological examinations, and men released from family obligations to sire offspring are the stuff of the worst male fantasies. But Nazi eugenics was a male fantasy predicated on a misdirected oedipalism resulting in the degradation of women. Understandably, such a program would have Hitler's sanction: "It was surely a reflection of this degradation, intensified by the conditions of his private life, that of the six women who were close to Hitler in the course of his life five committed or attempted suicide."[4]

Hitler's Supporting Cast

After Pearl Harbor, the studios no longer worried about invasion of privacy suits if they wished to feature Third Reich figures by name. In *Confessions of a Nazi Spy*, Martin Kosleck made an unbilled appearance as an unidentified Goebbels; in *The Hitler Gang* (1944), he received screen credit for his portrayal of the propaganda minister, who was identified by name. Paul Andor also played Goebbels in *Enemy of Women* (1944), Monogram's follow-up to *Women in Bondage*. Based on an original screen story by Alfred Zeisler, who also directed, *Enemy of Women* is fictionalized history, accurately depicting Goebbels as a failed man of letters who could not resist the charms of beautiful actresses. The plot revolves around his obsession with an actress called Maria Brandt, clearly modelled after Lida Baarova, the Czech actress with whom Goebbels had a much-publicized romance (until Hitler decided it had become too public for the good of the Reich).

Hitler himself was portrayed five times in the 1940s by Robert Watson, who made a career out of playing the Führer, in *The Devil with Hitler* (1942), *Hitler—Dead or Alive* (1943), *That Nazty Nuisance* (1943), *The Hitler Gang* (1944), and *The Miracle of Morgan's Creek* (1944). Ludwig Donath also portrayed Hitler in *The Strange Death of Adolf Hitler* (1943). While Rudolf Hess does not appear in *To Be or Not To Be*, his 1941 peace flight to Britain is the basis of a hilarious moment in the film. When a Polish actor in Hitler makeup parachutes onto a field in Scotland, a farmer spots him and says, "First Hess, now him."

The assassination of Reinhard Heydrich, "the beast of Prague" (a title he acquired when he became Reich Protector of Bohemia and Moravia), was dramatized in two 1943 releases, *Hangmen Also Die* and *Hitler's Madman*. Although *Hangmen Also Die* is reputedly the better film because the director was Fritz Lang and the screenwriter Bertolt Brecht (with the help of John Wexley),[5] it takes so many liberties with the facts that the assassination it depicts bears no resemblance at all to what took place on 27 May 1942. The film shows

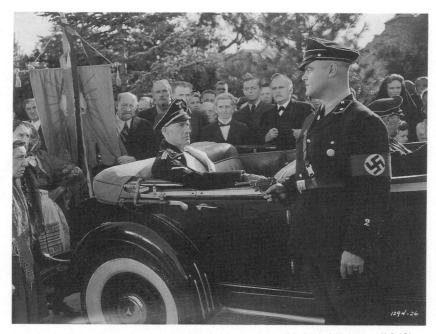

Heydrich (John Carradine) in his black Mercedes in Hitler's Madman *(1943).
Courtesy* MGM/UA

Heydrich killed on a Prague street. What really happened, however,
is recorded more or less faithfully in *Hitler's Madman*, another case
of the lesser film being the more accurate. The producer, Seymour
Nebenzal, received his information from Eduard Benes and Jan Ma-
saryk, president and foreign minister, respectively, of the Czech government in exile. *Hitler's Madman* may have embellished the facts,
but at least the embellishments are consistent with Heydrich's character.

· *Hitler's Madman* shows the assassination occurring, as it in fact
did, on a road outside Prague. When the car in which Heydrich was
being driven slowed down at a turn in the road, two British-trained
Czech operatives, who knew his itinerary, ambushed the car—one
of them hurling a grenade into it. Since the film emphasizes Heydrich's sadistic treatment of women, it was poetic justice to include
a woman in the assassination plot. Thus in the film, by prearrange-
ment with the assassins, a girl bicycles into the center of the road,

forcing the driver to brake and distracting Heydrich, who muses that "a beautiful girl means a beautiful day," at which point the resistance fighters emerge from their hiding place.

Hangmen Also Die ends with the execution of the hostages taken in reprisal for Heydrich's murder. Historically, there were no hostages; again, *Hitler's Madman* is closer to the truth. Hitler retaliated by ordering the razing of the Czech village of Lidice; the men were killed and the women and children (except for a few deemed racially fit for adoption) were shipped off to the camps. The powerful coda of *Hitler's Madman* is a recitation of Edna St. Vincent Millay's "The Murder of Lidice" by a ghostly chorus.

The Nazi that caused screenwriters the most trouble was Field Marshal Erwin Rommel, who was too civilized for caricature, too tragic for vilification. In *Five Graves to Cairo* (1943), Erich von Stroheim made Rommel such an extension of himself that Rommel hardly seems responsible for the heroine's death. Stroheim did the same in *Grand Illusion* (1937) playing the World War I squadron commander, Rauffenstein; when Rauffenstein has to shoot Boeldieu, one pities Rauffenstein, not Boeldieu, who before dying admits that Rauffenstein has done his duty.

After the war, Rommel ceased being a wit and became a tragic figure. In *The Desert Fox* (1951), Erwin and Frau Rommel (James Mason and Jessica Tandy) seem more like Shakespeare's Brutus and Portia than a Nazi and his wife. Rommel's initiation into Operation Valkyrie, the code-named plot to assassinate Hitler, recalls Brutus' joining the conspiracy to kill Caesar. Just as Brutus must be convinced there is no way to stop Caesar short of murder, Rommel must have proof that Hitler's refusal to make peace with the Allies is the result of madness before he supports the plot. Just as Cassius goads on Brutus, Dr. Karl Strolin prods Rommel, until he realizes, as Rommel does also, that the one thousand–year Reich will not last beyond 1944.

Hitler survived the abortive Operation Valkyrie; suspecting Rommel's complicity, he gave Rommel the choice of a cyanide capsule or a treason charge. Rommel chose the former. His action merited a tribute from Churchill, heard at the end of *The Desert Fox*, in which he is lauded because "he came to hate Hitler and all his works, and took part in the conspiracy to rescue Germany by displacing the maniac and the tyrant." One would think from such a eulogy that Rommel had carried the briefcase with the bomb that exploded under the table at the Wolf's Lair on 20 July 1944. While Rommel is a modern Brutus, there is a difference between the German and the

The leading members of The Hitler Gang *(1944). Courtesy* MCA

Roman: Brutus struck a real blow for freedom; Rommel only lent moral support. Rommel's real tragedy was that his rise and fall paralleled Germany's; after Normandy, both Rommel and Germany went into irreversible decline.

In 1943, B.G. ("Buddy") DeSylva, then production head at Paramount, saw a German propaganda film about the Boer War that was aimed at South American audiences: in an attempt to win South American sympathy for the Axis, the film portrayed the British as ruthless imperialists. DeSylva decided that Hollywood could do a better job of propaganda (as if Hollywood hadn't been doing it already) by explaining the origins of Nazism to both North and South Americans, on the (correct) assumption that while moviegoers knew a great deal about Nazis, having seen them on the screen for four years, they knew little about their leaders. The result was *The Hitler Gang*. The film was a bit out of character for Paramount, although its atypicalness was not unprecedented (e.g., *Wake Island* was also a Paramount film).

While *The Hitler Gang* garnered respectable reviews and a spread in *Life* magazine, it was not a popular success. Perhaps its length (over two hours) and lack of stars worked against it; but more likely, it was a matter of timing. Its conclusion, that Germany would lose the war, was no longer prophetic in the spring of 1944. Yet *The Hitler Gang* did something no previous film had done: it assembled the leaders of the Third Reich in one movie: Joseph Goebbels, minister of Popular Enlightenment and Propaganda; Rudolf Hess, deputy führer; Captain Ernst Röhm, head of the Brownshirts (SA); Heinrich Himmler, SS head; Hermann Göring, chief of the Luftwaffe; Reinhard Heydrich, the SS security chief who implemented the Final Solution; Alfred Rosenberg, National Socialism's official philosopher; and Adolf Hitler himself, impersonated by the ubiquitous Robert Watson.

Although *The Hitler Gang* may have been the most informative (though not always accurate) film Hollywood made about Nazism, it is also one of the least cinematic. The Frances Goodrich and Albert Hackett screenplay is really a chronicle in which the unity is thematic, the characterization minimal, and the suspense virtually nonexistent. What matters, however, is the composite portrait of the Third Reich.

While the prologue paints the familiar picture of a Germany that embraced National Socialism because of its humiliation at Versailles, the rest of *The Hitler Gang* does not traverse familiar ground, preferring to treat incidents previously unfilmed, such as the Munich Putsch of 1923 and the 1934 Night of Long Knives. Since its purpose is to trace Nazism from an idea to an ideology, it confines itself to a sixteen-year period, from 1918 to 1934, with a montage epilogue that brings everything up to date.

Although Hollywood tended to regard Hitler as a madman, *The Hitler Gang* views that madness as perverted messianism, which is in keeping with the evidence in *Mein Kampf*, the screenwriters' primary source (despite press releases boasting that they had access to government archives). The film opens just before the World War I armistice, with Hitler hospitalized for temporary blindness from a gas attack at Ypres but raving that he has lost his sight, as he would again—and again temporarily—after hearing that Germany surrendered. That is his epiphanic moment, the moment he decides to enter politics. It is the familiar combination of battle shock and revelation, of wound and vision. The coals that burn in his eyes are his lightning from heaven, his sign.

Once they have presented the mad messiah, Goodrich and Hackett introduce the rest of the gang, withholding each member's identity until the end of the scene in which he first appears. This may not be the subtlest kind of introduction, but it can be effective if the audience is unprepared for it. For example, in Mary Renault's *The King Must Die* (1956), Theseus encounters a child in the palace of Minos who promises to love him forever. Not knowing he has just met his nemesis, he asks her name. "Phaedra," she answers, the one-word reply bringing the chapter to a chilling close. Similarly, when Gregor Strasser decides to join Hitler's party, he says, "Put my chauffeur down, too. Heinrich Himmler." Another enthusiast signs up: "Hess. Rudolf Hess."

The screenwriters manage—and quite well—with material unambiguous enough to be dramatized in a straightforward manner. The Munich Putsch emerges as the comic fiasco it was, with Hitler bursting into the beer hall and shooting at the ceiling like an outlaw in a western saloon, demanding to be made head of the Bavarian government. Göring receives a wound in his thigh that makes him a morphine addict, and the failure of the coup results in Hitler's being sentenced to a five-year prison term, nine months of which is served in a cell that doubles as a study where, amid floral tributes, he dictates *Mein Kampf* to Rudolf Hess.

The Hitler Gang is also accurate in its depiction of the Night of Long Knives when, on 30 June 1934, the Blackshirts (ss) rid the Reich of the troublesome Brownshirts (sA)—the offspring organization killing the parent. Goodrich and Hackett knew that sA leader Ernst Röhm had not been slain but imprisoned and given the choice of shooting himself or being shot; he chose the latter. It is with the killing of Röhm that *The Hitler Gang* ends. Since 1934 seemed too early a conclusion for a 1944 movie, a montage connects the SA purge with the imminent purge of the Nazis by stringing together quotations from Roosevelt, Churchill, Chiang Kai-shek, and even Stalin, whose "scorched earth" speech of 3 July 1941 was ransacked for a suitable quotation about freedom.

It is when Goodrich and Hackett have to conjecture that they reveal their inability to do what writers of historical fiction and drama must do: conjecture so persuasively that the fictional hypothesis has the force of truth. It is imaginative hypothesis that makes historical drama superior to chronicle. Unable to make the leap from fact to fancy, *The Hitler Gang* remains on the level of chronicle. The failure to invent, to recreate what might have happened, which Aristotle considers the essential difference between tragedy and history (or between the mimetic and the nonmimetic) explains why there are so few historical films of worth. Whey they adhere to the facts, they are acceptable; when they assume, they become naive; hence the justifiable criticism of Hollywoodized history.

For some reason, perhaps because they felt the script needed some sensationalism, the writers decided to include the 1931 suicide of Hitler's niece, Geli Raubal, who may have been the only woman he really loved—even more than Eva Braun, of whom Geli was apparently jealous. Hitler was infatuated with Geli, although their relationship does not seem to have gone beyond Hitler's calf-eyed adoration. In the film, Geli commits suicide after Hitler accuses her of having a lover. Historically, Geli committed suicide; she also had several lovers. Furthermore, Geli received a Catholic funeral despite the rule forbidding suicides to be buried in consecrated ground. This irregularity intrigued Goodrich and Hackett, who made much of it in the film; yet it was not quite the scandal it seemed since there were rumors that Geli's death was accidental (the proverbial gun that went off) or the result of foul play.[6] What is really bizarre is the screenwriters' insinuation that Himmler, who at the time worshipped Hitler, persuaded Heydrich to court Geli in order to make Hitler jealous. Heydrich had just joined the ss a few months before Geli's suicide, after being courtmartialed for impregnating a girl and refusing to marry her. Heydrich might have been a Lothario, but he would never have gone so far as to become Hitler's rival. There was, however, a connection between Heydrich and Geli's suicide that the writers could have exploited: Heydrich knew that Emile Maurice (Hitler's chauffeur) and Geli had been lovers and planned to use that knowledge (which he kept in a file) to blackmail Hitler in case Hitler ever tried to oust him because of the rumor that Heydrich had a Jewish grandparent.

Perhaps *The Hitler Gang*'s chief defect is its failure to distinguish between Hitler's self-mythology as reflected in *Mein Kampf* and the Hitler myth created by others, especially Goebbels. For all its efforts to supply fresh insights into Nazism, *The Hitler Gang* only succeeds in dressing up the Hitler stereotype in historical accoutrements. The film is unwilling to concede that Hitler had oratorical gifts (which he did) although, understandably, suggesting in 1944 that Hitler had anything going for him, even demagoguery, was anathema. Even so, Hitler did have his own ideas, all of which were formed by the time he was in his early twenties. But the film portrays him as having no ideas of his own and entirely dependent on the suggestions of others. He is not even credited with selecting the scapegoat for Germany's economic depression. Rosenberg recommends Christianity, but Hitler feels the Church is too strong. Hess

Ronald Reagan as a captured American pilot in Desperate Journey *(1942).*
Courtesy MGM/UA

proposes Communism. Finally, Himmler comes up with the Jews, a suggestion that sends Hitler into a state of rapture. The obsequious Hess cries, "Adolf, that is an inspiration."

It really wasn't. Hitler was an anti-Semite long before he met his gang.

The (Almost) Light Side of Nazism

To the screenwriter with a sense of humor, Nazism was a comic idiosyncrasy; but whether it provoked laughter or fear, it was still dangerous. Thus, if it was to be treated lightly, it had to be within the framework of a seriocomic plot. Farce was another alternative; but farce, Hollywood farce particularly, tends to flatten characters that were never round to begin with, reducing a stereotype to a lumbering grotesque who is more of a nuisance than a threat.

Screenwriters have no difficulty turning out melodrama; a fist can be made in a second, but deftness of touch takes years to acquire. It was deftness that anti-Nazi comedy required. It was one thing to confound the Nazis, as Ronald Reagan does in *Desperate Journey* (1943), by making up names of airplane parts (thermotrockle, dermodyne) when he is questioned about his aircraft. That is verbal befuddlement. Wringing humor from evil, however, is something else. That requires skill—rare skill. Thus, literate anti-Nazi comedy was rare; during the war, it barely existed except for *Once Upon a Honeymoon* and *To Be or Not To Be*, both 1942 releases.

The screenplay of *Once Upon a Honeymoon* was written by Sheridan Gibney, a liberal who, when he became president of the Screen Writers Guild in 1948, challenged the blacklist and ended up being a victim of it. Thus Gibney was not the sort to write an anti-Nazi comedy strictly for laughs; he worked in references to Polish fifth columnists, Austria's capitulation, and the Third Reich's sterilization program. Despite the title, he knew the film had to be more than a fairy tale. Gibney was thinking more along the lines of a historical fable. Since it is also a comic fable, it has to open on a seriocomic note—not with a solemn foreword or footage of Axis conquests, but something lighter: a pop version of the "fall of countries montage" in the form of a clock with a swastika dial (a witty variation on the familiar transitional device of the clock with the spinning hands) that moves every time Baron von Luber (Walter Slezak) visits a country and it immediately falls to the Nazis.

Once Upon a Honeymoon operates on the premise that if all is human, nothing is sacred; thus there can be humor in an Irish-American show girl's being taken for Jewish in Nazi-occupied Poland. Katie O'Hara (Ginger Rogers), the show girl, is the baron's fiancée; taking pity on her Jewish maid,she trades passports with her so the maid can leave Poland. To the Nazis, then, Katie O'Hara is Anna Sarah Beckstein.

Gibney does not allow Katie's newly acquired Jewishness to become a running gag like "Concentration Camp" Ehrhardt in *To Be or Not To Be*; but he does make it a gag line, which is something quite different. Patrick O'Toole (Cary Grant) convinces the baron he will deliver a radio address that will endear the baron to the world; what the baron does not know is that O'Toole plans to commend him for his magnanimity in marrying a Jewish American, thereby disgracing him in the eyes of the Reich. Next comes the punch line. Katie and the baron are on a ship bound for the United States when she pushes him overboard. Just as the captain is about to turn the ship around and rescue the baron, Katie says, "He can't swim." Then it's full speed ahead to the U.S.A.

While *Once Upon a Honeymoon* is a fable, *To Be or Not To Be* is a conceit: theatre as life, turning in on itself and becoming its own converse, life as theatre. The conceit starts as soon as the film begins. Voice-over narration gives the time and place: August 1939, Warsaw. But Hitler is there, walking the streets. Why are storm troopers heiling Hitler and why is Hitler heiling himself? A play about the Third Reich is about to be performed, and the Polish actor playing Hitler is so determined to give a realistic performance that he has gone out into the street in costume, only to be stopped and asked for his autograph. "And that's how Adolf Hitler came to Warsaw in August 1939."

If the conceit had ended with the prologue, theatre would have surrendered to reality, and the metaphor would have played itself out. Instead, the film keeps juggling theatre and reality, art and life, until they come to rest naturally. But first August 1939 must give way to September 1939; then theatre must give way to reality—for the moment. Circumstance ordains that the actors will perform their play about the Reich not on the stage but in their own city. The leading actress of the company, Maria Tura (Carole Lombard), can finally play a femme fatale; Bronski can play Hitler, this time convincingly; and Joseph Tura (Jack Benny) can show his versatility by impersonating both a Polish traitor and a Nazi colonel, "Concentration Camp" Ehrhardt, whose sobriquet prompts the line, "We do the concentrating, and the Poles do the camping."

That line still causes some moviegoers to wince;[7] they feel it is out of place in an Ernst Lubitsch film, that it represents a misapplication of the Lubitsch touch. The line apparently did not bother Lubitsch; although he did not write the screenplay (that was the work of Edwin Justus Mayer), he was the film's director and coproducer and could therefore have had it deleted. Even so, the line is not a blight on the film. The Lubitsch touch does not mean an immaculate movie. Lubitsch lapses occasionally, sometimes with a double entendre that backfires (e.g., the play on "plumbing" in *Cluny Brown*, 1946). Yet Lubitsch's work was rarely tasteless; he was too busy elevating taste, and when he was not elevating it, he was kidding it with a wryness that stops short of perverseness. The line may have been a lapse, but a lapse of rhetoric—not of taste. It is a play on words, perhaps the wrong words, but in no way does it diminish the art of a superbly executed conceit.

To Be or Not To Be is the closest Lubitsch came to revealing his theory of art and the secret of his touch. The touch is a grasping of reality, a holding on to life before life slips into illusion; then a reshaping of life so that it ceases to be what it was and becomes something better. His realism may have been soundstage realism, but that too can have the semblance of reality. War-ravaged Warsaw, the bombed out theater, the gutted shops are as we see them; but they have been made part of a canvas of terrible beauty; they have acquired the look of art.

When the actors pursue the traitor through the auditorium, a spot tracking him through the rows, shots ring out; as the curtain rises, the traitor stands in the middle of the stage, his hand raised in the fascist salute. Then he collapses. It all seems real, but it is also theatre; and to complete the metaphor, it is theatre enacted in a theater.

Lubitsch's Nazis are not the usual chowderheads but the bumblers of operetta; in fact, the plot with its jealous husband, dashing suitor, and mustached villain evokes *Die Fledermaus*; even the blustering Ehrhardt recalls Frosch, the jailer, in the Strauss operetta. Only Lubitsch could make an anti-Nazi operetta without music, where the lilt is in the dialogue and the images. But there is also plangency in operetta; one hears it in the *Fledermaus* czardas and in the sweet sadness of "*The Merry Widow* Waltz." In *To Be or Not To Be*, it is in Greenberg's reciting Shylock's "If you prick us do we not bleed" speech from *The Merchant of Venice* at a time when his race was being bled to death.

The Amoral Nazi

Although Hollywood found little variety among Nazis, at least it managed to come up with an alternative to the sadist and the buffoon: the amoral Nazi. Sometimes, characters who seem to be amoral (Mame Dennis of *Auntie Mame*, Sally Bowles of *I Am a Camera/Cabaret*) are merely unconventional; if they were amoral, they would never have become so endearing. Mame and Sally are free spirits, encouraging audiences to be as uninhibited as they. Nazis, on the other hand, made audiences feel doubly moral, as if they had to make up for the Nazis' lack of morality by augmenting their own.

Moral indifference is even apparent in the language with which the Nazis described the New Order; there was utter insensitivity to syntax and meaning. Hitler's "artless lack of confidence in language,"[8] as evidenced in his tortured expression, glaring contradictions, and malapropisms, was really contempt for language as humankind's primary means of communication, deriving, in turn, from a contempt for humankind. In the movies, apologists for the New Order speak in a tangle of metaphors more mangled than mixed. In *Address Unknown*, "the thick band of despair" that girdled Germany after Versailles is "thrown aside like an old cloak" as "the future sweeps toward us like an overwhelming wave." Images of encirclement, clothing, and nature—none appropriate and all clichés—compete with each other to characterize the Third Reich. Infantilism is at the heart of bad rhetoric. The indiscriminate yoking together of words, often resulting in inappropriate pairings, suggests a childlike use of language, in which words are repeated purely for their sound or the image they conjure up. It is this kind of mindless rhetoric that wins Martin Schulz (Paul Lukas) over to Nazism in *Address Unknown*. After Schulz visits Munich in 1933, he turns off the light, as Charles Foster Kane does in *Citizen Kane* (1941) when he dictates his declaration of principles, leaving the past in darkness. Schulz hears the voices of Woden and Thor so clearly that he refuses to save his Jewish friend's daughter, Griselle, from an angry mob.

The most powerful scene in the film occurs when Griselle (K.T. Stevens), appearing in a Max Reinhardtlike production, delivers a speech about the twelve beatitudes that the censor had previously wanted cut. When the censor publicly calls Griselle a "Jewess," those in the audience turn into bacchants, climbing on the stage and slashing their way through the curtain. Griselle escapes through an expressionistic forest, her hands bleeding and her legs caked with dirt. Framed between two birch trees in an unforgettable shot, she sees salvation in the distance: the Schulz home. As she stands in front of it, her face is framed again—but ominously—between the bars of the iron gate. Schulz, now the confirmed Nazi, prevents her from entering; Griselle is only able to get her hand inside the door, leaving her bloody fingerprints on the wall. The door closes, the sound of gunfire confirming the inevitable.

While Nazism leaves Schulz without compassion, he is not as desensitized as Willy (Walter Sleazak), the U-boat captain, in Hitchcock's *Lifeboat* (1943). Nor is he as bright. Willy belongs to that rarest of species, the intelligent Nazi, who to some moviegoers is worse than the good Nazi—the argument being that since Nazis are not good, they cannot be intelligent. Yet a U-boat captain would have to know more about seamanship than passengers on a lifeboat. Willy is like the *servus callidus* of Roman comedy, the clever slave who is shrewder than anyone in the household. But the beery gemütlichkeit with which Sleazak plays him and the discrepancy between Willy's pleasantly porcine face and the moral vacuum it conceals are genuinely disturbing.

One of several points argued in the film is that a Nazi's virtues are no justification for his Nazism. Willy can perform an amputation; he knows to advise the patrician Constance (Tallulah Bankhead)

Griselle (K. T. Stevens) seeing refuge in the distance but barred from reaching it. Courtesy Columbia Pictures

that if she wants to attract the proletarian Kovac (John Hodiak), she must first rid herself of her diamond bracelet, which Kovac considers a manacle of capitalism. Willy can row for long stretches, while the others tire easily; he is not prone to anger like the rest. Yet he yawns when a mother, inconsolable over her baby's death, is tied down to a rocking chair. Willy is a survivor, and he would have survived if Gus, the amputee, had not discovered he had a water flask.

Willy throws Gus overboard, and the others retaliate by doing the same to Willy. Since Gus cannot be present at the vengeance ceremony, one of them strikes Willy with Gus's old shoe.

The survivors kill Willy because he has killed one of their own. In his revised final screenplay (29 June 1943), Jo Swerling described the killing of Willy as an "orgasm of murder. . . . You get the feeling it's a snake or some poisonous toad that's being killed rather than a man." Although Hitchcock realized Swerling's intentions, he could not accept the writer's suggestion for Willy's drowning. Swerling wanted a gurgling sound, perhaps a "Heil, Hitler," as Willy went under the waves; but that would have ruined the ambivalence Hitchcock was trying to create.

Willy's murderers feel no remorse. "What do you do with people like that?" Rittenhouse (Henry Hull) asks. You kill them, naturally, as you kill a fascist who impedes the work of the resistance (*Watch on the Rhine*) or a wife who turns out to be a Nazi spy (*The Hour before the Dawn*). *Lifeboat* justifies collective murder as an act of collective security. However, collective action, in which the individuals become of one mind, is also characteristic of totalitarianism. In a way that may have been too subtle for a forties audience, *Lifeboat* implies that collective action is a mixed blessing; it is achieved by the gradual erosion of amenities, the loss of status (Constance's typewriter, then her bracelet), and finally the absorption of the individual into the mass—the upshot being collective identity; the men shirtless or in undershirts, the women jacketless, all begrimed.

If collective action can end in collective murder, it is, to use Hitchcock's favorite phrase, because "things are not what they seem"; nor are people. Rittenhouse is so charmed by Willy's songs that he accompanies him on a flute. Just when a comparatively decent Nazi seems to have emerged, he acts inhumanly. Just when the survivors of a torpedoed ship seem to represent the voice of reason, they act irrationally. The world of *Lifeboat* is one without heroes or villains; if it is a microcosmic society (like the caravan of freaks in *Saboteur*), then who on the lifeboat is best suited to govern? Initially someone must take charge; because he is a shipping magnate, Rittenhouse does, only to be castigated by Kovac, the resident leftist. While an industrialist is not the ideal captain of the ship of state, neither is a petulant Marxist. When Kovac briefly takes over, he establishes a dictatorship of the proletariat, but an ineffectual one. If Hitchcock's chief obsession is original sin, *Lifeboat* is the prime example of Hitchcock's lower case catholicism. Since everyone on the boat is a product of original sin, one shudders at the prospect of any of them heading a government.

The Birds portrays an impersonal universe, and *Psycho* (1960) an unpredictable one. The universe of *Lifeboat* is both impersonal and unpredictable; it is one in which the need to behave rationally is challenged by a more compelling argument to act irrationally—a dilemma that can only be resolved by a deus ex machina in the form of a rescue ship.

The Camps

There are no extermination camps (*Vernichtungslager*) in the films of the war years, only concentration camps (*Kozentrationslager*); these are the camps depicted in *Beasts of Berlin*, *The Mortal Storm*, and *Escape*, which were all made well before Göring's 31 July 1941 directive to Heydrich to solve the Jewish question. The camps shown in *The Cross of Lorraine* (1943) and *The Seventh Cross* (1944) are also concentration camps; the one to which the Polish Jews are to be shipped in *None Shall Escape* (1944) is presumably a labor camp. Yet these latter seem more like extermination camps than internment or labor camps.

By June 1942 news of the systematic annihilation of Jews in German-occupied countries had reached the West. While most Americans refused to believe the accounts, Lester Cole, who wrote the screenplay of *None Shall Escape*, knew they were true; so, one suspects, did Ring Lardner, Jr., who coauthored *The Cross of Lorraine* screenplay, and Fred Zinnemann, who directed *The Seventh Cross*. Although Zinnemann was not a radical like Cole and Lardner, he was as antifascist and as politically knowledgeable as they were. Thus, while all three films are set prior to the Final Solution, they reflect an awareness of it that makes the concentration camps appear to be death camps.

In terms of the plot, the rounding up of the Polish Jews in *None Shall Escape* occurs in 1939, soon after the invasion of Poland. The way in which they are rounded up, however—marched down to the railroad station and herded into cattle cars—does not suggest 1939 at all, but 1941–42 when Jews were being transported to Auschwitz in cattle cars. In the film, the Jews never reach their destination. In one of the most powerful speeches ever delivered in a World War II film, their rabbi urges them to resist: "Let us prepare ourselves to face this supreme moment in our lives. This is our last journey. It doesn't matter if it's long or short. For centuries we have sought only peace. We have tried to take our place honestly, decently, alongside of all mankind, to help make a better world, a world in which all people would live as free neighbors. We have hoped and prayed, but now we see hope was not enough. What good has it done us to submit? Submission brought us rare moments in history when we were tolerated—tolerated! Is there any greater degradation than to be tolerated? To be permitted to exist? We have submitted too long. If we want equality, we must take our place along with all other oppressed peoples. . . . By our actions we will be remembered. It is our last free choice, our moment in history. I say to you, let us choose to fight here, now."[9] The rebellion ends at the foot of a cruciform signpost at the end of a railroad platform strewn with bodies, the rabbi's among them. Dying at the foot of a cross, the Jews find their moment in history, which iconographically harks back to another moment—the Crucifixion.

In *The Seventh Cross* and in *The Cross of Lorraine*, history is also at odds with itself—the time of the plot suggests one thing, the time of the film's release another. Even though the voice-over introduction to *The Seventh Cross* gives the year of the story as 1936 "when the war and the aggression had not yet begun but the concentration camps were full," the opening scene with its overtones of crucifixion—seven crosses prepared for seven escaped prisoners—would make a 1944 audience think of the present, not of 1936. The voice-over epilogue virtually insists that *The Seventh Cross* be taken as a World War II film since what it says of Germany applies only to the time when war and aggression have not only begun but are also in progress: "Even in this nation of beasts [goodness] must still live somewhere. Even in this Germany, among the cruellest people on earth, if you find one man with good in him, there is hope for the human race."

Camp life in *The Cross of Lorraine*, set in 1940, is equally barbaric. A rosary is taken away from a prisoner, a priest is shot while administering the last rites, and what befalls Victor (Gene Kelly) is uncertain. "We amputated his enthusiasm," the commandant boasts as the camera reveals Victor chained to the wall in a Christlike pose and scourged. This is not 1940 despite what the prologue claims. When a prisoner says, "The Germans don't bury you; they make soap out of you," he is not repeating a World War I myth but one that started being recirculated in 1942.[10] Concentration camps have become death camps; time, a cross-reference, a reverse prolepsis prefiguring what has already occurred.

The feeling the camps evoke is not one of tragic waste but of human waste. The Holocaust does not fit into the neat schema of Aristotelian tragedy because there is no tragic flaw, no self-knowledge except shame and guilt, and certainly no catharsis. But evil, even of the unnameable variety, fascinates. Thus the death camps became plot pegs but, in American films, rarely the basis of the entire plot.[11] The enormity of what the camps represent can only stun, and stunned moviegoers are a poor endorsement for a film. *The Last Stop* (1948), a Polish film released in the United States in 1949, is set entirely at Auschwitz. The impact was so numbing that it left many moviegoers nauseous or synaesthetic, experiencing a sense of grayness for days afterward.[12]

Hollywood first portrayed the camps as places of atrocities in *Sealed Verdict* (1948), the first American film to speak of the camps specifically as death camps and not merely as internment centers. A character describes the death of his family at Buchenwald: "My daughter was cremated. . . . All my daughters, three of them together, and my wife. My son's skull was crushed by ss men, his children buried in a mass grave. . . ." A father describes his daughter's degradation: "At the camp, they put whip in her hand. Push her into big room with many women, all naked. Her mother, too. . . . They force her to lash all the people, her mother. They all dance. Germans laugh. They dance till can't stand up; then Germans turn on gas."

Next, the camps became plot devices: a Belsen survivor assumes the identity of a dead inmate (*The House on Telegraph Hill*, 1951); a wife returns to the husband who does not recognize her (*Return from the Ashes*, 1965).

However, the lesson of the camps is a personal one that cannot be learned from a recitation of horrors or a return from the grave. The American film most successful at integrating that lesson with a real plot is *The Pawnbroker* (1965), in which the camp experiences are subliminal flashes of memory, shards of the past piercing the pawnbroker's consciousness and making him as desensitized as his persecutors. To return to the human race, he must pierce himself, giving himself stigmata to make him one with crucified humanity.

Eventually the camps yielded their own symbology. If they represent the debasement of others, they can also represent the debasement of self—the degradation being so vivid that remembering is not enough: it must be relived (*The Night Porter*, 1974). The view of the camp as an Eden for masochists is extreme, and the anger that *The Night Porter* continues to arouse is understandable, although the iconography—partly apocalyptic, partly expressionistic—suggests that the filmmaker aspired to something higher than sadomasochism.

Since the camps were the result of an ideology, they should eventually be portrayed as such. The only film to do this is not American but Italian: Lina Wertmüller's *Seven Beauties* (1975), which revolves entirely around the theme of prostitution—of self, others, and country. Pasqualino, who is so outraged at his sister's whorish ways, prostitutes himself in a camp where, to survive, he services the mountainous female commandant. But self-prostitution is symptomatic of national prostitution, of a country's reverting to whoredom by bedding down with fascism. *Seven Beauties* takes the camps out of the realm of horror and isolates that horror in ideological whoremongering.

9. California Comrades

        In the Fall of 1947, the House Committee on Un-
American Activities (HUAC) took up an item that was still outstanding on its prewar agenda and that, in light of the Cold War,
required immediate attention: the Communist subversion of the
motion picture industry, on the grounds that Soviet propaganda had
been injected into films in the guise of Stalinist tributes and barbs
aimed at the United States. HUAC chose not to remember that during the period when Russia was an ally, short lived as that was, Soviet support was at its highest level. Nor were Communist screenwriters the only Russophiles. Emmett Lavery was a Catholic who
was constantly being mistaken for a Communist because of his liberal views; he had included a sympathetic Russian in *Behind the
Rising Sun* (1943), as had Will Burnett in *Background to Danger*
(1943), although neither writer was even remotely radical. *Days of
Glory* may have been a paean to the Russian partisans, but the
writer, Casey Robinson, was a political conservative.

    The difference between *Days of Glory* and *Song of Russia* is im-
mense. *Song of Russia* is not so much Russophilia as Russomania.
Days of Glory arouses sympathy for a Russia under siege but not for
Stalinist Communism; *Song of Russia* is a Stalinist tract written by
Communist writers Paul Jarrico and Richard Collins,[1] with propa-
ganda taking precedence even over the plight of a besieged nation.

    Although Communist screenwriters frequently inserted refer-
ences to the Soviet Union into their scripts, the references were usually so recondite that only another comrade would pick them up.
For instance, in *Thousands Cheer* (1943), also written by Jarrico and
Collins, some soldiers are in their barracks, musing on where they
would like to be sent. One says Alaska; another England; a third—
Russia.

    The lyrics to the ballad that opens and closes *A Walk in the Sun*

211

were written by Millard Lampell, who was later blacklisted. The ballad has the rhythm of a union song; its point is that the men of the Forty-fifth Texas Division are no different from people fighting for freedom anywhere, and that their walk in the sun is merely a trek down a well-trodden road:

> It's the walk that leads down
> Through a Philippine town
> And it hits Highway Seven north of Rome.
> It's the same road they had
> coming out of Stalingrad;
> It's the old Lincoln Highway back home.

A Walk in the Sun ends with the lyrics appearing on the screen. Perhaps, in 1946, a couple of Party members might have nudged each other approvingly at the reference to Stalingrad or nodded assent at the expression of commonality, but most moviegoers were leaving the theater.

On the other hand, *Song of Russia* is so unashamedly Stalinist that certain scenes "left some [moviegoers] in pain," as *New York Post* critic Archer Winsten noted in his review. Yet the film was supposed to have been a love story, paralleling the romance between Greta Garbo and conductor Leopold Stokowski, or at least that is what director Gregory Ratoff thought: "Russian girl falls in love with American conductor who arrives in Russia to give concerts but gets involved in scorched earth policy."[2] That is not the way Jarrico and Collins wrote it, however; nor is it the way Anna Louise Strong, an ardent supporter of the Soviet Union and the film's technical adviser, envisioned it. The film was not only conceived as Stalinist; it was also to have been called *Scorched Earth*.

Most moviegoers had forgotten *Song of Russia* by 1947, but not Ayn Rand. On 20 October 1947, she appeared before HUAC as a friendly witness, eager to denounce the film that made her "sick." What sickened her especially was the way America faded out and the Soviet Union faded in. Rand claimed that a scene in which the conductor is leading his orchestra in "The Star Spangled Banner," with the American flag prominently displayed, dissolves into one in which a Soviet orchestra is playing the Soviet anthem with the U.S.S.R. flag in the background: "It [the dissolve] suggests literally and technically that it is quite all right for the American national anthem to dissolve into the Soviet."[3] For the record, the stars and stripes do not dissolve into the hammer and the sickle. *Song of Russia* is a flashback, framed by a Russian war relief concert. The newscaster's remark, "It was to Russia in 1941 that fate sent John Meredith," is the cue for the flashback to start. As the conductor makes his way to the podium, "The Star Spangled Banner" begins. The concert hall dissolves to the Moscow airport where an army band awaits the conductor's arrival.

In its unconstitutional way, HUAC was right; in her Russophobic way, so was Ayn Rand: there is something special about a left-wing script. Often it is a matter of tone; the left speaks more loudly and bluntly. *Pride of the Marines* (1945), *The Best Years of Our Lives* (1946), and *Till the End of Time* (1946) all deal with the problems of returning veterans; all are critical of American right-wingers and bigots, but in varying degrees. In *Best Years*, a boor buttonholes a double amputee, telling him that America was pushed into the war by a "bunch of radicals in Washington." In *Till the End of Time*, members of the American War Patriots, a rightist organization restricted to WASPS, tries to recruit three ex-marines in a bar while a black soldier looks on cynically. *Best Years* and *Till the End of Time* were written by Robert E. Sherwood and Allen Rivkin, respectively, both anti-Communist liberals. When a character speaks out against prejudice in *Pride of the Marines*, written by a Communist, Albert Maltz, he is not attacking bigots who tout an organization that excludes Catholics, Jews, and Negroes. Rather, he is a Jewish marine voicing his fear of returning to an America where he won't be hired because "my name is Diamond instead of Jones and I celebrate Passover instead of Easter."

While many films demanded an end to war, there is a difference between a flabby admonition and a marine's insisting there be "no more wars . . . no apples, no bonus marches, no doing business with any new Hitler" (*Pride of the Marines*); a difference between saying that on 7 December America received a "stab in the back" (*Remember Pearl Harbor*, 1942) and that America was "soft" (*Halls of Montezuma*, 1950, written by Michael Blankfort who, while not a Communist, was the theatre and film critic for the Communist *Daily Worker* [4]).

For all its zeal, the left was not free from error. Its obsession with fascism would lead to an occasional gaffe, the most conspicuous of which occurs in *Hotel Berlin* (1945), written by Alvah Bessie and Jo Pagano, in which a member of the Gestapo berates a Jewish woman for not wearing her star and orders her back to her "district" (i.e., ghetto)—in 1945 Berlin! While there were some Jews in Berlin in early 1945, the number was relatively small—perhaps a few hundred; but the writers would not have known this.[5] The truth of the matter was that Goebbels was annoyed that he had not exterminated all the Berlin Jews, despite his August 1943 boast that there were no Jews in Berlin. And the Jews who were in Berlin would hardly be roaming the city, much less wearing the Star of David.

The left could also be shrill and illogical. Although leftist screenwriters criticized the treaty of Versailles and American indifference to the threat of Nazism, the better writers made their charges within the context of the plot so that the allegations at least seemed natural. When fervor got the better of reason, the result was a tirade like the one in *City without Men* (1943), which derived from an original story by Budd Schulberg and Martin Berkeley, both Communists at the time (and later HUAC informants, Berkeley naming more names than any other informant). In the film, a lawyer compares the district attorney's reluctance to free an innocent man, who saw a German ship discharging Japanese passengers on the West coast five months before Pearl Harbor, with America's unwillingness to intervene in acts of foreign aggression. When the DA asks for time, the lawyer explodes: "Time, time, time! Ten years ago, when Hirohito marched into Manchuria, we could have knocked his big teeth down his throat with a backhand slap. But China was far away. We had time. Six years ago, when Hitler marched into the Rhineland, we could have put him in a lunatic asylum. But the Rhineland was far away, too."

This is the left at its worst, tossing history on a Procrustean bed and stretching the facts, or lopping them off, until they fit the thesis that everything is interconnected: Manchuria, the remilitarization of the Rhineland, and the hero's fate.

At its best, the left could deepen a plot by giving it a political or social slant, as Ellis St. Joseph and Howard Koch did in their screenplay of *In Our Time*, so that the characters emerge as individuals working for the perfection of society. It seems that Koch, who imparted a political dimension to *Casablanca*, did the same for *In Our Time*.[6]

While *In Our Time* was advertised as a romance, it is a romance kept within the borders of history, rather than history banished to the borders of romance. Yet it is a particular kind of romance—one between people from two different classes: a Polish count (Paul Henreid) and a British commoner (Ida Lupino) whose bipolar backgrounds are a metaphor for a similarly divided Poland. One of the chief problems facing Poland in 1939, and one that explains why the Poles could not repel the German invasion, was class polarization: aristocratic landowners, oppressed peasants, and a cavalry (the uhlans) equipped for heroics but not for battle. The coldness with which the count's mother greets Jennifer the commoner is indicative of the disdain the Polish aristocracy felt toward its social inferiors. But once the nobleman and the proletarian wed, the class barriers vanish in their marriage as well as on their estate. The couple effect radical change: they mingle freely with the peasants, teach them modern farming methods, give them a share of the profits, and open their manor to them for the harvest celebration.

In Our Time is as much a historical chronicle as a reflection of the screenwriters' utopian socialism. The title derives from Neville Chamberlain's tragic boast after his return from Munich: "I believe it is peace for our time." As might be expected, given the title, the film disparages appeasement, but not with the gracelessness of the lawyer's plea in *City without Men*; instead, a baron deplores the willingness with which the world digs itself deeper into the sand; a Chamberlain-like aristocrat, in his eagerness to keep Poland out of war, goes boar hunting with Göring.

In Our Time works from a polarized society toward a vision of what that society might have been. It invites the viewer to consider how Poland might have fared if it were socially unified instead of factionalized; if the count's estate were the norm, not a noble experiment. But the film is not so naive as to maintain that agrarian reform would have solved Poland's problem of military unpreparedness. The count, who goes off to battle splendidly attired, returns in rags, pitifully describing the fate of his brigade as it charged on horseback into a line of German tanks.

An adaptation often reveals a writer's politics better than an original screenplay, by providing grounds for comparison. In 1949, when Carl Foreman adapted Arthur Laurents's Broadway play, *Home of the Brave*, he changed the character of Moss from a Jew to a black. While anti-Semitism had already been portrayed on the screen in *Crossfire* (1947) and *Gentleman's Agreement* (1947), white racism had not— or, at least, not in the same way. Thus in 1949 (a year before Joseph L. Mankiewicz used "coon" and "boogie" in *No Way Out*, 1950) Foreman put "yellow-bellied nigger lover" into the mouth of T.J. (Steve Brodie), one of a four-member reconnaissance mission in the South Pacific. The other three are a fair-minded cynic, Moss (James Edwards), and his white high school buddy Finch (Lloyd Bridges). The film is a flashback in which a doctor tries to discover the origin of Moss's amnesia and paralysis, both medically unexplainable. The cause is Moss's guilt over the death of Finch who, before he falls into the hands of the Japanese, starts to call Moss a "nigger" but catches himself and says "nitwit." Moss feels a moment of exultation when Finch dies, and then punishes himself for it, until he learns that such momentary feelings are common in war and that they are only relief at being alive though one's buddy is dead.

Home of the Brave did not endear itself to right-wingers with its charge that racism was America's legacy to blacks who themselves were scapegoats of insecure whites. However, Foreman was not just a radical pointing up America's shortcomings by exalting blacks over whites. Moss is far from blameless; he is filled with self-loathing and self-pity. There are few scenes in World War II movies as anguished as the one in which Moss cradles Finch's body in his arms as "Sometimes I Feel Like a Motherless Child" swells into a threnody on the soundtrack. Moss rocks Finch's body; then he flings it away, only to retrieve it and embrace it again. This act of love and hate, of guilt and atonement, is an expression of racism's two-edged sword that slashes each race, making it impossible for one to tend to the other's wounds.

Foreman continued to write balanced scripts, resisting disillusionment even when the blacklist drove him into self-imposed exile in England. In *The Victors* (1963), he showed the speed with which World War II turned into the Cold War by depicting the American occupiers as so hardened by combat that they are unable to deal with the Russians, who, in turn, because of their distrust of the West, are unable to deal with Americans. *The Victors* ends with two soldiers, an American and a Russian, killing each other over the right of way and dying side by side in the rubble because neither understands the other's language. There are no individual heroes or villains in Foreman's films (even the villain in *High Noon* (1952) is not one, but many—the community). Foreman's hero is humankind at its best; his villain, humankind at its worst. In between are just plain people.

While in England, Foreman wrote a draft of an adaptation of Pierre Boulle's novel, *The Bridge over the River Kwai* (1957), which another blacklisted writer, Michael Wilson, rewrote. Neither writer received screen credit; it went to Boulle, as did the Academy Award for best screenplay, thereby completing the travesty.* The screenplay brought out a theme that was only implicit in the novel: collaboration. When a British colonel (Alec Guinness) commits his men to building a bridge for their Japanese captors, he is guilty of collaboration, which to the left is the deadliest of sins. The colonel's argument is that the men need discipline and the Japanese need a lesson in Western efficiency. When he is told that what he is doing might be construed as collaboration, his reply is that, as prisoners of war, they cannot refuse work. The nature of the work does not matter. Work becomes *the* work, finally *a* work—a work of art, for that is

---

* On 23 March 1985, the widows of Foreman and Wilson were awarded the Oscars denied their husbands.

how the colonel perceives the bridge: as a monument to England made from the wood of trees similar to the elms that were felled for London Bridge. He even has a commemorative plaque made, proving that the bridge was built by British soldiers.

As the bridge becomes an obsession and its completion a necessity, the colonel confers with the camp commandant, Colonel Saito (Sessue Hayakawa), about increasing the work quota and daily output. The colonel even visits sick bay to recruit the infirm and the wounded. The bridge has become such a matter of pride that when he learns commandos plan to blow it up, he intervenes.

When the colonel and the American commando confront each other, each can only utter a shocked "you!"—the colonel realizing that the American who escaped from the camp is now the destroyer of the bridge, the commando that the colonel is responsible for its construction. The denouement is a deus ex machina, not the most imaginative type of conclusion, but here morally fitting as the colonel falls on the detonator, destroying his own creation.

The novel's thesis is that war is madness; the film's is that war may be madness, but collaboration is insanity. To the Hollywood left, loyalty was a cardinal virtue; betrayal and collaboration, unforgivable sins. Left-wing writers did not simply kill traitors; when possible, they tried them, allowing them a final but fruitless plea. The tribunal's location varied; it could be a restaurant, a cellar, or even a waterfront cafe as it is in *Cornered* (1945). This completely left-wing effort was produced by Party member Adrian Scott, directed by (then) Communist Edward Dmytryk, and written by another Party member, John Wexley. The screenplay was revised by screenwriter John Paxton, brought in to depoliticize Wexley's script, which accused Argentina of being a haven for Nazis and Peron's regime of being fascist. While the script may have been depoliticized, *Cornered* is by no means apolitical. Fashioned by the writer-director team that made *Murder, My Sweet* (1944), *Cornered* is hard-boiled espionage; it is the kind of film in which the Nazi hunter (Dick Powell), a French Canadian lieutenant tracking down the French collaborationist responsible for his wife's death, blacks out after a beating as the screen expands into a whirling bull's eye.

Cornered is not a typical manhunt film; manhunt films as a rule do not advance the theory that Nazism encourages humankind's propensity for evil while democracy tries to develop its passion for good. "You continue to attack the wrong things in the wrong way. We accept the evil in man; we find it good and fertile," the collaborationist argues. Manhunt films also do not blame the victors of World War I for letting "the fruits of victory decay in their hands."

What is ironic, however, is the collaborationist's charge that Nazism thrives on disaffection and poverty. "Wherever you have the hungry, you will find us" can also be said of Communism, although this is something no one responsible for *Cornered* would have admitted (except Dmytryk, whose experience with the film convinced him to leave the Party[7]).

In 1947, ten members of the Hollywood community, who had been subpoenaed to appear before the House Committee on Un-American Activities, were cited for contempt of Congress for refusing to answer two questions: Are you a member of the Screen Writers Guild? Are you or have you ever been a member of the Communist party? The ten stood on their First Amendment rights, maintaining that where Congress could not legislate (i.e., a person's politics), it could not investigate. Although the questions seemed unrelated, they were not—not to a committee that believed the Screen Writers Guild was a subversive organization and that screenwriters were primarily responsible for inserting Soviet propaganda into films. Of the ten, commonly known as the Hollywood Ten,[8] nine were screenwriters: Alvah Bessie, Herbert Biberman, Lester Cole, Ring Lardner, Jr., John Howard Lawson, Albert Maltz, Samuel Ornitz, Adrian Scott, and Dalton Trumbo; one, Edward Dmytryk, was exclusively a director.[9]

Although Adrian Scott is better known as a producer, he coauthored the script of a Cary Grant vehicle, *Mr. Lucky* (1943), with Milton Holmes. On the surface, *Mr. Lucky* is the familiar story of a con man/draft dodger. Con men as well as draft dodgers had appeared on the screen before, but Joe (Cary Grant) is unique. Unlike Lucky Jordan, who pays a woman to pose as his mother, Joe acquires the draft card of a dead man who was 4-F and assumes his identity. Joe's conversion to patriotism is brought about not by a regenerative woman (whom, in fact, he attempts to fleece) but by the discovery that he has taken the name of a Greek whose brothers died defending their village from the Germans. To continue their crusade against fascism, Joe enlists in the Merchant Marine. Films about assumed identity and the politicization of apathetic males are common, but because the writers were more interested in the politics of war than in war itself, *Mr. Lucky* is different: the protagonist takes on another's politics as well as his identity.

Because they were acutely aware of class distinctions, left-wing writers often resolved a situation by eradicating all differences between the classes—something quite different from the mere dropping of social barriers so upper-class boy can marry middle-class girl (*Easy Living*, 1937), or upper-class girl can marry middle-class boy

Cary Grant as the title character in Mr. Lucky (1943) and Laraine Day as the socialite he cons. Courtesy RKO Radio Pictures

(It Happened One Night, 1934). The left-wing writer was not aiming at an amalgam of the classes but at pure classlessness, expressed in easily understood concepts such as equality and commonality. Sam Ornitz even did it with young and old, making the child partisans of China's Little Devils the equals of adults, and their boy leader the guardian spirit of his elders after his death. In Three Faces West, for which Ornitz shared screen credit with F. Hugh Herbert and Joseph Moncure March, the plot begins heading toward a classless resolution when the Austrian heroine rejects her ties with the past, including her Nazi boyfriend, and becomes the consort of the Tom Joad figure (John Wayne), who, like his Steinbeck prototype, leads his community out of the dust bowl to the promised land of Oregon.

If there is a difference between MGM's Dr. Kildare series and RKO's Dr. Christian series, it is due, in large part, to the fact that Ring Lardner, Jr., helped create the character of Dr. Christian, making him the champion of the underdog in Meet Dr. Christian (1939) and The Courageous Dr. Christian (1940). The latter dramatizes the impact of a squatters' community on the local gentry. In *The Courageous Dr. Christian*, the solution to Hoovervilles is not relief, but low income housing; its solution to class antagonism is the elimination of fear. When the citizens realize the squatters are not a social menace but decent human beings, they rally to support them.

Because of his novel, *Johnny Got His Gun* (1939), Dalton Trumbo is the best known of the Ten. However, his World War II screenplays did not do him justice. *Thirty Seconds Over Tokyo* is poorly constructed; *A Guy Named Joe* (1943), in which Spencer Tracy returns from the dead to train pilots, alternates between fantasy and pretension, with a speech about the community of souls that is as rarefied as the air in which much of the action takes place. A better example of Trumbo's craft is his adaptation of Christopher Morley's novel *Kitty Foyle* (1940); Trumbo's Kitty is a true member of the working class and not just another dime store heroine. Trumbo also links each important moment in Kitty's life with a significant event (the depression, the New Deal, etc.) so that she is representative of her era.

Trumbo's most notorious screenplay is *Tender Comrade* (1943), remembered today because Leila Rogers testified to HUAC that her daughter Ginger had to deliver the line "Share and share alike; that's democracy," which obviously was Communist propaganda. Since *Tender Comrade* is about five servicemen's wives who rent a house together, "share and share alike" is the only way to manage. If Mrs. Rogers had remembered the context, she would have known that the character is really talking about sharing what's left after all the bills have been paid. That is not democracy; it's socialism.

Alvah Bessie was one of the three screenwriters responsible for *Northern Pursuit* (1943), in which the Nazis try to set up a miniature Luftwaffe in Canada. For a change, the Nazis are pursued on dogsled and skiis instead of in submarines and bombers. In a corporate screenplay, it is often difficult to isolate an individual writer's contribution. The average screenwriter would not have Nazis exploiting Indians or regarding them as *untermenschen*, however; someone working on a script about Nazis in Canada and aware of their attitude toward nonwhites would. Furthermore, the theme of guilt by association was, if not Bessie's idea, one that appealed to him (it recurs in *Hotel Berlin* in which a "hotel hostess," suspected of being a Nazi, has to prove herself to the underground before she can be trusted). In *Northern Pursuit*, a Canadian Mountie of German descent is suspected of being the one who helped a Nazi escape from an internment camp. To capture the escaped prisoner and thereby clear himself, he poses as a Nazi sympathizer.

John Garfield (left) as the historical Al Schmid just before a grenade blinds him in Pride of the Marines *(1945). Courtesy* MGM/UA

Bessie even left his mark on *The Very Thought of You* (1944), a slight service romance, which he coauthored with Delmer Daves and which features one of the most offensive families to appear during the war (the complete reverse of the sacrificing households of *The Human Comedy*, 1943, and *Sunday Dinner for a Soldier*, 1944). The soldier who comes to dinner in *The Very Thought of You* has to endure a civilian's wish that the war will continue because of the prosperity it has brought.

The Ten were not above criticizing an America that was reaping profits from the war, discriminating against Jews, and begrudging GIs their former jobs because replacements could be hired at less pay. Albert Maltz made these points in *Pride of the Marines*, which was inspired by the true story of Al Schmid. Serving in the Solomon Islands in 1942, he was left virtually blind by a Japanese grenade hurled into his machine gun emplacement.

Pride of the Marines has some unforgettable moments: Al meeting Ruth (Eleanor Parker) in total darkness when a fuse blows, a prefiguration of his blindness and her role in helping him accept it; Ruth and Al reading the funnies while Brahms's Fourth comes over the radio, soon to be interrupted by the announcement of the Pearl Harbor attack; Al responding to the perennial "Where's Pearl Harbor?" "I was never very good at geography." The camaraderie so typical of the films of the Ten is revealed in an especially candid scene when a group of hospitalized marines wonder whether they will ever know the same comradeship in civilian life that they did in the service.

Maltz was especially sensitive to racial and religious prejudice. In his "Suggestions for *Al Schmid, Marine*" (20 September 1943), he asked that an American Indian and a Jew be in the bunker with Schmid when the grenade explodes. Maltz's reasoning was that since Schmid was German-Irish, a racial mix would "show America in its best sense and . . . answer the woofish malice by which some people scorn each other on a racist basis."[10] He did not get his American Indian, but he did get LeRoy Diamond, who was Jewish and, like Schmid, an actual person.

Maltz revealed the same sensitivity in a Frank Sinatra short, *The House I Live In* (1945), in which Sinatra takes time out from a recording session to explain democracy to a group of kids beating up a boy who is obviously Jewish. Sinatra calls the kids "Nazis" because "religion makes no difference, only to a Nazi" and reminds them that some day their Aryan fathers may need non-Aryan blood.

Although John Howard Lawson came from New Playwrights, the most radical of the left-wing theatre groups, and was known as the idealogue of the Hollywood Communists, he never allowed ideology to adumbrate art.[11] This is not to say there are no propagandistic touches in his work; there clearly are. But a touch is not a brushstroke, and Lawson's touches were put in with a fine hand. Two of his films, *Sahara* (1943) and *Action in the North Atlantic* (1943), reflect the comradeship he found in the Communist party in the sense that the group, the community, is the real protagonist in both.

For *Sahara*, set during the 1942 desert war, he drew on a Soviet film, *The Thirteen* (1937), also a desert adventure. Lawson envisaged *Sahara* as an allegory of brotherhood, a common theme in the films of the Ten (the world soul view in *A Guy Named Joe*, the sharing and pooling in *Tender Comrade*, the "work together" philosophy of *Pride of the Marines*). To make the allegory as comprehensive as possible, Lawson devised an international cast: a Frenchman who had fought for Republican Spain in the civil war, an Italian who had been part of Rommel's Afrika Corps, a German aviator, an Australian, a Briton, a British Sudanese, and a couple of Americans—all under the command of Joe Gunn (Humphrey Bogart), their leader in the trek across the desert. Only the Nazi resists the call to comradeship; the rest respond, including the Italian whom the others motion to join them in a scene resonant with echoes from *Potemkin*, in which the insurgents beckon to their "brothers" in the Czarist cruiser. When a well is discovered, Gunn scoops out water in a tin cup, passing it around and giving everyone, including the Nazi, three swallows. The effect is that of a mass; the men form a circle as the cup passes from one to the next, with the celebrant—Gunn—drinking last.

Sahara is dialectic rendered as narrative: a heterogeneous military detachment resolves its political and cultural differences. That, however, is not the only miracle. The German shelling floods the wells, causing an outpouring of water. When the Nazis see what has happened, they lay down their arms, crying "Wasser!" as if they too yearn for what the water symbolizes—baptism into brotherhood and communion with one's fellows. The ending is not a conclusion but a synthesis; and the synthesis, in turn, is a miracle. The kind of brotherhood Lawson imagined would have to be miraculous.

Action in the North Atlantic is more political than *Sahara* because it is a prolabor as well as a war film; like *Mr. Lucky*, it also celebrates the Merchant Marine. The Hollywood left's interest in the Merchant Marine in 1943 was probably due to the fact that the merchant seamen's union was Communist controlled. Lawson, of course, could not emphasize that point (nor could Scott in *Mr. Lucky*); but those who knew could make the connection between the union and the union types in the film.

Lawson was again depicting the proverbial motley crew, which this time is not united by a Moses-like leader but by a common goal: transporting war matériel to the Russian port of Murmansk. Again it is a Soviet work, *Potemkin*, that gives the film its structure, imagery, and resolution. Since Lawson conceived *Action in the North Atlantic* in terms of Soviet montage (which was also the way director Lloyd Bacon shot it), the result was a Soviet-type film: no mise-en-scène, no long takes—just rhythmic cutting and tonal montage (gradation of light and shade).

Lawson even succeeded in duplicating *Potemkin*'s five part structure. Part 1, The Torpedoing of the *Northern Star*, has the same turbulence as the opening of *Potemkin*, with the rescue of the crew of the *Northern Star* paralleling the temporary victory of the sailors on the Russian battleship. Part 2, The Homecoming, contrasts a tranquil reunion between a husband and wife with the meeting of a seaman and a singer in a dive—the tender balanced by the tough. Part 3, The Gathering of the Ships, is an interlude, with a montage of graceful wipes and an animated map tracing the convoy's route as it

J. Carrol Naish, thinking he is being left behind in Sahara *(1943). Courtesy Columbia Pictures*

sets out in the early dawn through the same nacreous mist that hung over the harbor of Odessa at the beginning of Part 3 of *Potemkin*. The entire third part of *Action in the North Atlantic* is a study in tonal montage: the sky alternates between sunshot and sulphurous, bright and opaque; the Liberty ship shifts from proud vessel to ghost ship cutting through the fog.

Part 4, The U-Boat Attack, has the rhythmic montage of *Potemkin's* fourth and most famous part, the Odessa Steps Massacre. The rhythm accelerates with rapid cuts of torpedoes darting through the water, then subsides when the attack is over. The last part, The Arrival at Murmansk, is the synthesis. One ally, threatened by the enemy, has brought aid to another ally besieged by the same enemy. The allies are now one, so much so that a seaman looks up at the planes overhead and cries, "They're ours"—"ours" being "Soviet." This is Soviet propaganda at its most artful, as "their" becomes "our." Likewise, when the people of Murmansk greet the seaman as comrade, he returns the greeting joyously—another echo of *Potemkin*, in which, at the end, the mutinous sailors cry "Brothers!" to the Czarist crew who respond by waving to them, forgetting (or ignoring) their ideological differences. In one brief scene, *Action in the North Atlantic* evokes what happened when Hitler's invasion of the Soviet Union gave the Western democracies a new ally.

Three of the Ten—Herbert Biberman, Lester Cole, and Alvah Bessie—anticipated the end of the war on film. Biberman in *The Master Race* showed the Germans preparing for World War III after Normandy has convinced them they have lost; Cole put them on trial in *None Shall Escape*, thus anticipating Nuremberg; Bessie had them heading for Argentina in *Hotel Berlin* on the supposition that old Nazis never die; they go to South America and spawn a new cycle of films (e.g., *Notorious*; *The Marathon Man*, 1976; *The Boys from Brazil*, 1978).

Of the three films, *The Master Race* is the weakest both as prophecy and as cinema. It is difficult to quarrel with Biberman's thesis that, even with the end of the war, Nazism did not abate, as neo-Nazism has shown. Nor is the story line unpromising: a Nazi colonel assumes the identity of a dead Belgian patriot and returns to the patriot's village to breed dissension and perpetuate the scapegoat mentality that once rallied Germans around Hitler. Furthermore, the notion that the liberated can turn on their liberators is fascinating, if diabolical. The approach, however, is ponderous (Biberman also directed). Good and evil are stretched to such extremes (a faultless American at one end, a depraved Nazi at the other, and collaborationists, guerrillas, and townspeople in between) that there is no room for both a good Nazi and a Russophile; the Nazi doubles as Russophile, attributing his conversion to the bravery he witnessed at Kiev ("The Russians didn't fight like vermin").

While Lawson and Maltz could work a tribute to Russia into the script naturally and promote an unforced spirit of commonality, Biberman had Belgian Catholics assembling for a service in a bombed out church with a menorah on the altar and a Protestant chaplin in the pulpit, which in 1944 would have set a new high for ecumenism.

Although *None Shall Escape* traces the path from Versailles to Munich, the one who has traversed it is a war criminal whose story is told in flashback by witnesses to the crimes he has committed against humanity. Since the final script was ready by July 1943, it is clear that Cole was looking ahead to the war's end and the time of reckoning. The trial is not the usual recitation of horrors; *None Shall Escape* is considerably more restrained than *Hitler's Children* or *Behind the Rising Sun*. The defendant, Wilhelm Grim (Alexander Knox), is an embittered World War I veteran who returns to the Polish village where he had taught before the war. Although he had fought for the Kaiser, the Poles bear him no animosity and even give him his old job back. Yet Grim continues to brood over Germany's defeat and his bleak future as a provincial schoolmaster. With the rise of National Socialism, Grim becomes progressively more inhumane. He commits rape and drives his victim to suicide; then he betrays his socialist brother, sending him to a concentration camp; finally he becomes a Reichscommissioner stationed in the same Polish village, where, it is intimated, he implements the Final Solution.

In contrast to the syncretic church service in *The Master Race*, there is the natural blending of religious motifs in *None Shall Escape*. After the rabbi urges his people not to enter the cattle cars, he is killed with the others, dying in the shadow of a crossbar that makes his death, and that of his people, a crucifixion.

Cole's best known World War II script is the doubly controversial *Objective, Burma!* (1945). First, the British objected to the impression it gave of the Burmese campaign being an American operation.[12] Originally the opening title was a quote from General Stillwell that was a sort of "back to Burma" promise on the order of MacArthur's "I shall return." To appease the British, another title was substituted, which claims that while "the actors are Americans . . . they enact experiences common to British, Indian and Chinese forces who victoriously fought the grim jungle war"; the end title dedicates the film to the same "American, British, Chinese, and Indian armies without whose heroic efforts Burma would still be in the hands of the Japanese."

The British objection was niggling since the Burmese campaign is not the substance of the plot, only its point of departure. Furthermore, the British are ignored neither in the plot nor in the credits, which list a major from the British Indian Army as technical ad-

Janina (Dorothy Morris) soon to be forced into prostitution at a Nazi officers' club in None Shall Escape (1944). Courtesy Columbia Pictures

viser. However, the objection raised by Cole and Alvah Bessie, who wrote the original story on which Cole based his screenplay, was not niggling. The writers vehemently opposed the addition of a speech written, it would seem, by Ranald MacDougall, who received co-screenplay credit. The speech is the worst example of anti-Japanese invective to appear on the screen. It is not even good vituperative rhetoric, but merely an ugly diatribe unworthy of the film and of the character who delivers it, a journalist (played sympathetically by Henry Hull). When the journalist sees the body of a mutilated GI, he exclaims, "I thought I've seen or read about everything one man can do to another, from the torture chambers of the middle ages to the gang wars and lynchings of today. But this—this is different. This was done in cold blood by people who claim to be civilized. Civilized! They're degenerate, moral idiots. Stinking little savages. Wipe them out, I say. Wipe them off the face of the earth. Wipe them off the face of the earth."

In the original story, Bessie had Nelson (Errol Flynn) answer one of the men who calls the Japanese "beasts" by saying, "There's nothing Japanese about [torture]. You'll find it wherever you find fascists. There are even people who call themselves Americans who'd do it too."[13] In a strongly worded memo (2 December 1944) to producer Jerry Wald, Bessie argued his and Cole's position: There should be no indictment of the Japanese people because "in a film that so sedulously avoids political statement of any kind, this one . . . sticks out like a sore thumb."

Bessie and Cole were right; the speech, an ugly excrescence in any script, is a blight on *Objective, Burma!*, which, unlike most films written by leftists, is not political. While *Sahara* is an exodus, *Objective, Burma!* is an odyssey: a platoon's journey through the Burmese jungle, after having destroyed a Japanese radar station, to await rescue by the Air Force. What was to have been a simple mission becomes a struggle for survival when the absence of a landing field makes rescue impossible. Finally, the remnants of the platoon reach a hilltop where they manage to attract the attention of an American plane.

The journalist's speech aside, there is much to admire in the film: Franz Waxman's Prokofiev-like score, alternately martial and elegiac; the unaffected earnestness of Flynn's performance; Raoul Walsh's epic direction in such scenes as the retreat, in which the men wade through a stream carrying their dead on makeshift stretchers; the marchlike advance toward the radar station; the cutting of a swath through the underbrush, orchestrated by the slash of metal and the call of birds.

The strongest scene in the film is the one in which the men reach a Burmese village and discover that some of their party have been tortured to death or mutilated beyond recognition. Joe Breen invoked Article 12.3 of the Code ("brutality and possible gruesomeness"), insisting that there be "no attempt to photograph [the bodies] directly."[14] Walsh did not have to be told how to shoot the scene; he was too professional to succumb to the lure of the horrific. When Nelson sees his best friend lying in the doorway, begging to be killed, only his legs are in frame. It is mutilation by suggestion: a pleading voice and a half-concealed body, with the rest of the details to be supplied by the imagination. Hence, the journalist's outburst on seeing the torture victim is gratuitous; the camera has made it clear that what was done defies description.

The Ten were a mixed yarn; sometimes, they could be obvious and painfully naive; at other times, insightful and amazingly subtle. But the yarn had enough common strands to make it distinctive. What was distinctive about the Ten was their passion for unity—not the "united we stand" sort that holds up group effort and collective action as the ideal. The Ten's unity was different; it was the unity of collective responsibility as well as collective action; it was party loyalty translated into solidarity—the group conceived as a cadre. The goal was not the clichéd winning the war but winning the class war. Hence, they saw American anti-Semitism and white racism as manifestations of the same mentality that classifies people as *Übermenschen* and *untermenschen*, Aryan and non-Aryan. The alternative—to them, the only alternative—was an abolition of the classes so the distinction could never be made again.

While the Ten did their share of flagwaving, they did not portray an America bedewed with God's grace or one where a family scrimps for a week to invite a soldier to Sunday dinner; where a teenager is torn between doing a play and doing war relief work (*Chip Off the Old Block*, 1944); where a boy welcomes the buddy of his dead brother as a heaven-sent surrogate (*The Human Comedy*). Their America is the underside of America the Beautiful; not America the Ugly, but America the selfish, the bigoted; yet also America the redeemable. They imagined a future where people would be as free as the air (*A Guy Named Joe*); they believed, like Lee in *Pride of the Marines*, that "we can make it work in peace as we did in war."

The Ten could not make it work in peace. Their war, their finest hour, was World War II. The peace that followed, also known as the Cold War, was their nemesis.

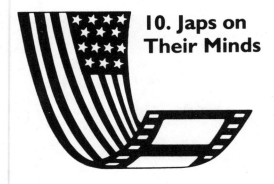

10. Japs on Their Minds

"All I want to do is get me a Jap. Just one Jap."
—*Bataan (1943)*

"I wouldn't wish this on a Jap."
—*Since You Went Away (1944)*

Hollywood's revilement of Japan after its "unprovoked and dastardly attack" on Pearl Harbor is unparalleled in movie history. There is no real analogue, not even the Yellow Peril serials of the teens like the anti-Japanese *Patria* (1917) or *Pearl of the Army* (1916), in which "peerless, fearless" Pearl White saves the Panama Canal from Oriental spies. "The Jap" is neither a white slaver nor a warlord, bottom lit to look as if he has just emerged from the nether world; instead the Jap is subhuman, a lethal object, a thing that, when incinerated, becomes "fried Jap" (*Air Force, God Is My Co-Pilot*).

Hollywood wasted no time in implementing America's "Slap the Jap" policy. By the spring of 1942, the racial epithets were flying fast; "monkey" was the most common, along with its variants, "monkey people" and "ringtails." When "rat" was used, it was prefixed by "yellow" or "slant-eyed." Even *The Sullivans* is not beyond a bit of name calling: "They can't fight," one of the brothers observes; "they close their eyes when they fire off a gun." That is mild compared to the allegation in *Flying Tigers*: "I hear those Japs glow in the night like bugs." Though mercenaries, the Tigers take a patriotic view of their salary: "Every check you've cashed in is a Jap cashed in, too."

Perhaps the most charitable exchange about the Japanese occurs in *Thirty Seconds over Tokyo*, (the screenwriter is Dalton Trumbo, who was not known for his wrath):

TED LAWSON (Van Johnson): My mother had a Japanese gardener once. He seemed like a nice little guy.
BOB GRAY (Robert Mitchum): You know, I don't like Japs—yet. Funny, isn't it. I don't hate 'em. But I don't like 'em.
TED: I guess I don't either. You get kind of mixed up.

Trumbo is magnanimous compared to most writers who endorsed the national position that hatred of Japan is an inalienable right.

In contrast to the "good German" and the occasional good Nazi, good Japanese were almost unheard of. When they finally appear in *Behind the Rising Sun*, they are a parody in reverse, simpering and guilt-ridden instead of sadistic and amoral. Even so, there is no attempt to individualize them; because of their country's treachery, they too have forfeited the right to individuation.

Since the Japanese are sneaks, they fit the enemy as gangster image, like the Nazis. The main difference is one of appearance; the Nazi hood is thickset and humorless; the Japanese, slight of build, smiling, and—most important—a wearer of hornrim glasses that create a saucer-eyed look.

One of the earliest bespectacled villains is Joe of *Across the Pacific*. If Joe seems as jaunty and extroverted as Charlie Chan's Number One Son, it is because the same actor, Victor Sen Yung, had been playing that part since 1938. (The dearth of Oriental actors necessitated their shuttling back and forth between our Chinese allies and our Japanese enemy.) At first Joe seems likeable; but after he demonstrates his judo ability, he holds his glasses before his eyes, which proceed to take an Cyclopean proportions.

Whether they smiled dementedly or scowled, Hollywood's Japanese were doubly dangerous because they were in league with the Third Reich; as a result, a web of Nazi-Nipponese espionage stretched from southeast Asia to the west coast of the United States. Not only were the Nazis and Japanese partners in espionage; they also knew in advance about Pearl Harbor, which, according to Hollywood, was one of the biggest open secrets in history. Except for slumbering Americans, everybody seems to have known about it; even Japanese students at Texas A & M (*We've Never Been Licked*, 1943) know "striking time is two weeks away." The Japanese soldier who bums a cigarette from Alan Ladd in *China* knows. A Nazi and an American fifth columnist in the Philippines speak of the plants in Hawaii that are ready for harvest (*Remember Pearl Harbor*). In *Salute to the Marines*, a shopkeeper in the Philippines, who always has something good to say about Japan and is therefore suspect from the beginning, dons his swastika armband after Manila is bombed and cries "Heil, Hitler" to a Japanese officer, who returns the Nazi salute but replies, "Banzai Nippon." The most blatant example—and one supposedly drawn from history—of the mythical collaboration between Japan and Germany occurs in the purge trials sequence in *Mission to Moscow*, in which Trotsky's plot to partition Russia between Japan and Germany is disclosed. The partition, however, was a trumped-up charge designed to play upon Soviet hatred of Hitler.

The screenwriters who were busily promoting the grand alliance between Germany and Japan should have realized that Japan's joining the Axis did not mean it had joined forces with Hitler. The Third Reich's racial policies would make any alliance between Japan and Germany purely one of expediency. Similarly, there was no evidence that Japan intended to include Germany in the Greater East Asia Co-Prosperity Sphere. In their haste to come up with a script, writers often fell victim to speculation and rash judgment or latched on to a news item before it could be verified. Hastily drawn conclusions were symptomatic of the times, especially after the attack on Pearl Harbor when paucity of information caused some papers, like the *Chicago Times*, to infer that "had it not been for Adolf Hitler, Japan would never have ventured on such a suicidal course."[1] If, as New York's P.M. (8 December 1941) alleged, "the Nazi Government is master minding the Japanese policy," then a writer might conclude that the Nazi government was masterminding Japan's espionage policy as well. As it happened, whatever espionage went on at Oahu was legal: "There is no record that the Japanese ever stole or photographed classified information. They violated no law in pausing to look at the imposing spectacle of men-of-war moored in Pearl Harbor. In fact, the base was an open book by its very nature."[2]

Although Japan showed its colors on 7 December, Hollywood wanted further evidence of duplicity. Ingratitude would do for a starter: Japanese using the education they had received in the United States against the country that educated them. "I have spent many years in your country" soon became a cliché. One gets the impression that the top brass of Japan's imperial army studied in the United States, and at such institutions as Stanford (*Betrayal from the East*) and the University of Washington (*Three Came Home*).

Generally, when a film was set on a college campus, the school was given a fictitious name. But *We've Never Been Licked*, which Walter Wanger produced for Universal, identifies the college: Texas A & M, to which the film is dedicated. Spanning the period from 1938 to 1942, *We've Never Been Licked* illustrates the impact of Japanese culture on a career officer's son. Because of his affinity for

Japan, the young man befriends two Japanese students planning to "apply the best of American civilization" not to their own country but to China, which Japan is gradually absorbing. And if Japan's conquest of China appears cruel, the students have a maxim to cover it: "If, sometimes, it is necessary to choke the dog to give it medicine, it's for the dog's own good."

In addition to being duplicitous, the Japanese are barbaric. Hollywood made a careful distinction between Nazi sadism and Japanese savagery. The Nazis brand, lash, crucify, and perform mass executions. The Japanese blind and cut out tongues (*Manila Calling*); for sport, they toss Chinese babies into the air and bayonet them (*Behind the Rising Sun*).

Behind the Rising Sun (1943), RKO's companion film to *Hitler's Children* by the same director-screenwriter team, Edward Dmytryk and Emmett Lavery, hit a new high in atrocities; within eighty-nine minutes, the Japanese, in addition to bayonetting children (when they are not giving them opium), rape women, strike them to the ground if they dare use the same sidewalk, and insert needles under their fingernails; they burn men on the chin with lighted cigarettes, and string them up by the wrists until the vessels in their arms burst. When criticized, the Japanese reply that the Germans behaved worse in Poland.

However, the significance of *Behind the Rising Sun* does not lie in its astonishing catalog of horrors but in its setting—prewar Japan. Since 1939, films about the Nazis had been set in prewar Europe, but none about the Japanese had been set in pre-Pearl Harbor Japan, but only in China and the Philippines. Having ignored Japanese expansionism during the thirties, Hollywood had no prologue to the war in the Pacific on which to build. Audiences were familiar with the rise of the Third Reich but not with the evolution of the Japanese defense state. *Behind the Rising Sun* does little to add to their knowledge except to derive Japanese imperialism from feudalism and lay the blame on the great families, an antidemocratic elite that created puppet parliaments that were easily dissolved. Japanese nationalism is explained in terms of a geography lesson geared to third graders: "Japan center of universe. Best air lanes lie to north—Russia, Europe. The East is the heartland. Who holds the heartland holds the world. Who is best fit to hold the world?" As if one doesn't know.

Behind the Rising Sun also features the first "good Japanese": a limpid-eyed secretary who gushes over America ("Is it really as wonderful as people say?" "Can anyone get to be president?") and a former imperialist who sees the light and is so consumed with self-

The killing of Takahashi in Behind the Rising Sun *(1943). Courtesy* RKO *Radio Pictures*

loathing that he commits hara-kiri, calling on "whatever gods that are left in the world [to] destroy us as we have destroyed others."

The only other film of the war years that takes place in pre-1941 Japan is *Blood on the Sun* (1945). Lester Cole's screenplay, set in 1929, includes two familiar types, the gangster and the newsman (James Cagney), but with a twist: the gangsters are Japanese, and the newsman's scoop is the discovery of Japan's blueprint for conquest—the Tanaka Plan, also called the Tanaka Memorial and the Tanaka Memorandum after its alleged author, General Tanaka Giichi, Japan's prime minister from 1927 to 1929.

Prelude to War also makes much of the Tanaka Plan, chiding the world for ignoring it. The reason it was ignored was simple: it probably never existed; although throughout the thirties and during the war, there were those who considered it authentic. *Blood on the Sun* attempts to equate the Tanaka Plan with *Mein Kampf*. There is a difference, however: *Mein Kampf* was published; the Tanaka Plan, which the film's opening title admits "depended upon secrecy for success," was not.

In Cole's original ending, the newsman and the heroine bring the Tanaka Plan to the League of Nations at Geneva, only to discover that China is already lost.[3] Their realization that the plan is being implemented would have been a powerful ending, but it also would have been an insult to Generalissimo Chiang Kai-shek; it would have implied that Chiang's anti-Communism weakened China's ability to resist Japanese expansionism. Since an ally cannot be discredited, the producer, William Cagney (the star's brother), brought in another screenwriter to revise the ending so that no one goes to Geneva. Instead, when a Japanese invokes the biblical exhortation to forgive one's enemies, the newsman replies, "Forgive your enemies, but first get even"—a good one-liner but a petty philosophy. Cole's ending is the better one; it would have brought the action to a sobering conclusion.

When World War II ended, there had still not been a single film that explained Japanese imperialism as clearly as *Beasts of Berlin* and *The Hitler Gang* explained Nazism; there had not even been a Japanese *Mortal Storm*. Like the Roosevelt administration, Hollywood adopted a "Europe first" policy; not that it favored the European war over the Pacific (although Europe provided the better plots), but it found the war in Europe easier to portray. Japan was an alien country, linguistically and culturally different from the United States. Japan, as *Betrayal from the East* charges, "had spit upon Western civilization"—the civilization the United States and Germany had in common. The bond of Western civilization made it easier for strange bedfellows to share even a narrow bed.

Although budget constraints, tight shooting schedules, and a dearth of technical advisers—all of which characterized moviemaking on Poverty Row—ordinarily work against a film, they sometimes had the opposite effect, forcing writers to conjure up a plot from their imaginations. When the imagination was fertile, the result was the equivalent of good pulp fiction, making up in style for what was lacking in sophistication. Thus one finds among the films of the forties the occasional programmer that is more inventive than the standard "A" movie of the major studios.

Early in 1942, *Prisoner of Japan* went into production at PRC under the direction of Arthur Ripley, who coauthored the screenplay. When Ripley was unable to complete the film, Edgar G. Ulmer, who wrote the original story, took over the direction and, it seems, the script. Whatever its defects, *Prisoner of Japan* at least does not have the marines trying to hold an island or prisoners of war being subjected to ghoulish tortures.

Instead of wresting a plot from a battle, Ulmer coaxed one out of a myth—the myth of the tyrannized island, like Circe's Aeaea or the island of Dr. Moreau. The island tyrant of *Prisoner of Japan* is the satanic Matsuru; his prisoner, a weak-willed astronomer. With the arrival of the tarnished but patriotic heroine, the astronomer comes down to earth and, after making contact with the navy and disclosing the island's location, dies with the heroine. The couple's self-willed death is a righteous suicide, the kind that was sanctioned in the 1940s: one could choose to die if it meant the enemy would, too.

Although Ripley is credited as *Prisoner of Japan*'s director, Ulmer's presence pervades the film, both in the pared-to-the-bone plot and the shoestring production with its hazily lit miniatures (anticipating the postcard sets of turn-of-the-century Paris in Ulmer's *Bluebeard*, 1944).

Executive Order 9066

On 19 February 1942, President Roosevelt signed Executive Order 9066, which gave Secretary of War Stimson and the military commander to whom Stimson delegated authority, Lieutenant General John L. DeWitt, the power to remove or evacuate individuals from areas considered vulnerable to espionage and sabotage. In effect, the order meant exile for West Coast Japanese-Americans. By the spring and summer of 1942, they had been interned in relocation camps in remote areas of California, Arizona, Idaho, Wyoming, Colorado, and Arkansas. From the newsreels, one would think the evacuation was moving day: "Seattle's Japanese are packed and ready, awaiting Uncle Sam's order," the *Paramount News* narrator announces as spirited background music and close-ups of children smiling naturally, and of adults smiling courteously, convey the impression that 120,000 people are just changing residence.

Since the first anti-Nippon films did not reach the screen until the spring of 1942, they could not have contributed to the internment decision. Yet they reflected the same mentality that led to Executive Order 9066: the belief that the West Coast was a hotbed of espionage and that, if it were attacked, the ethnic Japanese would turn saboteur as they allegedly had at Pearl Harbor. That sabotage at Pearl Harbor was discounted immediately after the attack and that there was no documented sabotage or fifth column activity by West Coast Japanese-Americans or resident aliens was no more important to General DeWitt than it was to Hollywood. If the War Department could designate the West Coast a theater of operations, declaring it,

Residents of Los Angeles's Little Tokyo proclaiming their patriotism to no avail in Little Tokyo, USA *(1942). Courtesy Twentieth Century-Fox Film Corporation*

in effect, a war zone, Hollywood could declare it a center of Japanese espionage on the assumption that wherever there is a war zone, there are spies. Since Los Angeles' Little Tokyo was one of the "military areas" that was evacuated, it must have been riddled with Japanese agents. Such is the premise behind Fox's *Little Tokyo, USA* (1942), which appeared five months after the signing of Executive Order 9066.

The OWI was appalled by the film, but Fox insisted that it reflected government policy (which it did) and that the script was based on the records of the Dies Committee. Reviews of *Little Tokyo, USA* were poor; at least one critic, Cecil Smith of the Chicago *Tribune*, had the courage to accuse it of "cheaply and viciously" trivializing the war effort. The opening narration is a recitation of untruths, delivered with stentorian self-righteousness. "For more than a decade Japanese mass espionage was carried on in the United States and her territorial outposts, while a complacent America literally slept at the switch. In the Philippines, in Hawaii, and on our

Pacific Coast, there toiled a vast army of volunteer spies, steeped in the traditions of their homeland—Shintoists, blind worshippers of their Emperor—all-out believers in Kipling's immortal lines, 'East is East and West is West and never the twain shall meet.' This film document is presented as a reminder to a nation which, until December 7, 1941, was lulled into a false sense of security by the mouthings of self-styled patriots, whose beguiling theme was 'it can't happen here.'"

Little Tokyo, USA not only trivializes the war effort; it also argues that anyone who does not believe an "Oriental Bund" is operating in Los Angeles is a fool. Japanese hoods are in league with the Nazis, and Japanese businessmen have enough clout to get a detective transferred from Little Tokyo to Hollywood because he believes "there is a direct line between Big Tokyo and Little Tokyo." The detective is really a racist who, at one point, enumerates his gripes: the Japanese monopoly of the vegetable crop (which means they could spray the produce with arsenic), the location of Japanese-owned farms next to airplane factories and dams (which means they could go next door and commit sabotage), and the ill-boding presence of Japanese engineers in the Department of Water and Power (which means they could poison the water).

At the end, the detective is proved right. Newspaper headlines fill the screen: ALL JAPS TO BE EVACUATED/MANZANAR SETTLEMENT FOR JAPANESE EVACUEES IN OWEN'S RIVER VALLEY. Long shots of the evacuees, empty stores, and deserted streets follow. Then the heroine, once a liberal and now a Yellow Peril convert, delivers the envoi: "And so, in the interests of national safety, all Japanese, whether citizens or not, are being evacuated from strategic military zones on the Pacific Coast. Unfortunately, in time of war, the loyal must suffer inconvenience with the disloyal. America's attitude toward this wholesale evacuation can best be summed up, I believe, in the last four lines of a poem by Robert Nathan, entitled 'Watch, America': 'God who gave our fathers freedom/God who made our fathers brave,/What they built with love and anguish/Let our children watch—and save.' Be vigilant, America."[4]

It may be possible to excuse a 1942 film for promoting the myth of West Coast espionage by Japanese-Americans, but not a 1945 release like *Betrayal from the East* and certainly not one that is introduced by columnist Drew Pearson, swearing to its accuracy and warning audiences that what they are about to see "must not happen again" when they should have been warned that it never happened at all. An example of *Betrayal from the East*'s accuracy is the claim that "Tokyo has set up a complete espionage and sabotage organization to cripple all our defenses from Seattle to San Diego in one simultaneous blow when war comes." While most films confine espionage to one location, *Betrayal from the East* has the Japanese working out of Los Angeles's Little Tokyo, Panama, and San Francisco—and always in league with the Nazis. The ballroom of the Little Tokyo Club doubles as a classroom for saboteurs on the supposition that if Bundists can gather in Yorkville cafes, Nisei saboteurs can meet in the West Coast equivalent.

Perhaps the greatest irony of the Exclusion Order is that Nisei units, the 442nd Regimental Combat Team and the 100th Batallion, were among the most decorated of the war—a fact that Hollywood finally acknowledged in *Go for Broke* (1951). But it was not until 1960 that the plight of the Japanese-Americans was actually dramatized in an American film—*Hell to Eternity*.[5] Directed by Phil Karlson, *Hell to Eternity* is the true story of Marine hero Guy Gabaldon (Jeffrey Hunter), who was orphaned at an early age and spent his adolescence as the ward of a Japanese-American family in the years before World War II. When his adoptive parents are interned, Guy angrily asks why the same fate did not befall German- and Italian-Americans. Yet *Hell to Eternity* it not a polemic; it is a war film made memorable by long shots of such breadth that it seems as if Karlson had to stretch the frame to compose them. Karlson's battlefields are vistas of death. Long shots of hand-to-hand combat are intercut with close-ups of bloodied bayonets catching the morning light; battle chants and muffled cries provide the only sound. Later, in the sun's glare, a detachment of Marines silently searches for wounded comrades as the camera pans rows of bodies—the Japanese fallen indistinguishable from the American dead.

Slouching toward Revisionism

With the end of the war, Hollywood adopted a different attitude toward the defeated—one that was somewhere between a victor's compassion for the vanquished and a judge's reconsideration of a criminal. Again the policy was "Europe first," with Germany's case being rescheduled before Japan's. Several factors determined the order of priority. Because of Pearl Harbor, many Americans viewed World War II primarily as a conflict between the United States and Japan—the war in Europe being one that America entered after it had begun in 1939. A character in *The Very Thought of You* remarks, "If we'd stop fooling around in Europe and take care of those Japs, we'd be better off." Joe Bailey in Gore Vidal's novel *Washington,*

D.C. (1967) was not alone in maintaining that "the Japanese are the real enemy, not the Germans. . . . You might even say we're on the same side as the Germans because they're against the Commies and so are we."

Since the war blew cold in Europe before it blew hot in Asia, the United States discovered that once the iron curtain came down, West Germany was standing at the footlights, having moved downstage just in time. In addition to sharing a common cultural and linguistic heritage, West Germany and the United States had a common adversary—Communism, once fascism's scourge and now, it seemed, its synonym.

The Soviet army's rape of Berlin also induced sympathy for the Germans. As with Nanking, the image of sexual violence was fitting. "Do you know what it was like to be a woman when the Russians came in?" asks Berliner Erika von Schluetow (Marlene Dietrich) in *A Foreign Affair* (1948). The question is rhetorical because the women of Berlin had already answered it.

Billy Wilder's *A Foreign Affair* is the first postwar film to express a tolerant, although not necessarily forgiving, attitude toward former Nazis who are able to explain themselves. Erika is able to; she is a survivor who even managed to endure Soviet barbarism, which in itself is partial penance for having been the mistress of a high-ranking Nazi. By casting Marlene Dietrich as Erika, Wilder capitalized on the Dietrich persona: the star who once donned fatigues to entertain GIs at the front lines now plays the ex-consort of a Nazi-at-large. Thus, whatever Dietrich/Erika has done cannot be thoroughly reprehensible. When Erika is about to be sent to a labor camp, the MPs assigned to escort her are so taken by her charms, as thousands of servicemen were by Dietrich's, that it is obvious she will never get there.

Gradually, Hollywood's good Germans and good Nazis became decent Germans and victimized Nazis. They began to acquire an idealistic fervor that extended to their appearance: Oskar Werner in *Decision before Dawn* (1951), his flaxen hair shining with sincerity; Marlon Brando in *The Young Lions* (1958), reverting to his *Julius Caesar* haircut and his *On the Waterfront* integrity to portray a character who, although he fought for the Fatherland, is devastated when he learns about the death camps. The days of Martin Kosleck and Helmut Dantine were over; their replacements were clean-cut types like John Gavin in *A Time to Live and a Time to Die* (1958) and Van Johnson in *The Last Blitzkrieg* (1958).

It took Hollywood longer to come to terms with Japan. At first, the industry softened the Japanese stereotype by reconstructing characters that were salvageable. The logical candidate for reconstruction would be a cultivated Japanese like Colonel Suga in *Three Came Home* (1950), whose sympathy for Western values would make him superior to his grinning, buck-teethed fellows.

Three Came Home, the first postwar film to portray a Japanese soldier sympathetically, was part of Fox's revisionist minicycle, which also includes *Twelve O'Clock High* (1949), *The Desert Fox, Decision before Dawn*, and *Five Fingers*. Based on Agnes Keith's account of her three years in a Japanese prison camp, *Three Came Home* is generally faithful to its source except for the author's rape, which becomes "an attempted criminal assault." The heart of the book remains intact: the bond between the literate Colonel Suga (Sessue Hayakawa) and the literary Mrs. Keith (Claudette Colbert).

Hayakawa was the Japanese Erich von Stroheim; just as Stroheim could never play an evil Nazi, Hayakawa could never play an evil Japanese. Thus, when Colonel Suga tells Mrs. Keith that his family has been killed at Hiroshima, one is genuinely saddened. Since Mrs. Keith holds nothing against him, neither can the viewer.

Three Came Home was written and released before the Korean War began on 24 June 1950. Since Asia had turned into a battlefield again and Asians (North Koreans) had become the enemy, an enlightened attitude toward Japan was impossible for the duration. Admittedly, there was no connection between Japan of 1941–45 and Korea of 1950. But it was a matter of expediency rather than logic. With the studio system in its twilight and the threat of television having become a reality, the industry could not rally around a police action in Korea as it had around a world war; it did not have the screenwriters (many of whom had been blacklisted), the finances, the stars, or the stamina to do so. The Pacific war would have to do double duty and evoke Korea until Hollywood could turn out some Korean War potboilers in the interest of relevancy (*The Steel Helmet*, 1951; *Fixed Bayonets*, 1951, etc.).

One such double duty film is *An American Guerrilla in the Philippines* which, although released five months after the Korean War began, could just as well have been made in 1945 when it was customary to hear the hero exclaim, as he does in the 1950 movie, "That was our first moment of real satisfaction. . . . We had killed our first Jap!" The *Variety* reviewer sensed that the "current Asiatic turmoil" would give the film a special appeal; Bosley Crowther in his *New York Times* review (8 November 1950) wrote that the film's "contemporary graphicness" was attributable to the presence of "Americans . . . in another Far Eastern land."

While *Halls of Montezuma* (1950) admits that war is hell on the nerves, it perpetuates the image of the shifty-eyed Jap, not only by featuring one but also by basing the plot on Japanese duplicity. The film's premise is that, since the Japanese invert everything, the rocket-launching base the marines are trying to locate is not on the reverse slopes, as they think, but on the forward slopes.

With the end of the Korean War, the Japanese stereotype softened into mush as the Japanese came to be perceived as lovable and even tragic. *The Teahouse of the August Moon* (1956) is a Japanese *Bell for Adano* with the conqueror learning from the conquered; in *Sayonara* (1957), the conqueror commits hara-kiri with the conquered. It is as if *The Mikado* had been crossed with *Madame Butterfly* with a bit of Grand Kabuki thrown in for local color. But the one event that brought the United States into war with Japan—Pearl Harbor— was still unexplained.

While films like *The Search* (1948) and *The Big Lift* (1950) were portraying a war-ravaged Germany trying to pick up the pieces, Japan, which had more pieces to pick up, was being ignored. Hollywood had already stated its position on Hiroshima in *The Beginning or the End* (1947): if Japan had had the A-bomb first, it would have used it on the United States. At least the United States had dropped warning leaflets on Japan ten days before it dropped the bomb—"ten days more than they gave us at Pearl Harbor." *The Beginning or the End* calls atomic energy a gift from God: "God has not shown us a new way to destroy ourselves. Atomic energy is the hand He has extended to lift us from the ruins of war and lighten the burdens of peace." Although the explosion at Los Alamos looks like a malignancy, with spirals of smoke bursting out of each other, it will not prove fatal: "We have found a path so filled with promise that when we walk down it, we will know that everything that went before the discovery of atomic energy was the Dark Ages."

Having glorified the force that brought Japan to its knees, Hollywood was loath to return immediately to the days when Japan was a colossus. It would be too inconvenient. Pearl Harbor was doing nicely as a narrative semaphore, a foreshadowing technique, visual shorthand. Whenever "Pearl Harbor" or "December 7" appeared on the screen, audiences would react like Greeks watching a play about a myth they already knew. When the camera tilts up to a Pearl Harbor signpost after Burt Lancaster and Deborah Kerr say their goodbyes in *From Here to Eternity*, one knows the real climax is yet to come. *In Harm's Way* (1965) opens with an elaborate tracking shot; the camera moves along the grounds of the commissioned officers' mess at Pearl Harbor, past a sign announcing a dinner dance for 6 December, along the pool where couples are seated at tables, and on to the dance floor where an officer's wife dances uninhibitedly. When the drunken wife rushes off to spend the night on the beach with her lover, one knows she will awaken the next morning to the roar of Japanese planes overhead.

Eventually, Hollywood gets around to making a movie about everything, including Pearl Harbor from the Japanese perspective. But that was not to happen until almost thirty years after Flight Leader Mitsuo Fuchida cried *"Tora! Tora! Tora!"*—the code signal that Japan's surprise attack had succeeded.

Early in 1950, Edward P. Morgan, a Washington attorney, and Spyros Skouras, president of Twentieth Century–Fox, discussed the possibility of a movie about the bombing of Pearl Harbor, a subject on which Morgan was particularly well informed. A former FBI agent, Morgan had been assistant counsel in 1946 at the Joint Congressional Committee Investigation of the Pearl Harbor Attack and had played a major role in drafting the committee report. Naturally, Zanuck was attracted to the proposal, but at this stage he was not so much interested in a war movie (and certainly not a *"March of Time* recital of the events")[6] as in one that would dramatize the problems Morgan faced with he joined the committee. For example, there had been an attempt on the part of some anti–New Deal senators to expunge all references to Roosevelt from the report so that the omission of his name would cast a pall over his presidency and indirectly make his administration responsible for America's unpreparedness. A film about a man's attempt to be impartial and maintain his integrity at the same time would make a good semi-documentary, the kind Zanuck particularly favored.

Before the Pearl Harbor script could even be written, the studio would have to secure permission from those who would be portrayed in it by name. One of the main characters would necessarily be Admiral Husband E.Kimmel, commander in chief of the U.S. Pacific Fleet, whom the Roberts Commission charged with dereliction of duty. When Zanuck wondered whether Kimmel would agree to be impersonated in a film about the event that ruined his career, Morgan replied that Kimmel might want to be vindicated, particularly if he were shown as the victim of an antiquated chain of command.

Morgan wanted desperately to be involved in the project, and insisted there would be few legal deterrents because the information had all been documented in the committee report. But there still loomed the possibility of an invasion of privacy suit, which was always one of Hollywood's fears. Fox's legal adviser, George Wasson, wrote to Zanuck on 27 February 1950 and, without mentioning Kimmel by name, reminded Zanuck that if a film were to cause embarrassment to an individual depicted in it, the individual could sue and the courts might decide in the plaintiff's favor.

A month later, Zanuck sent a memo ("Subject: Confidential Pearl Harbor File") to his assistant Molly Mandaville along with all the material that had accrued on the project: "Keep these in your file. I may want to refer to it again. It is the Pearl Harbor story."

If Zanuck referred to the file again, it was not until 1963 when the publication of Gordon Prange's "Tora! Tora! Tora!" in *Reader's Digest* revived Zanuck's interest in a Pearl Harbor film. Prange, who had been chief of the Historical Section in Japan under MacArthur, was hired to prepare a day-by-day chronology for 1940–41; but Prange was such a thorough historian that he even provided hour-by-hour breakdowns for particular days. Zanuck regarded *Tora! Tora! Tora!* (1970) as another *House on 92nd St.*—a semi-documentary for the nuclear age, a point he emphasized in full-page ads in the *New York Times* and the *Washington Post* on 16 June 1969, a year before the film was released: "The basic reason for producing the film . . . was to arouse the American public to the necessity of preparedness in this acute missle age where a sneak attack could occur at any moment. You cannot arouse the public by showing films where Americans always win and where we are invincible."

Zanuck had another reason for taking out the ad: to rebut the charge made by some members of Congress that he was producing a film glorifying the enemy. "Glorify" is too strong a term, but there was no doubt that *Tora! Tora! Tora!* would reflect a point of view never before expressed on the American screen—the Japanese.

By 4 April 1966, Larry Forrester had completed a first outline treatment of *Tora! Tora! Tora!* with more exposition than dialogue. From the treatment alone it was evident that the "Slap the Jap" days were gone. Even at this stage, the "sleeping giant" speech of Admiral Yamamoto, commander in chief of Japan's Combined Fleet and the initiator of the Pearl Harbor attack, was included, although Forrester had not yet decided where it should be delivered; its summary nature made it a natural coda, which is what it finally became. Forrester's treatment and continuity step outline (6 April 1966) made it apparent that the film would not only reflect the Japanese point of view but reflect it sympathetically. To humanize Yamamoto, Forrester had him visiting a geisha house "where he calls upon the beautiful Kikuji . . . and a deep bond is forged between them."

Forrester was not to be the only screenwriter; he ended up sharing credit with Hideo Oguni and Ryuzo Kikushima. Zanuck was so eager for another *Longest Day* that he wanted the same format: multiple direction, with the directors drawn from the countries represented in the film, each shooting only those sequences pertaining to his country; and a multiple screenplay, created by writers from the countries depicted in the film. The latter was a goal Zanuck had been only partially able to realize in *The Longest Day* since he was unable to find a British screenwriter (he supposedly wanted Noël Coward) and did not even bother with a German one.

Zanuck was more successful with *Tora! Tora! Tora!*—theoretically, at least. Richard Fleischer was hired to direct the American sequences, Akira Kurosawa to direct the Japanese. But after three weeks, Kurosawa collapsed from nervous exhaustion; his contribution up to that point consisted of 7½ minutes of unedited film at a cost of $1.5 million. Toshio Masuda and Kinji Fukasaka replaced Kurosawa, but the film needed Kurosawa's genius, which neither replacement could provide.

Zanuck tried again. This time, rather than use one basic screenplay with additional episodes by other writers, he commissioned Kurosawa, Oguni, and Kikushima to write their own script, intending to fashion a composite screenplay from theirs and Forrester's. But the Japanese screenplay (9 June 1967) disappointed Zanuck; pencilled over the title page were such criticisms as "doesn't seem dramatic," "no drama," "more interest in Larry script."

While Forrester's script was sympathetic to Japan, the Japanese script was sympathetic to America. There was even something quaint about the way the Japanese wanted to end the film: with a reverential forties shot of Roosevelt, back to camera, dictating his "day of infamy" address to his secretary, Grace Tully, while a crowd sang patriotic songs outside the White House. Although such a crowd did gather and sing on the evening of 7 December, ending a Pearl Harbor movie with "God Bless America" was exactly what a Hollywood director would have done in the 1940s. Forrester knew how it should end—with Yamamoto's speech, which the Japanese writers omitted completely.

Eventually Zanuck got his composite script, but only after much rewriting. He also made his film, at a cost of more than twenty million dollars. *Tora! Tora! Tora!*, released in the late summer of 1970, was the first American film to explain the events that led up to Pearl Harbor, thereby correcting the Hollywood version of that "dastardly and unprovoked" attack. That version went something like this:

On 7 December, just as Fay Bainter is about to celebrate her birthday (*The War against Mrs. Hadley*), just as John Garfield and Eleanor Parker are about to sit down to Sunday dinner (*Pride of the Marines*), just as Mildred Natwick is about to rent a room to Robert Young and Hillary Brooke (*The Enchanted Cottage*, 1945), just as John Wayne is relaxing in Manila (*They Were Expendable*), just as Dana Andrews and Susan Hayward are watching the Giants play the Brooklyn Dodgers at the New York Polo Grounds (*My Foolish Heart*, 1949), the first bombs start falling on Pearl Harbor.

"Hey, the Japs bombed Pearl Harbor!" (*The Sullivans*). "Pearl Harbor! Most of us didn't know what it was, let alone where it was" (*So Proudly We Hail*). "Jim, where's Pearl Harbor?" "Pearl Harbor? Oh, it's down the Jersey coast, near Atlantic City, someplace" (*Pride of the Marines*).

America had been "stabbed in the back" (*Remember Pearl Harbor, Wing and a Prayer*), "hit from behind with a blackjack" (*Betrayal from the East*). While the Pacific fleet was being bombed, those "oily gents" (*Air Force*), "those dressed-up, four-eyed monkeys" (*Salute to the Marines*), that "no good dirty stinking pair" (*The Sullivans*)—Japanese ambassador Admiral Kichisaburo Nomura and special representative Saburu Kurusu—sat in the diplomatic waiting room at the State Department to keep their appointment with Secretary of State Cordell Hull, after having "assured the press that Japan's intentions are wholly peaceful" (*Air Force*).

"They knew all the time!" (*The Sullivans*).

They really didn't. The Sullivans, who were reading the Sunday paper when the news of Pearl Harbor came over the radio, heard about it approximately forty minutes after Nomura and Kurusu did; and Hull knew fifteen minutes before he received Nomura and Kurusu in his office at 2:20 p.m.

Their appointment with Hull was originally scheduled for 1:00 p.m.; the timing was critical. During that fated weekend, Tokyo cabled a fourteen part message to the United States government, which Nomura and Kurusu were to deliver by 1:00 EST, 7 December. The United States already knew what was contained in the first thirteen parts, which had been intercepted and translated by Signal Intelligence Service (SIS). The fourteenth, and crucial, part had been translated by 7:30 a.m., 7 December, about a half hour before it arrived at the Japanese embassy. The final part was not a formal declaration of war but rather a diplomatically worded cessation of discussion ("The Japanese Government regrets . . ."). Still, the conclusion was inevitable: a showdown was imminent.

If the message had been delivered as planned (i.e., at 1:00), Washington would have received Japan's "regrets" twenty-five minutes before the bombs started falling. But the way in which Tokyo transmitted the message precluded the possibility of a 1:00 delivery. Tokyo did not take human fallibility into consideration; it did not appreciate the significance of Sunday in America; it did not realize that the employees of the Japanese embassy were not on war alert. Tokyo did not know that the embassy secretary, Okumura, was a poor typist; that, when the message was not ready for presentation by 1:00, Nomura had to request a delay from Hull; and that by the time it was finally typed, Pearl Harbor was being bombed.

Colonel Rufus S. Bratton, head of the Far Eastern Section, realized the meaning of the 1:00 deadline (7:30 a.m. in Hawaii); he wanted to warn all the field commanders in the Pacific but he had no authority. Bratton had to track down General Marshall, who was out horseback riding; and when Marshall finally wrote out his 1:00 warning alert, it was in longhand. Bratton had to get it typed, which meant another delay. When the message reached Honolulu, it was pigeonholed for regular delivery because it was not marked "priority"; four hours after the attack began, it arrived in Oahu.

What *Tora! Tora! Tora!* does that no previous film did is to show that the attack on Pearl Harbor was the culmination of more than a year of security bungles, errors of judgment, miscalculations, military feuds, and attempts at secrecy that backfired; and a weekend of messages received but not acted on, of messages acted on but too late, of appointments made and rescheduled, of authority withheld or not delegated. All the while a Japanese task force is shown moving relentlessly, inexorably toward its destination, executing a plan that seemed to be ratified by fate. *Tora! Tora! Tora!* captures that air of inexorability, the feeling that 7 December was the culmination of a spiral of events that could not occur in any other way, not even if a god were to descend from the machine. There were too many forces at work to generate a simple narrative. The causes were manifold; the effects, international. To achieve an atmosphere of participatory destiny, of control slipping out of human hands and into the grip of fate, the action cuts back and forth between the Japanese armada, Washington, and Oahu, resulting in a sense of simultaneity, as if everything is happening concurrently. Through associative montage, events that are similar but temporally distinct are conjoined by an image or an allusion. The scene in which former navy minister Yoshida voices his fear about an embargo is followed by one in which "a full embargo on all trade with Japan" is announced. In his cabin on the Japanese flagship *Nagato*, "Gandhi" says, "We'll attack on a weekend;" cut to Rear Admiral Bellinger in Kimmel's office on Pearl Harbor discussing the possibility of a weekend attack. As Bratton is slowly typing out Marshall's 1:00 warning, Okumura is pecking away at the Japanese embassy, trying to get the fourteen-point message into final form. In his bomber, Fuchida picks up the same soothing music that Major Landon is listening to in his B-17.

Montage gives *Tora! Tora! Tora!* the semblance of tragedy but not its essence. In tragedy, there is poetry; there is hamartia or the tragic error. In tragedy, there is a hero who dismisses the obvious or defers the inevitable until the obvious can no longer be ignored or the inevitable postponed. But Pearl Harbor has no one hero; it has a myriad of heroes—hence a myriad of errors, some big and some small. *Tora! Tora! Tora!* is simply prose. (However, it did not deserve Vincent Canby's "Tora-ble, Tora-ble, Tora-ble" review in the *New York Times*, 4 October 1970.)

It is certainly possible to respect the film for what it tried to accomplish. The problem is the fragmentation of the narrative, which in turn fragments the characters, who seem to get cropped by all the crosscutting. What the film really needs is not crosscutting but cross resonance, so that the characters have more in common than hearing the same music or picking up the same cues.

It is also possible to admire the screenwriters for trying to make Yamamoto and Kimmel doubles—the former regretting Washington's receiving the message fifty-five minutes after the attack, the latter receiving it when the attack is over. However, the doubling is not sustained. Pearl Harbor is Yamamoto's cross; the film belongs to him and ultimately to Japan. Thus it ends with Yamamato's prophecy: "I feel all we have done is to awaken a sleeping giant and fill him with a terrible resolve."

Kimmel's fate is quite different from Yamamoto's. Kimmel's is not that of someone ignorant of the past and therefore doomed to repeat it; but of someone unable to control the present and therefore doomed to be part of it. Kimmel is history's victim; Yamamoto, history's agent. Kimmel has to face a weekend that only a poet of ironic vision could have appreciated; seeing the bombing of Pearl Harbor from one's own backyard must have been as shattering as watching Birnam wood come to Dunsinane.

Like the weekend it delineates, *Tora! Tora! Tora!* suffered from fatal mistiming. When it reached the theaters, audiences had already seen *M*A*S*H* and *Patton*, both favorites of the antiwar young, who regarded them as antiwar films. *M*A*S*H* is an antiwar film revealing the folly of war; *Patton* reveals the folly of the warrior while, at the same time, praising that folly because it is the Pattons who win the wars—a point that seemed to elude the student activists in their eagerness to find nonexistent analogies with Vietnam. Yet the ads dubbing *Patton* "A Salute to a Rebel" were clearly aimed at the college rebels; their elders knew George S. Patton was not a rebel, or certainly nothing like the campus rebels of the late sixties. Patton belongs to that breed of epic warrior whose conduct, like Achilles', vacillates between reason and paranoia, compassion and revenge, pettiness and magnanimity. Patton can tenderly pin a Purple Heart to the pillow of a wounded GI and then strike an enlisted man for weeping. But that is the way epic heroes behave— weeping like children for their lost armor and bursting with childlike joy when they receive a new shield. Patton is a quixotic militarist, as the final scene discloses with great subtlety. Walking across a field where a windmill turns slowly, Patton looks like a Quixote too weary to tilt at the vanes.

Even without the competition of M*A*S*H and *Patton*, 1970 would have been too late for *Tora! Tora! Tora!* To achieve its aim and present moviegoers with a corrected version of the Pearl Harbor legend, time would have had to stand still. If the studios had been in their pride of place in the entertainment world, with each of the majors releasing about thirty movies a year; if the neighborhood theaters had not been converted into supermarkets or banks; if home entertainment were still radio; and if the "Slap the Jap" mentality still prevailed, the film could have made its point. But in 1970, Fox made only fourteen films; Columbia Pictures had become a division of Columbia Pictures Industries; Universal was a spoke of the MCA umbrella; Paramount was a subsidiary of Gulf + Western; Republic, PRC, and Monogram were defunct; George C. Scott could say "shit" in *Patton*, and there was no Joe Breen to scream "Code!"

All *Tora! Tora! Tora!* could do was to make amends and correct the impressions of veteran moviegoers who thought Nomura and Kurusu were smiling on 7 December because they had helped plunge the dagger in America's back; and perhaps the film could offer a different perspective to the generation that learned about World War II from Saturday afternoon television or the Late Show. But the film did nothing for the 120,000 Japanese-Americans who had been interned in 1942. They had to wait until 1976 for their vindication; and when it came, ironically, it came from television, in the form of that hybrid creation, the TV movie—*Farewell to Manzanar*, a deeply affecting account of a Japanese-American family's attempt to survive their exile with dignity.

In the fullness of time, the scales of justice are balanced. But as T.S. Eliot asks in "Gerontion," "After such knowledge, what forgiveness?"

11. Remembering Pearl Harbor

Some moments are metaphors; others, epiphanies. Still others are both, such as the moment in which one recognizes a relative in a painting or finds oneself in a character, or when strands of thought that have been hanging loose in the mind suddenly pull together and form a pattern.

For me, it was the Saturday afternoon I saw *Fighting Coast Guard* at the West Side in 1951. It was a Republic programmer, that ordinarily would have appeared as a second feature of a double bill, along with a chapter of a serial, a short, a cartoon, and a newsreel.

It had been well over a year since I was at the West Side, having forsaken it for our short-lived art theater and the downtown movie houses, which seemed more fitting for a student at Scranton's only college preparatory school. I am not certain why I went that Saturday, except perhaps that I needed a break from the geometry theorems I had been memorizing for an exam.

I was unprepared for the change in the theater, in the audience, and most of all, in myself. The marquee had been streamlined; stripped of its jazzy border of colored bulbs, it had the look of a billboard. The auditorium still smelled of disinfectant, but now it had a sweetly heady aroma, like rose-scented Lysol. Although, like "all children over twelve," I had been paying an adult admission for three years, now I finally felt like an adult, entering a historic restoration of a childhood haunt.

Fighting Coast Guard is a movie about World War II, but the audience was not a World War II audience. The kids manifested their disinterest by using the main aisle as a grand promenade or talking over the dialogue, which soon disappeared beneath the overlapping conversations.

Who could blame them? This was not their war, only an event in

Republic continues fighting the war in Fighting Coast Guard *(1951) despite overage stars.*

their lifetime, not remote enough to have any allure or fascination. They did not know that Brian Donlevy and Ella Raines were ten years too old for their parts, that the stars were trying to resurrect their forties' selves as if the intervening decade had been a sleep and a forgetting. Neither did I, really, but I sensed it. I sensed something else, too: the war as I had experienced it in the movies was over.

But that has not stopped Hollywood from making movies about it. Yet, for the most part, that is all they are—movies about World War II rather than World War II movies. The American World War II film has its own themes, plots, and iconography, which have become such a permanent part of American culture that they have acquired the status of native archetypes. To paraphrase Pope, to copy World War II is to copy them.

The Longest Day did not copy them, nor did its successors (e.g., *Battle of the Bulge*, 1965; *A Bridge Too Far*, 1977), which mingle epic length, mammoth casts, and documentary detachment. The World War II film does not clutter the screen with needless print, introducing characters by titles or translating foreign dialogue by subtitles. These more recent productions are the World War II film made intellectually respectable but robbed of the reckless spontaneity that made it distinctive. These films may be better documented, but they also call attention to their documentation. While they may have more facts, they have no myths.

The American World War II film has its own mythology, based on the paradox of a nation involved in global war but never attacked. The miraculous unity the movies reflect is only possible in a country that has not been invaded or occupied; without such unity, inconvenience would never have taken on the air of deprivation. Furthermore, the industry could never have functioned as efficiently as it did; a Hollywood under siege would no longer be Hollywood. But Hollywood was as blessed as America, the divinely protected nation on which God shed His grace (it seemed more like the mist that shielded Brigadoon from the outside world). As Americans lived out that myth, Hollywood captured it in a cycle of films that became paradigmatic.

Since the paradigm has a basis in both history and myth, it has to be approached from a dual angle and with a double vision that no lens can produce. The explanation for the paucity of good American World War II films is the same as that for the scarcity of good historical fiction. While there are many historical novels, there are few historical novelists worthy of the name. Recreating an era so that the characters embody it in appearance, idiom, and mores requires someone who can write as a novelist but think as a historian. Such beings are rare—in literature as well as in film.

When writers cannot recreate an era, they restage a battle, reduce the war to a setting, use it to preach pacifism or inveigh against military corruption—in which case any war will do. For example, *Attack!* (1956) uses the Battle of the Bulge as the background for a clash between a heroic lieutenant (Jack Palance) and a craven captain (Eddie Albert). The clash could have taken place during any war; World War II happens to be the setting of the play on which the film is based—Norman A. Brooks's *Fragile Fox* (1954). Yet visually there is little about *Attack!* that suggests the American World War II film.[1] In fact, it seems as if director Robert Aldrich went out of his way to keep the viewer from thinking of *Attack!* as a World War II movie. Everything looks either bone white or chalky; sometimes the lens appears to have been sprinkled with powder. Aldrich shot through gratings and doorways, masking the frame or casting bars over it so that the screen becomes reality's sieve instead of its mirror.

Even Aldrich's imagery is alien to the war film. The cannon of a German tank enters the frame from the left, like the beak of a prehistoric monster that has been severed but continues to move. The lieutenant's corpse looks petrified, like a body preserved by the lava of Vesuvius, a silent scream coming from his gaping mouth.

In a typical World War II film, the villain is the enemy who is either killed or punished; in *Attack!*, the villain is an American—the captain whom the lieutenant kills. A typical World War II film celebrates group action; *Attack!* celebrates group murder, with each man's firing a bullet into the captain's corpse so that his death becomes a collective act (which, however, does not prevent the captain's receiving the Congressional Medal of Honor posthumously). By inverting the conventions of the American World War II film, *Attack!* ceases to be one, having more in common with fifties' exposés of hypocrisy like *The Great Man* (1956), *A Face in the Crowd* (1956), and *Sweet Smell of Success* (1957) than with the war movie.

Simply because a movie is a World War II film does not mean it portrays everything about the war as sacrosanct. It does portray the war as a just one and true heroism as unassailable, but also shows that false heroics merit contempt (*A Medal for Benny*, 1945) or satire (*Hail the Conquering Hero*, 1944), depending on the degree of fraudulence. In *A Medal for Benny*, the father of a dead war hero refuses to accept his son's Congressional Medal of Honor in the house provided by local politicians who feel his hovel will give the press a poor impression of the town. The father's reasoning is that a home, not a house, makes a hero. In Preston Sturges's *Hail the Conquering Hero*, a group of marines comes to the aid of the despondent 4-F Woodrow Lafayette Pershing Truesmith (Eddie Bracken). Through their machinations, Truesmith returns to his home town as a hero, stirring up such pride in the people that they elect him mayor. Just when the film seems to be a sendup of America's mania for heroes, it becomes a tribute to American magnanimity. When Truesmith confesses the truth, he is so sincere that the people want him to stay in office. Any ambiguity that may have existed earlier disappears at the end when Truesmith whispers "Semper Fidelis" as the marines who have made his dream possible depart. *Hail the Conquering Hero* may mock jingoism and hero worship, but not patriotism and heroism.

I Want You (1951), one of the few films of any worth about the Korean War, also distinguishes between real and bogus patriotism, but within the context of another distinction: duty and patriotism. During World War II, duty and patriotism were virtually synonymous, but Korea could not inspire the same feelings. Korea had to appeal to a sense of duty, to an obligation to defend America against "godless atheistic" Communism, as it was redundantly called. As *Hail the Conquering Hero* has shown, a little pretense could be tol-

Mr. Lucky (James Garner) meets Mrs. Miniver (Julie Andrews) in The Americanization of Emily *(1964). Courtesy MGM/UA*

erated during World War II when patriotism abounded; but not during Korea. In 1951, there was nothing poignant about a father's claiming to be a war hero when he spent the war as a general's orderly; on the eve of his son's departure for Korea, it seems obscene. The most powerful moment in *I Want You* occurs when the mother clears the mantel of her husband's "war trophies," Lugers and swords that were bought in a New York pawnshop.

Bogus heroism is also the subject of *The Americanization of Emily*. But though it was made in 1964, *Emily* is a genuine American World War II movie. It is as if Mrs. Miniver and Mr. Lucky, the regenerative woman and the impassive man, have been reunited. Even the stars suggest the personas of their predecessors, with Julie Andrews (Emily) exuding Greer Garson's propriety and James Garner (Lieutenant Charles Madison) projecting Cary Grant's darkly cool insouciance.

Yet on the surface the film appears to have more in common with *Attack!*—not as an indictment, but as a satire, of hypocrisy. Based on Paddy Chayefsky's adaptation of William Bradford Huie's novel,

The Americanization of Emily concerns the navy's scheme to erect
a Tomb for the Unknown Sailor in honor of the first seaman to die
on Omaha Beach during the Normandy invasion. The honored,
Charlie Madison, turns out not only to be alive, but a coward to
boot.

Like *Hail the Conquering Hero*, *The Americanization of Emily*
works according to the principle of transvaluation. Generally, it is
transvaluation of values, as it is in Erasmus's *Praise of Folly*, in
which a virtue is evaluated in terms of its opposite, contraposed
with it, examined from various angles, and continually redefined
until a new value, superior to the original, emerges. In *Emily*, it is a
vice that is transvaluated: Madison's cowardice, which, when contrasted with the navy's self-aggrandizement, is really love of life, the
desire for survival. Similarly, in Sturges's film, Truesmith's decep-
tion, viewed in terms of the town's sense of inferiority, which has
made it hero-mad and publicity-hungry, appears to be a manifesta-
tion of genuine patriotism and civic responsibility.

In keeping with the World War II tradition, the regenerative
woman redeems the apathetic man; in keeping with the tradition of
transvaluation, she acquires his values. Emily's Americanization
consists of her imbibing some of Madison's zest for living—but only
after she converts him from a cynic into a realist. To his insistence
that war is a fraud, Emily replies, "War isn't a fraud; it's very real.
It's the virtue of war that's a fraud."

War is not a virtue in the American World War II film; it is, to use
a recurring word, a job[2]—a job that must be done for reasons ranging
from the desire to abolish war in general (*The Story of G.I. Joe, Halls
of Montezuma*) to the desire to insure the happiness of all (*Over
Twenty-one*, 1945); and, in between, the desire to return to such
prewar pleasures as dancing at Roseland (*Lifeboat*), wearing black
negligees (*So Proudly We Hail*), and eating fresh vegetables (*Destination Tokyo*).

What is virtuous, however, is valor, which deserves praise wherever it exists—among Russian partisans, on doom-ridden Bataan, in
a Czech village, among Chinese children, in occupied Norway, in
the o.s.s., in the American home. In response to the allegation
that, of the 1,313 movies released between 1942 and 1944, only "a
few dozen . . . accomplished anything of significance for the war effort at home or abroad,"[3] one can only answer that Hollywood did
not consider itself an educator but a moral mythographer whose
outstanding creation was a world that complemented our own—a
world running on mirror time, peopled by exemplary beings acting
out the myth of a united America for the edification and enjoyment

of a world running on clock time and peopled by mortals. When mirror time and clock time coincide, as they do in film where the only time is the running time, myth becomes reality.

The vicar in *Mrs. Miniver* is only partially correct: World War II may have been a war of the people, but it was also a war for the movies. It might even be called the movies' war.

 **Afterword**

Between 1940 and 1945, the war had been worked
into practically every genre except science fiction (which would have
challenged the most imaginative filmmaker). Even such unlikely
types as the musical and the horror film rallied to the Allied cause.
The Rita Hayworth musical *Tonight and Every Night* (1945), set in
London during the Blitz, did not spare the lives of two of the secondary characters. Wartime London was also the scene of *Return of the
Vampire* (1944), in which the Dracula figure (Bela Lugosi) roamed
the city with a werewolf. Since the true horrors of the war would
not be revealed until later, the familiar mad scientist easily became
a Nazi type like Bela Lugosi, who performed plastic surgery on Japanese saboteurs to make them resemble respectable Americans (*Black
Dragons*, 1942), or like John Carradine, who created zombies for the
Third Reich (*Return of the Zombies*, 1943).

In Hollywood, once an event becomes a plot peg, it lands on the
story line rack. By the time America celebrated the fiftieth anniversary of the war's end in 1995, the conflict had either formed the
basis of—or figured prominently in—films about the rise of Nazism
(*The Searching Wind*, 1946; *Ship of Fools*, 1965; *Cabaret*, 1972; *Julia*,
1977), pre-Pearl Harbor America (*Brighton Beach Memoirs*, 1986;
Radio Days, 1987), and the homefront (*Summer of '42*, 1972; *Class
of '44*, 1973; *Baby Blue Marine*, 1976; *Racing with the Moon*, 1984;
Swing Shift, 1984).

There was also no dearth of interest in combat films (e.g. *Battle
Cry*, 1955; *Battle Hymn*, 1957; *The Naked and the Dead*, 1958; *Heroes of Telemark*, 1965; *Battle of the Bulge*, 1965; *Tobruk*, 1967;
Patton, 1970; *Midway*, 1976; *MacArthur*, 1977; *Memphis Belle*, 1990)
or in those dealing with postwar adjustment and the problems facing returning veterans (*From this Day Forward*, 1946; *The Best Years
of Our Lives*, 1946, remade for television in 1975 as *Returning Home*;

257

The Blue Dahlia, 1946; *Till the End of Time*, 1946; *The Guilt of Janet Ames*, 1947; *Winter Meeting*, 1948; *The Men*, 1950; *Bright Victory*, 1951; *Japanese War Bride*, 1952; *Desert Bloom*, 1986).

The avenging hero was not limited to the western, as films like *Cornered* (1945), *Act of Violence* (1948), and *Captain Carey, U.S.A.* (1950) showed with protagonists seeking satisfaction for wartime betrayal. Perpetuating the notion that war turns boys into men were the films *Between Heaven and Hell* (1956) and *The Big Red One* (1980).

Prison camps provided the setting for *Stalag 17* (1953), *The Bridge on the River Kwai* (1957), *Seven Women from Hell* (1961), *The Great Escape* (1963), and *Victory* (1981); and the American occupation served as the setting for *A Foreign Affair* (1948) and *The Teahouse of the August Moon* (1956). The end of the war also introduced a new character type: the Nazi hunter (e.g., *Rogues' Regiment*, 1948; *Boys from Brazil*, 1978).

Performers who entertained the troops had been celebrated in such films as *Follow the Boys* (1944) and *Four Jills in a Jeep* (1944), and the tradition continued in *Interrupted Melody* (1955) and *For the Boys* (1991). Another tradition also continued: the wartime romance, a variation on the women's film (e.g., *About Last Night*, 1954; *Sea Wife*, 1957; *Until They Sail*, 1957; *Yanks*, 1979; *Hanover Street*, 1979). Finally, Hollywood insisted there was a comic side to the war that could be reflected in slapstick (*Up Front*, 1951; *Willie and Joe Back at the Front*, 1952; *Kelly's Heroes*, 1970) and screwball comedy (*I Was a Male War Bride*, 1949; *The Producers*, 1968; and the anemic remake of *To Be or Not To Be*, 1983).

Several *films noirs* implied a connection between the war and a character's behavior and values (*Crossfire*, 1947; *Dead Reckoning*, 1947; *In a Lonely Place*, 1950). *Crossfire* suggested that life in the military inhibited a soldier's anti-Semitism, which erupted upon his return to civilian life and eventually lead to the senseless murder of a Jew; *Dead Reckoning* that combat creates bonds between men that are stronger than heterosexual attraction; and *In a Lonely Place* that a screenwriter's penchant for violence was the direct result of his wartime experience. With the growing awareness of the genocide—the "war within the war" as it is sometimes called—the Holocaust film became a full-fledged genre (*The Juggler*, 1953; *The Diary of Anne Frank*, 1959; *Judgment at Nuremberg*, 1961; *The Pawnbroker*, 1963; *Voyage of the Damned*, 1976; *Sophie's Choice*, 1982; *Schindler's List*, 1993).

Science fiction, which Hollywood classified 4-F for the duration, was conscripted in the 1950s to usher in the nuclear age with a rash of movies about the aberrations caused by atomic testing, such as the mutants like giant ants in *Them!* (1954) and the prehistoric creatures restored to life in *The Beast from 20,000 Fathoms* (1953). It took a while, however, for Hollywood to dramatize the psychological effects of nuclear testing on humans (*Desert Bloom* and *Blue Sky*, 1994) and to move away from the pieties of *The Beginning to the End* (1947) to tell the real story of the bomb that gave its name to an age (*Fat Man and Little Boy*, 1989). But then, the studios largely ignored the internment of Japanese Americans during the war until *Come See the Paradise* (1990), assuming that television had already made amends with *Farewell to Manzanar* (1976).

For filmmakers, World War II was America's most versatile conflict. Since audiences associated it with exemplars of courage and survival, character types like prison camp inmates, homefront heroines, and callow recruits who mature into fighting men were already familiar. The mold had been created; it had only to be filled.

This was not an easy task, however. The films of the war years were very much products of their time; hence, only a handful qualify as world class cinema. Yet as cultural artifacts and indices of American sentiment, they are exceptional. By creating an America that was part real, part myth—and marketing it as the lost template of a Platonic form that film had discovered—Hollywood was able to tap into the American consciousness, feeding aspirations and dreams that everyone had but would never express quite so extravagantly as did the movies.

Since these films were spawned directly by the war, relevance and immediacy were never an issue. While historical fact may have been occasionally skewered, the films were accurate in such details as dress, language, ambiance, and mores—superficial elements to some, but, ironically, the most difficult for later filmmakers to reproduce. Idioms and slang were especially troublesome. "Swell" was the 1940s what "groovy" was to the 1960s, "awesome" to the 1970s, and "cool" to the 1980s and 1990s. When "swell" was heard on the screen in the 1940s, it never occasioned guffaws. Today, students in particular tend to laugh when they hear it in a movie of the period because, to them, it represents their grandparents' generation.

Neil Simon's *Biloxi Blues* (1988) and Woody Allen's *Radio Days* are outstanding examples of the art of evoking a period without exactly replicating its idioms. In each film, the dialogue is marked by simplicity and directness—qualities that have become synonymous with World War II America. The trick is to sound authentic, not archaic—a decision Joseph L. Mankiewicz made regarding *Cleopatra* (1963). Mankiewicz wanted language that sounded classical but not affected; thus he opted for mock Shakespeare in certain scenes, flavoring the dialogue with a touch of rhetoric. By contrast, Ben Barzman, Basilio Franchina, and Philip Yordan wrote a script for *The Fall of the Roman Empire* (1964) that sounded like a literal translation of a Latin text (e.g., "Let us fall upon the Romans, killing them!").

In *Radio Days*, Aunt Bea (Dianne Wiest) invites a man she has been dating to come into the kitchen, where she offers him a glass of milk; no other beverage would have occurred to her. Anticipating a proposal, she engages her suitor in conversation. Gradually, he confesses that he will always remain loyal to the memory of his dead fiancé. When he speaks of the fiancé in the third person masculine, Bea registers a look of compassion tempered by resignation to hide her deep disappointment. The disclosure—made at a kitchen table over a glass of milk—is marked by an ingenuousness typical of an age when Warner Bros. could release a movie with the title *The Gay Sisters* (1942) and audiences would assume it was about happy siblings.

As present becomes past, which is then enshrined as history, recreating the past becomes increasingly complex. Of course, it can always be done badly, as scores of films about antiquity have shown. The serious filmmaker, however, must deal with three forms of accuracy: historical, linguistic, and, most important, visual.

Historians may disagree, but unless one is making a documentary or a combat film about a particular battle, factual accuracy is the easiest to achieve. It is simply a matter of research. In a fiction film, the war is merely a background against which a human drama is taking place. The facts should disappear within the interstices of the visual text, becoming part of the *mise en scéne*. A fact-heavy film like *Tora! Tora! Tora!* calls attention to its documentation and seems more like a history lesson than a movie. Frankly, the best World War II films used only a few random facts because their narratives transcended the time of the main action. If *Mrs. Miniver, The Bridge on the River Kwai,* and *The Americanization of Emily* have not become dated (while *Guadalcanal Diary, Wing and a Prayer,* and *A Walk in the Sun* have), the reason is that their themes (courage in time of adversity, blinding obsession, and false heroics, respectively) were not limited to World War II. And if a film like *Hell in the Pacific* (1968)—in which two men find themselves alone on an island in the Pacific, each unable to speak the other's language because one is American and the other Japanese—seems even more relevant in a climate of racial and ethnic tension, it is because communication has become more complex than it was at the time of the movie's release.

The best World War II films had more than outstanding scripts. The script is only the framework in which the characters move and speak in language evocative of the time and place. What matters most is visualization, and that is the task of the filmmaker, not the writer. In *Sophie's Choice*, director Alan J. Pakula, like his central character, also made choices—artistic ones. Although *Sophie's Choice* was shot in color, Pakula decided that the Auschwitz flashback should look dramatically different from the main action. For the Auschwitz scenes, Nestor Almendros, one of film's greatest cinematographers, reduced the spectrum to brown, black, gray, and white—the colors of the inmates' surroundings and uniforms.

Steven Spielberg, on the other hand, chose to film *Schindler's List* in black and white, with color only at the beginning and the end. His decision to use a format associated with the 1940s newsreel and documentary heightened the realism of *Schindler's List*, so that one was never conscious of watching a movie but of experiencing a historical event. But there are other factors to consider here; the film's art derived from a number of choices: location shooting, a cast without stars who were household names, a visual style that could alienate fans of colorization, and Spielberg's refusal to reduce the Holocaust to a catalog of horrors that would have overshadowed Oskar Schindler's humanity and de-emphasized the will to survive even in a hell that Dante himself could not have envisaged.

The second point—the cast—merits further consideration. *Schindler's List* is flawlessly cast with actors in the principal roles (Liam Neeson, Ralph Fiennes, Ben Kingsley) who were far from screen icons. But such casting worked to the film's advantage. Lacking a persona, the actors were not saddled with the baggage of their screen image.

It was quite the opposite with blockbusters that purported to recreate a battle, substituting screen icons for drama: Henry Fonda, Charlton Heston, and Robert Mitchum in *Midway*; Henry Fonda, John Wayne, Robert Mitchum, and Richard Burton in *The Longest Day*; and Henry Fonda in *Battle of the Bulge*. Icons are all these films offered; corporate Hollywood would call such movies "actioners." No matter how realistic they may seem, theirs is the realism of elaborately staged battle scenes. As Aristotle noted in the *Poetics*, spectacle is the least important element in drama.

Directors must take two factors into consideration when shooting a World War II related script: the period itself, which can be recreated independently of the movies made during it, and the period reincarnated with as many of the conventions (cinematic and cultural) of the 1940s as are transferable to the present—in other words, a "forties movie" about the forties.

Only a genuine filmmaker can bring off the latter with a cast that first heard about World War II in high school. Woody Allen succeeded in *Radio Days* because he had built up a stock company primarily of character actors about whom audiences had no preconceptions. Even when Alan Alda became a member of the company, he could play off his image without throwing the film off kilter. For *Radio Days*, Allen also had a production designer Santo Loquasto, who affectionately recreated the period, and director of photography, Carlo DiPalma, who softened the hues to suggest a gilded past. Then, too, was Allen's judicious choice of music (popular 1940s songs like "You'd Be So Nice to Come Home To") that are either heard in the background or sung in the film itself—but always unobtrusively.

When Mike Nichols undertook the screen version of Neil Simon's *Biloxi Blues*, he said he wanted the film to have the look of a Norman Rockwell painting, meaning that he wanted an aura of innocence, a word that has often been used to describe the era. Thus Nichols, his director of photography Bill Butler, and production designer Paul Sybert gave the movie a rotogravure tonality, as if the colors had faded to sepia, with the images taking on the look of the pictures in a family album. Although *Biloxi Blues* was filmed in color, it had such a desaturated look that it closely resembled black and white, or perhaps one should say brown and white, since various shades of brown (the recruits' brown hair, their khaki uniforms) appear. In the mess hall, for example, the browns are set against the white of the wall, the vapor from the steam table, and the gray of the posts.

Biloxi Blues succeeded on all counts. Nichols conjured up the past with such 1940s touches as dissolves and the incorporation of a *Movietone News* as part of the bill in a local movie theater. With non-icons Matthew Broderick and Christopher Walken in the leads, and a supporting cast that could smoke a cigarette naturally (not holding it as if it were a deadly prop to be discarded with relief when the director called "Cut!"), Nichols achieved the authenticity he desired. Naturally, the language was stronger that what would have been heard on the screen in the 1940s (but not so strong as to result in an R rating). It was the contemporary equivalent of the forties vernacular, vulgar and tangy enough for the PG-13 rating, despite a scene between Broderick and a prostitute that came as close as possible to suggesting intercourse but without the writhing and posturing a less sensitive director would have insisted on. This was forties sex, nineties style.

A textbook case in how not to replicate the past is the 1990 *Memphis Belle*. There was no reason to remake William Wyler's magnificent documentary about a B-17's final mission half a century later as a fiction film—except that producer David Puttnam and Wyler's daughter, Catherine, wanted to. No one, however, was up to the task; the cast looked and spoke as if it were 1990. In the lead, Matthew Modine, who was so memorable as Joker in Stanley Kubrick's *Full Metal Jacket* (1987), seemed to be in the wrong war.

Film accuracy is not the same as scholarly documentation or photographic reproduction. The chief opponents of film's incursion into history are academics who want to restrict the authentic to the factual; hence the uproar over Oliver Stone's *JFK* (1990) and *Nixon* (1995). Yet Stone is no different from the historical novelist or playwright who traditionally appropriates the past for his or her own end. Stone is not recreating history but creating his version of it. Stone's post-Camelot America is one beset by fear, paranoia, and self-righteousness—emotions that continue to thrive because of a distrust of the federal government and a belief in a conspiracy spiral that resembles the inverted cone of Dante's hell.

Henry King's America was the other extreme. King, one of Fox's best contract directors, specialized in films that idealized America (*State Fair*, 1933; *In Old Chicago*, 1938; *Jesse James*, 1939; *Maryland*, 1940; *Margie*, 1946), just as Stone specializes in ones that demythologize it. Assigned to direct Darryl Zanuck's tribute to his idol Woodrow Wilson (*Wilson*, 1944), King, abetted by screenwriter Lamar Trotti, created a heroic figure who, at the film's end, is still campaigning for the League of Nations, although 1944 audiences knew the League had proved a failure. But Hollywood has always counted on audiences with three kinds of memory: no memory, a selective memory, or a memory flexible enough to suspend disbelief for the movie's duration.

Because of film's ability to evoke one era while depicting another, 1944 audiences viewed *Wilson* within the context of the World War II film, regardless of the period in which the action was set. *Wilson* confirmed the vision of a president (who died twenty years before the film was released) that might eventually come to pass with something like the United Nations. Woodrow Wilson was the closest Zanuck could get to Franklin D. Roosevelt. Zanuck wanted a voice to echo what he thought were American convictions and used a film about a former president to express them.

Film authenticity is a complex matter. Authenticity means a screenplay about events and situations that could have occurred—or actually did—during the period; dialogue suited to the era without idioms that have become archaisms; actors who can inhabit their characters without looking like anachronisms; a visual style that defines the era without calling attention to the various processes used to achieve the effect; and a soundtrack that, if it does not include period music, at least offers the sort that might have been heard at the time.

The narrator of Graham Swift's *Waterland* (1983) calls history "the impossible thing: the attempt to give an account, with incomplete knowledge, of actions undertaken with incomplete knowledge." The war's perennial appeal to filmmakers suggests that some of them are trying to add to that knowledge, not in the factual but in the interpretive sense, realizing that an event like World War II can never come close to closure but only to a state of being better understood.

The 1985 edition of *The Star-Spangled Screen* included an appendix that listed the 16 mm. distributors of films discussed. Since then, the number of distributors has shrunk considerably as video has begun to replace 16 mm., even in the classroom. At present, Facets Video (1517 West Fullerton, Chicago, IL 60614) has the most comprehensive collection of World War II videos including documentaries and the work of both American and international filmmakers.

 **Notes**

1. Prologue to Pearl

1. Frank Capra, *The Name above the Title: An Autobiography* (New York: Macmillan, 1971), 346.

2. Richard W. Steele, "The Greatest Gangster Film Ever Filmed: *Prelude to War*," *Prologue* 9 (Winter 1979): 232–33. Steele cites other reasons for the OWI's opposition to commercial release, including the fact that it had produced its own "prelude," *World at War*.

3. On the series, see William Murphy, "The Method of *Why We Fight*," *Journal of Popular Film* 1 (1972): 185–96; Thomas W. Bohn, *An Historical and Descriptive Analysis of the "Why We Fight" Series* (New York: Arno Press, 1977).

4. David Culbert, "'Why We Fight': Social Engineering for a Democratic Society at War," in *Film & Radio Propaganda in World War II*, ed. K.R.M. Short (Knoxville: University of Tennessee Press, 1983), 178.

2. The War that Dared Not Speak Its Name

1. For the background, see Nancy Lynn Schwartz, *The Hollywood Writers' Wars*, completed by Sheila Schwartz (New York: Knopf, 1982). Since this book is not as detailed as it would have been if the author had lived to complete it, it should be supplemented by Larry Ceplair and Steven Englund, *The Inquisition in Hollywood: Politics in the Film Community, 1930–1960* (New York: Doubleday, 1980).

2. Donald Ogden Stewart, *By a Stroke of Luck* (New York: Paddington Press, 1975), 218. Stewart became such a convert that in 1939 he proposed a foreword for what became *Pacific Blackout* (1942) showing the bombing of Barcelona during the Spanish civil war, and included a defense demonstration drill during which a Spanish mother is asked, "Have your children received drill instruction?" The mother replies, "I don't think, sir, that will be necessary; they lived in Barcelona." Stewart's suggestions, which were never used, are in the *Pacific Blackout* file in the Paramount Collection at

the Margaret Herrick Library of the Academy of Motion Picture Arts and Sciences (hereafter cited as Herrick Paramount Collection).

3. The original narrator was Orson Welles, whose voice was too theatrical.

4. Fuentedueña was probably not the socialist utopia portrayed in the film. As John Dos Passos has noted in *Journeys between Wars* (1938), there was friction between the socialists and the anarchists, whom the socialists regarded as fascists and loafers.

5. The production history of *Love under Fire* derives from material in the Fox archive in the Theater Arts Library at the University of California at Los Angeles (hereafter cited as Fox archive–UCLA).

6. This scenario was the reverse of what really happened. The Spanish Republic authorized the transfer of almost three-fourths of Spain's gold reserves to the Soviet Union to keep them from falling into Franco's hands.

7. "Conference with Mr. Zanuck (on Revised Final Script of 3/10/37)," 15 March 1937, p. 2, in *Love under Fire* production file, Fox Collection–University of Southern California (USC).

8. Production information concerning *The Last Train from Madrid* has been obtained from material in the Herrick Paramount Collection.

9. Marjorie Valleau, *The Spanish Civil War in American and European Films* (Ann Arbor, Mich.: UMI Research Press, 1982), 15.

10. On the making of the film that became *Blockade*, see Larry S. Ceplair, "The Politics of Compromise in Hollywood: A Case Study," *Cineaste* 8, no. 4 (1977): 2–7.

11. Robert Stanley, *The Celluloid Empire: A History of the Motion Picture Industry* (New York: Hastings House, 1978), 279.

12. John Howard Lawson, *Film in the Battle of Ideas* (New York: Masses and Mainstream, 1953), 9.

13. Hugh Thomas, *The Spanish Civil War*, rev. ed. (New York: Harper & Row, 1977), 410. The running of the blockade was a short-lived triumph; Bilbao was bombed June 8–9 and surrendered on June 20.

14. Ibid., 299.

15. Ibid.

16. Ibid., 298.

17. Robert Buckner and Charles Grayson, "A New Cure for 'The Desert Song' (8/26/41)," in *The Desert Song* production file in the Warner Bros. archive at the Archives of Performing Arts, University of Southern California (hereafter cited as Warner archive–USC). The film's production history is based on material in this archive.

18. Dick Richards imitated the scene in *March or Die* (1977).

19. In *The Autobiography of Cecil B. DeMille*, ed. Donald Hayne (Englewood Cliffs, N.J.: Prentice-Hall, 1959), 375–76, DeMille states that Macpherson worked on the screenplay for 6½ months until a request from John Hay Whitney to make a never-to-be-filmed Latin American epic ended DeMille's association with the project. Although there is no script in the DeMille Collection at Brigham Young University, there is Macpherson's plot synopsis along with an "analysis"—half treatment, half suggestions—which is summarized in the text.

20. The subsequent production history of *For Whom the Bell Tolls* is based on material in the Herrick Paramount Collection.

21. So his daughter, actress K.T. Stevens, believes; see Tony Thomas, "Sam Wood," in *The Hollywood Professionals*, vol. 2 (New York: A.S. Barnes, 1974), 173.

22. *Time*, 2 August 1943, 60.

23. Gene D. Phillips, S.J., *Graham Greene: The Films of His Fiction* (New York: Teachers College Press, 1974), 31.

24. The production history of *Confidential Agent* derives from material in the Warner archive–USC.

25. On the differences between the play and the film, see Bernard F. Dick, *Hellman in Hollywood* (Cranbury, N.J.: Fairleigh Dickinson University Press, 1982), 108–18.

26. *Ernest Hemingway: Selected Letters, 1917–1961*, ed. Carlos Baker (New York: Charles Scribner's Sons, 1981), 456.

27. The production history of *The Angel Wore Red* has been compiled from the production files at MGM/UA in Culver City, California.

3. Hollywood as Premature Antifascist

1. Much of my thinking concerning the thirties' antifascist film has been influenced by Andrew Bergman, *We're in the Money: Depression America and Its Films* (New York: New York University Press, 1971).

2. Rossen left the Party about ten years later; see Alan Casty, *The Films of Robert Rossen* (New York: Museum of Modern Art, 1969), 5.

3. For an anticapitalist reading of *Marked Woman*, see Karyn Kay, "Sisters of the Night," reprinted in *The Velvet Light Trap* 17 (Winter 1977): 48–52.

4. Richard Maurice Hurst, *Republic Studios: Between Poverty Row and the Majors* (Metuchen, N.J.: Scarecrow Press, 1979), 68.

5. Ibid., p. 4.

6. I am grateful to Professor Raymond E. White of Ball State University for calling my attention to *Range Defenders*.

7. Quoted in Hurst, *Republic Studios*, 91.

8. The production history of *Confessions of a Nazi Spy* is based on material in the Warner archive–USC.

9. *New York Post*, 21 June 1938, 1, 12, 13.

10. "Warners was considered very daring to undertake the *Confessions* film, and the producer, Robert Lord, carried a pistol all through the production period, in a serious belief of the necessity for defending himself from Nazi agents. The brothers Warner were themselves very worried about their daring in making this film. . . . It was just a nervous time for any Semitic persons. . . ." Robert Buckner, letter to author, 30 December 1982.

11. John Davis, "Notes on Warner Brothers Foreign Policy, 1918–1948," reprinted in *The Velvet Light Trap* 17 (Winter 1977): 20. On the portrayal of Germans in World War I movies, see Michael T. Isenberg, *War on Film: The*

American Cinema and World War I, 1914–1941 (Cranbury, N.J.: Fairleigh Dickinson University Press, 1981), 145–60.

12. Jack L. Warner, with Dean Jennings, *My First Hundred Years in Hollywood* (New York: Random House, 1964), 249.

13. Hal Wallis and Charles Higham, *Starmaker: The Autobiography of Hal Wallis* (New York: Macmillan, 1980), 71.

14. Wallis to Ebenstein, memo, 25 March 1939, Warner archive–USC.

15. Senta De Wagner to Warner Bros., 11 May 1939, Warner archive–USC.

16. Details of the filming of *Espionage Agent* are from the Warner archive–USC.

17. Jack Warner to Hal Wallis, memo, 27 March 1939, Warner archive–USC.

18. The censorship problems are recounted in Gene Fernett, *Hollywood's Poverty Row, 1930–1950* (Satellite Beach, Fla.: Coral Reef Publications, 1973), 101–3; and Donald Miller, *"B" Movies: An Informal Survey of the American Low-Budget Film 1933–1945* (New York: Curtis Books, 1973), 199–201.

19. Traube also directed *Street of Memories* (1940), *For Beauty's Sake* (1941), and *The Bride Wore Crutches* (1941) for Fox.

4. Hollywood as Neutral Interventionist

1. Gordon Sager, "Hollywood Carries On for Neville," *TAC: A Magazine of Theatre, Film, Radio, Music, Dance* (October 1939): 14.

2. "I immediately closed up our offices and exchanges in Germany, for I knew that terror was creeping across the country." Warner, *First Hundred Years*, 249.

3. David Stewart Hull, *Film in the Third Reich: A Study of the German Cinema 1933–1945* (Berkeley and Los Angeles: University of California Press, 1969), 178.

4. According to the *Jahrbuch des Reichsfilmkammer* (1939), cited in M.S. Phillips, "The Nazi Control of the German Film Industry," *Journal of European Studies* 1 (1971): 48, n. 40.

5. Ibid., 63, n. 96.

6. The production history of *The Mortal Storm* is based on material in the production files at MGM/UA.

7. That Mankiewicz was responsible for the mild anti-Nazism in *Three Comrades* is the conclusion of Gore Vidal, who has examined the various drafts of the screenplay at MGM/UA; see Gore Vidal, "Scott's Case," *New York Review of Books*, 1 May 1980, 18.

8. Fred Laurence Guiles, *Hanging on in Paradise* (New York: McGraw-Hill, 1975), 159.

9. William Dozier to Kenneth MacKenna, memo, 16 November 1938, MGM/UA.

10. Kenneth MacKenna to producers, memo, 20 February 1939, MGM/UA.

11. Phyllis Bottome to Sidney Franklin, 7 February 1940, MGM/UA.

12. Damon Runyon, "Foreword," in Darryl F. Zanuck, *Tunis Expedition* (New York: Random House, 1943), 16.

13. Zanuck, "Notes on a Conference on Treatment," 11 November 1939, in *Four Sons* production file, Fox archive–UCLA. The production history of *Four Sons* is based on material in this file.

14. William L. Shirer, *The Rise and Fall of the Third Reich: A History of Nazi Germany* (New York: Fawcett Crest, 1960), 23.

15. The entire speech is quoted in Charles Chaplin, *My Autobiography* (New York: Simon and Schuster, 1964), 400.

16. According to Donald Spoto, *The Dark Side of Genius: The Life of Alfred Hitchcock* (Boston: Little, Brown, 1983), 233–35, Hitchcock's belief that the Battle of Britain was imminent resulted in Ben Hecht's being called in to write the fadeout speech. However, one suspects Wanger had much to do with it, also. The correspondent's peroration harks back to Marco's in *Blockade* and anticipates Bishop Coombes's in *Sundown* (1941), also a Wanger production.

17. David Chierichetti, *Hollywood Director: The Career of Mitchell Leisen* (New York: Curtis Books, 1973), 147.

18. *Hearings before a Subcommittee of the Committee on Interstate Commerce United States Senate Seventy-Seventh Congress First Session on S. Res. 152: A Resolution Authorizing an Investigation of War Propaganda Disseminated by the Motion Picture Industry and of any Monopoly in the Production, Distribution, or Exhibition of Motion Pictures, September 9 to 26, 1941* (Washington, D.C.: United States Government Printing Office, 1942), 329.

19. Isenberg, *War on Film*, 101.

20. Story outline dictated by Zanuck, 25 October 1940, in *A Yank in the RAF* production file, Fox archive–UCLA. Production history is based on material in this file.

21. "Notes on Story Conference," 23 November 1940, Fox archive–UCLA.

22. "Notes on Story Conference," 13–14 January 1941, Fox archive–UCLA.

23. "Notes on Story Conference," 22 February 1941, Fox archive–UCLA.

24. "Notes on Story Conference," 2 April 1941, in *Confirm or Deny* production file, Fox archive–UCLA.

25. Mel Gussow, *Darryl F. Zanuck: Don't Say Yes until I Finish Talking* (New York: Pocket Books, 1971), 6.

26. For a summary of the hearings, see n. 18. Page references in the text are to this transcript.

27. "Nye Assails Film War Propaganda," *St. Louis Globe–Democrat*, 2 August 1941, p. A.

28. *The Hollywood Reporter*, 9 September 1941, p. C.

29. Peter A. Soderbergh, "The Grand Illusion: Hollywood and World War II, 1930–1945," *University of Dayton Review* 5 (1968): 14. In Appendix II of his otherwise excellent *An Analysis of Motion Pictures about War Released by the American Film Industry, 1930–1970* (New York: Arno Press,

1976), Russell Earl Shain lists fifty movies made between 1939 and 1941 that presumably are meant to be Wilkie's fifty. But many of them (*Top Sergeant Mulligan, You'll Never Get Rich, Here Come the Marines,* etc.) can hardly qualify as films about "issues" or "ideological beliefs."

30. The invasion of Finland also figures in Fox's comedy, *Public Deb No. 1* (1940), in which an heiress, introduced to Communism by her butler, sees the light after the Soviet Union's invasion of Finland.

31. Similar to this category, although less obvious, is the Warner Bros. historical drama (e.g., *The Life of Emile Zola,* 1937; *Juarez,* 1939); its veiled antifascism even appears in a swashbuckler like *The Sea Hawk* (1940), according to Colin Shindler, *Hollywood Goes to War: Films and American Society 1939–1952* (Boston: Routledge & Kegan Paul, 1979), 13.

32. François Truffaut, *Hitchcock* (New York: Simon and Schuster, 1967), 98.

33. Stuart Kaminsky, *John Huston: Maker of Magic* (Boston: Houghton Mifflin, 1978), 32, states that Huston, learning he had been drafted into the Army Special Services, in less than a day "hammered out a wild scene with Bogart and Astor trapped in a plantation in Panama by Greenstreet" and "purposely did this as a joke on whoever took over direction of the film." All Huston really did was change the ending from Hawaii to Panama, with a corresponding change of target (Panama Canal instead of Pearl Harbor). Furthermore, a similar plantation exists in Carson's story, and it is there that the climax occurs. *Across the Pacific* follows Carson's story more closely than has been supposed.

34. Robert Carson, "Aloha Means Good-By," *The Saturday Evening Post,* 5 July 1941, 75.

5. Hollywood Mobilizes

1. *The 1938 Film Daily Year Book of Motion Pictures,* p. 1143.

2. The production history of *A Yank on the Burma Road* has been compiled from the files at MGM/UA.

3. The best example never reached the screen. It was to have been in Fox's *The House on 92nd St.* (1945). A Nazi spy tells an American undercover agent to check the latest issue of a *New Yorker*–type magazine ("I saw a gag you might like"). The "gag" is a picture of a pair of dice with the numbers 12, 5, and 7.

4. The production history of *China Girl* derives from the Fox archive–UCLA.

5. "Notes on Treatment," 31 January 1942, MGM/UA.

6. Ibid.

7. Ibid.

8. The production history of *Secret Agent of Japan* is based on material in the Fox archive–UCLA.

9. Gordon W. Prange, *At Dawn We Slept: The Untold Story of Pearl Harbor* (New York: McGraw-Hill, 1981), 561.

10. Letters of protest and the studio's reply are in the *Air Force* production file in the Warner archive–usc.

11. Lawrence Howard Suid, ed., *Air Force*, Wisconsin/Warner Bros. Screenplay Series (Madison: University of Wisconsin Press, 1983), 26.

12. The extent to which the owi influenced movie content, if at all, is highly debatable. The best discussion is that of Gregory Black and Clayton R. Koppes, "What to Show the World: The Office of War Information and Hollywood, 1942–1945," *Journal of American History* 54 (1977), 87–105. On Walter Wanger's criticism of the owi, see Garth Jowett, *Film the Democratic Art: A Social History of American Film* (Boston: Little, Brown, 1976), 308–9.

13. Don Whitehead, *The FBI Story: A Report to the People* (New York: Random House, 1956), 185.

14. The eight Nazi saboteurs who reached America in June 1942 were apprehended before they could commit actual sabotage. Thus, the FBI could rightly say in 1942 that no *act* of sabotage was foreign directed.

15. Production information for *Margin for Error* has been obtained from the Fox archive–ucla.

16. Gabe Essoe, *Tarzan: A Pictorial History of More Than Fifty Years of Edgar Rice Burroughs' Legendary Hero* (New York: Citadel Press, 1968), 115.

17. On the nature of Lord Haw-Haw's broadcasts, see Charles J. Rolo, *Radio Goes to War* (New York: G.P. Putnam's Sons, 1940), 66–80. He appears as a character in RKO's *Passport to Destiny* (1944), yearning to leave Germany and admitting he only went there when he received no recognition in Britain.

18. Truffaut, *Hitchcock*, 105.

19. David Kahn, *The Codebreakers: The Story of Secret Writing* (New York: Macmillan, 1967), 530.

20. President Truman commuted the sentence in 1948, and Dasch was deported.

21. Fox clearly saw the connection between the two films, rereleasing *They Came to Blow Up America* a few months before *The House on 92nd St.*

22. The case is discussed in Whitehead, *The FBI Story*, 193–94.

23. *The Secret History of the Atomic Bomb*, ed. Anthony Cave Brown and Charles B. MacDonald (New York: Delta Books, 1977), 206–9.

24. Ibid., xiv–xvi. By 1942 the Soviet Union was receiving information from u.s.–based atomic spies; see David J. Dallin, *Soviet Espionage* (New Haven: Yale University Press, 1955), 458 ff.

25. *Life*, 20 January 1947, 115.

26. Breen to Col. Jason S. Joy, memo, 17 May 1946, in Fox's Story Files.

27. Production details for *Cloak and Dagger* are taken from the Warner archive–usc.

28. Peter Bogdanovich, *Fritz Lang in America* (New York: Praeger, 1969), 70.

29. Paramount was a studio dear to Donovan's heart; Stanton Griffis, a

top Paramount executive, was Donovan's special agent to Finland. As a result, Paramount helped defray the cost of espionage activity in Finland and Sweden; see R. Harris Smith, oss: *The Secret History of America's First Intelligence Agency* (New York: Delta Books, 1973), 15, 199.

6. Plotting the War

1. From the *Winged Victory* production file, Fox archive–UCLA.

2. The production history of *Wake Island* is based on material in the Herrick Paramount Collection.

3. W. Scott Cunningham, with Lydel Sims, *Wake Island Command* (Boston: Little, Brown, 1961), 46. The book is also interesting for its discussion of Mrs. Cunningham's feud with Paramount (pp. 254–58) after *Wake Island* was released. She complained that the film gave the impression a marine was commanding officer while it was really her husband who was—Commander Winfield Scott Cunningham, U.S.N.

4. *Best Film Plays of 1943–1944*, ed. John Gassner and Dudley Nichols (New York: Garland, 1977 reprint), 90.

5. Before reaching New York, it was performed in Los Angeles as *Cry Havoc*.

6. The production history of *Fighter Squadron* is based on material in the Warner archive–USC.

7. On the filming of *The Longest Day*, see Steven Jay Rubin, *Combat Films: American Realism 1945–1970* (Jefferson, N.C.: McFarland, 1981), 43–78.

8. Gussow, *Zanuck: Don't Say Yes*, 207.

9. William Wellman, *A Short Time for Insanity: An Autobiography* (New York: Hawthorn Books, 1974), 82.

7. The People's War

1. Henri Michel, *The Shadow War: European Resistance 1939–1945*, trans. Richard Barry (New York: Harper and Row, 1972), 190.

2. Ibid., 358.

3. "I knew Breda, and his name may have been in the back of my mind when I wrote HOSTAGES." Stefan Heym, letter to author, 23 June 1982.

4. For the texts of both speeches, see François Kersaudy, *Churchill and de Gaulle* (New York: Atheneum, 1982), 78, 85.

5. Allan Dwan's *Friendly Enemies* (1942) might qualify if it were better. It has a World War I plot that is unambiguously World War II in sentiment, with references to "madmen dreaming of power," meetings in Bundist cafes, a spy ring, and an attempt to blow up the Brooklyn Navy Yard and level Washington, D.C. The film charts the transformation of a naturalized German millionaire (Charles Winninger) from an uncritical champion of the

kaiser to a true American who learns to call the enemy by the hated name of "Hun" and to sing "My Country 'Tis Of Thee."

6. Joel E. Siegel, *Val Lewton: The Reality of Terror* (New York: Viking, 1973), 149.

7. This may be the reason screenwriter Irwin Shaw would not assume responsibility for the script, claiming it was "severely tampered with by persons unknown," as Bosley Crowther reported in his *New York Times* review, 14 January 1943. The "persons unknown" may have heard about Operation Jupiter and decided to anticipate it, not knowing it would never materialize.

8. Richard Petrow, *The Bitter Years: The Invasion and Occupation of Denmark and Norway April 1940–May 1945* (New York: Morrow Quill Paperbacks, 1979), 133–37.

9. The novella and the play appeared almost concurrently, the novel in March 1942, the play in April.

10. Production details for *Edge of Darkness* are taken from information in the Warner archive–usc.

11. King Vidor completed the film when Arzner became ill.

12. The film's history has been documented by David Culbert in the introduction to his edition of *Mission to Moscow*, Wisconsin/Warner Bros. Screenplay Series (Madison, Wis.: University of Wisconsin Press, 1980); and in Idem, "Our Awkward Ally: *Mission to Moscow* (1943)," in *American History/American Film*, ed. John E. O'Connor and Martin A. Jackson (New York: Ungar, 1979), 121–45.

13. On the film's history, see Dick, *Hellman in Hollywood*, 97–107.

14. Robert Blees, letter to author, 3 September 1982. Blees is a screenwriter, and was Robinson's best man.

15. M.R.D. Foot, *Resistance: European Resistance to Nazism 1940–1945* (New York: McGraw-Hill, 1977), 230.

16. Rudy Behlmer, *America's Favorite Movies: Behind the Scenes* (New York: Ungar, 1982), 154–76; Charles Francisco, *You Must Remember . . . : The Filming of Casablanca* (Englewood Cliffs, N.J.: Prentice-Hall, 1980); Howard Koch, *Casablanca: Script and Legend* (Woodstock, N.Y.: Overlook Press, 1973); Idem, *As Time Goes By: Memoirs of a Writer* (New York: Harcourt Brace Jovanovich, 1979), 76–84.

17. Koch's embellishments were political. Behlmer, *America's Favorite Movies*, 165, credits Koch with having Rick fight for the Loyalists and with being "more interested in the characterizations and the political intrigues with their relevance to the world struggle against fascism" (p. 169).

18. For the text of Robinson's memo, which is in the *Casablanca* file in the Warner archive–usc, see Behlmer, *America's Favorite Movies*, 165–67. The memo has also been noted by Joanne Yeck and Gaylyn Studlar, "The Warner Brothers Collection," *The usc Spectator* 3 (1983): 5.

19. Russell Merritt, "Nickelodeon Theaters 1905–1914: Building an Audience for the Movies," in *The American Film Industry*, ed. Tino Balio (Madison, Wis.: University of Wisconsin Press, 1976), 73.

20. On the various types of women featured in movies, see Marjorie Ro-

sen, *Popcorn Venus* (New York: Avon Books, 1974), 139–200; Carol Traynor Williams, *The Dream beside Me: The Movies and the Children of the Forties* (Cranbury, N.J.: Fairleigh Dickinson University Press, 1980), 41–80, 120–61.

21. John Belton, "Frank Borzage," in *The Hollywood Professionals*, vol. 3, (New York: A.S. Barnes, 1974), 82.

22. Al Block to Ben Goetz, telegram, 13 April 1943, in *Hitler's Madman* production file, MGM/UA. Production information is taken from material in this file.

23. On the genesis of *Mrs. Miniver*, see Axel Madsen, *William Wyler: The Authorized Biography* (New York: Crowell, 1973), 212–18.

8. The Masters of the Race

1. Robert Edwin Herzstein, *The Nazis*, in *World War II* (Alexandria, Va.: Time-Life Books, 1981), 104.

2. Joachim C. Fest, *The Face of the Third Reich: Portraits of Nazi Leadership*, trans. Michael Bullock (New York: Pantheon, 1970), 274.

3. Ibid., 273.

4. Ibid., 275.

5. On the screenplay's disputed authorship, see Lotte H. Eisner, *Fritz Lang* (New York: Oxford University Press, 1977), 231–38.

6. John Toland, *Adolf Hitler* (New York: Ballantine Books, 1977), 348.

7. It also made some reviewers wince in 1942; see Lester D. Friedman, *Hollywood's Image of the Jew* (New York: Ungar, 1982), 112.

8. Rudolf Olden, *Hitler*, trans. Walter Ettinghausen (New York: Covici, Friede, 1936), 146. Olden's rhetorical analysis of Hitler's style (pp. 144–47) is still valid.

9. In his autobiography *Hollywood Red* (Palo Alto, Calif.: Ramparts Press, 1981), 203, Lester Cole recalls the scene differently, stating that for the rabbi's speech he "plagiarized" La Pasionaria's famous "It is far better to die on your feet than to live on your knees." In both the final shooting script (21 June 1943) and in the actual film (rarely shown but screened on 1 November 1983 at the Public Theater in New York as part of a Columbia Pictures retrospective), the rabbi's speech does not contain that exhortation. Cole may have planned to include it, but the speech requires nothing more than Cole has given it—certainly not a line that would call attention to itself and to its source.

10. Walter Laqueur, *The Terrible Secret: Suppression of the Truth about Hitler's "Final Solution"* (New York: Penguin Books, 1982), 9.

11. Although *Playing for Time* (1980) seems to be an exception, it is really a TV movie.

12. On *The Last Stop* and other Holocaust films, see Annette Insdorf, *Indelible Shadows: Film and the Holocaust* (New York: Random House, 1983).

9. California Comrades

1. Collins left the Party and turned informant, naming twenty-three names.

2. Salka Viertel, *The Kindness of Strangers* (New York: Holt, Rinehart and Winston, 1969), 268.

3. Eric Bentley, ed., *Thirty Years of Treason: Excerpts from Hearings before the House Committee on Un-American Activities, 1938–1968* (New York: Viking, 1971), 112.

4. Blankfort later cooperated with HUAC but did not name names; see Victor S. Navasky, *Naming Names* (New York: Viking, 1980), 101–2.

5. The story was finally told by Leonard Gross, *The Last Jews in Berlin* (New York: Simon and Schuster, 1982).

6. In *As Time Goes By*, 93–95, Koch describes his role in the writing of *In Our Time* as more "peacemaker and insurer than writer" in order to get Ellis St. Joseph screen credit (Warner Bros. had found the script too literate). Yet Koch does not deny that he gave the film political depth: "Although Ellis is politically sophisticated, I was perhaps more actively concerned with social and political problems—and still am—so that I may have brought emphasis to the story's political implications." Howard Koch, letter to author, 17 January 1984.

7. Bentley, *Thirty Years of Treason*, 384.

8. It is probably more accurate to speak of the Hollywood Nineteen or the "Unfriendly" Nineteen, eight of whom (Richard Collins, Gordon Kahn, Howard Koch, Lewis Milestone, Larry Parks, Irving Pichel, Robert Rossen, and Waldo Salt) were never called to testify. Of the remaining eleven, Bertolt Brecht admitted to the committee that he was not a Communist and left the United States. Hence, only ten took the First Amendment and refused to answer both questions. There are many books about the blacklist, but none has covered the October 1947 congressional investigation as well as Ceplair and Englund, *The Inquisition in Hollywood*, 254–98.

9. For the screen credits of the Hollywood Nineteen, see Schwartz, *Hollywood Writers' Wars*, 301–19.

10. The production history of *Pride of the Marines* is based on material in the Warner archive–USC.

11. See the excellent Gary Lee Carr, *The Screen Writing of John Howard Lawson, 1928–1947: Playwright at Work in Hollywood* (Ph.D. diss., University of Texas, 1975).

12. Britain's role is memorialized in the British documentary *Burma Victory* (1945), which Warners distributed the following year, thus offering moviegoers the factual and fictionalized versions of the Burma campaign at the same time.

13. Production information for *Objective, Burma!* comes from the Warner archive–USC.

14. Breen to Jack Warner, memo, 19 April 1944, Warner archive–USC.

10. Japs on Their Minds

1. Quoted in Prange, *At Dawn We Slept*, 583.
2. Ibid., 80.
3. Cole, *Hollywood Red*, 219–20.
4. Secretary of the Treasury Henry Morgenthau had the poem printed on circulars promoting war bonds.
5. *Bad Day at Black Rock* (1955) is often called the first film to deal with the internment of Japanese-Americans, but that is inaccurate. The film is set in 1945 a few months after the war's end and concerns an attempt on the part of the inhabitants of a mythical town in the American Southwest to keep a stranger (Spencer Tracy) from learning that on the day after Pearl Harbor one of their number killed a Japanese farmer. The irony is that the farmer was the father of the soldier who saved the stranger's life in the war.
6. Zanuck to Jo Eisinger, memo, 22 February 1950. This and subsequent information about the 1950 "Pearl Harbor Story" comes from the *Tora! Tora! Tora!* production file in the Fox archive—UCLA.

11. Remembering Pearl Harbor

1. Lawrence H. Suid, *Guts and Glory: Great American War Movies* (Reading, Mass.: Addison-Wesley, 1978), 175, assumes that lack of military co-operation resulted in a film that "visually . . . lacked the authentic feel of men in combat." But *Attack!* was not meant to be realistic; it was meant to have an alien look, as if it had been excavated rather than filmed or found under ancient rubble and placed on exhibit without first being cleaned.
2. This is also the view of director and World War II veteran Sam Fuller, who is quoted (*Time*, 28 May 1984, 28) as saying, "We were just doing our job."
3. Dorothy Jones, "Tomorrow the Movies III. Hollywood Goes to War," *The Nation*, 27 January 1945, 95. It should be remembered that Jones, who headed the Film Reviewing and Analysis Section of the OWI's Hollywood office, was unsympathetic to movies as a mass medium and approached them condescendingly and pedantically.

Bibliographical Essay

To evaluate a film as a work of art, one need not go beyond the film itself. If the film is unavailable, the cutting continuity—the dialogue transcript with the shots and transitions labelled—is second best. Less satisfactory, although sometimes the only alternative, is the shooting script, which, as its various forms ("final script," "revised final," etc.) attest, is not impervious to change. The shooting script may contain scenes that never appear in the actual film, or it may lack scenes that were added in that often undocumented period between the final screenplay and its realization.

To evaluate a film as a cultural document, the film itself is not enough. One must return to its origins, to its genesis within the studio, to the era—and at times, to the very year—that saw its birth. One must ignore the graduate school distinction between primary and secondary sources and treat memos and drafts, histories and biographies, interviews and letters, not as secondary sources but as written means to a visual end. In the case of the American World War II film, these means include the following:

Archival Materials

A film is more than the visualization of a screenplay; ultimately, it is the visualization of everything that has gone into that screenplay—the treatment, the drafts, the suggestions in memos, the credited revisions and uncredited changes: in short, the collaborative efforts necessary to produce a collaborative work of art. When production material is available, it is either in a studio's story files or in the studio-donated holdings at a research center such as the University of Southern California (USC), which houses the Warner Bros. archive, or the University of California at Los Angeles (UCLA), which has the Fox and RKO collections.

The major collections of archival materials have all been profiled in the AFI (American Film Institute) *Education Newsletter*. These include the UCLA Film, Television, and Radio Archives; the UCLA Theater Arts Library; the Museum of Modern Art; the Wisconsin Center for Film and

Theater Research; the University of Southern California Archives of Performing Arts; the Library of Congress, Motion Picture, Broadcasting, and Recorded Sound Division; and the Louis B. Mayer Library of the American Film Institute. Since these profiles describe resources and holdings, they are invaluable. Although the AFI's Education Department has been disbanded, copies of the *Newsletter* or of the Profiles may still be available from the AFI, Kennedy Center, Washington, D.C. 20566. Otherwise, *The Whole Film Sourcebook*, edited by Leonard Maltin (New York: New American Library, 1983), pp. 197–229, should be consulted along with the Archives column in *Quarterly Review of Film Studies*.

The chief archives used for this study were the Warner Bros. and Universal collections at USC, the Republic collection in UCLA's Department of Special Collections, the Fox archive at UCLA, the Paramount collection in the Margaret Herrick Library of the Academy of Motion Picture Arts and Sciences, the story files at Twentieth Century–Fox studios, and the production files at MGM/UA studios.

Archives are always fascinating. Where else can one learn that it was Hal Wallis who gave *Casablanca* its title in a 31 December 1941 memo ("The story that we recently purchased entitled 'EVERYBODY COMES TO RICK'S' will hereafter be known as . . . . 'CASABLANCA.'")? Where else can one read the crank mail Warner Bros. received about *Confessions of a Nazi Spy*, including a letter from a "loyal American" who suggested a companion film, *I Am a Communist*, "starring Eddie Cantor and a few other Communist Jews in order to let the public know what progress the Communists are making in this country"?

In a production file, quality often means quantity. The *Confessions of a Nazi Spy* files at USC are exhaustive; they even include the Turrou articles that inspired the film. Yet others are disappointing (e.g., *Across the Pacific*, *The House on 92nd St.*).

Histories of World War II

For the nonspecialist, by far the best history is the multivolume *World War II* published by Time-Life Books. Clearly written and superbly illustrated, often with pictures that have not appeared elsewhere, the series is the perfect ancilla to the World War II film. The illustrations often enable one to verify a film's accuracy. (In the volume entitled *The Nazis*, the reproduction of Nazi emblems makes it possible to show that the badges worn by the henchmen in *Range Defenders* were inspired by SS Civilian Dress Insignia.)

Although the text of *The American Heritage Picture History of World War II* (1966) is sketchy, reminiscences and eyewitness accounts make it worth owning. The best one-volume work is James L. Stokesbury's clear and vigorous *A Short History of World War II* (New York: William Morrow, 1980), which can be used as a supplementary text for a course in the films of World War II. The maps, however, are far from a cartographer's dream.

While film scholars may speak generally of the "war years," their chief concerns are specific years and particular days. For this purpose *The Britannica Book of the Year* is especially useful because of its summary nature and its daily calendar of events. A unique chronology in the sense that it is only concerned with military operations is *The Army Air Forces in World War II: Combat Chronology 1941–1945*, comp. Kit C. Carter and Robert Mueller (Washington, D.C.: u.s. Government Printing Office, 1973). The best overall chronology is Robert Goralski's *World War II Almanac 1931–1945: A Political and Military Record* (New York: G.P. Putnam's Sons, 1981). Daily summaries in sentence form are interspersed with short paragraphs on war-related topics (Soviet women in combat, the internment of Japanese-Americans), maps, photographs, and lists of statistics.

Although not exclusively devoted to World War II, Thomas M. Leonard's *Day by Day: The Forties* (New York: Facts on File, 1977) approaches the decade from ten points of view, including, as one would expect, the war (European and Pacific war zones) but also politics, economy and environment, and culture. Different from the almanac and the standard history is *The Historical Encyclopedia of World War II* (New York: Facts on File, 1980), translated from the French. The attention given some entries and the lack of attention given others may strike Americans as eccentric (e.g., Pearl Harbor gets the same amount of space as Pétain). But the entries on the atomic bomb and the resistance are models of encyclopedic learning and encyclopedia writing.

It is always illuminating to read popular works published during the war and compare them with later studies. The gulf between the transitory and the permanent can be seen in a comparison of Blayney F. Matthews, *The Specter of Sabotage* (Los Angeles: Lymanhouse, 1941) and Douglas Miller, *You Can't Do Business with Hitler* (Boston: Little, Brown, 1941) with William L. Shirer, *The Rise and Fall of the Third Reich: A History of Nazi Germany* (New York: Simon & Schuster, 1959; Fawcett Crest, 1960) and Gordon W. Prange, *At Dawn We Slept: The Untold Story of Pearl Harbor* (New York: McGraw-Hill, 1981). Although Shirer called Miller's book "must" reading, Shirer's, which places Hollywood Nazism in its natural setting, is really the "must." Similarly, Prange's work must be the yardstick against which the anti-Japanese films of the 1940s are measured.

Studies of the World War II Film

Pre-1941. Andrew Bergman, *We're in the Money: Depression America and Its Films* (New York: New York University Press, 1971) offers the best general account of the thirties antifascist film. However, since Bergman is discussing various genres (musicals, social consciousness films, screwball comedy, etc.), he cannot cite all the antifascist films of the decade. For an overview of the thirties that includes a sentence, and often more, about every film of the period, obscure and renowned, see Roger Dooley, *From Scarface to Scarlett: American Films in the 1930s* (New York: Harcourt

Brace Jovanovich, 1981), especially chapters 49 and 50 on the film of ideas. The decade is also well served by Nick Roddick, *A New Deal in Entertainment: Warner Brothers in the 1930s* (London: British Film Institute, 1983), which combines studio and cultural history.

Fear of losing the German market is often given as the reason for the paucity of antifascist films in the late thirties. An article that gives the number of American films shown in Germany between 1933 and 1938 and therefore deserves to be better known is M.S. Phillips's "The Nazi Control of the German Film Industry," *Journal of European Studies*, 1 (1971): 37-68.

Post-1941. The virtues of Garth Jowett, *Film the Democratic Art: A Social History of American Film* (Boston: Little, Brown, 1976) are many, but Chapter XII, "Hollywood Goes to War, 1939–1945," is a classic summation. One cannot say the same of Dorothy Jones's frequently cited article, "The Hollywood War Film: 1942–1944," *Hollywood Quarterly* 1 (1945): 1–19. Jones headed the Film Reviewing and Analysis Section of the OWI's Hollywood office, and Jowett (p. 319) has rightly inferred that her bias against film was partly irritation that the industry failed to heed OWI suggestions. That she misunderstood movies and moviegoers is evident from such statements as *"Blondie for Victory* . . . belittled the seriousness of civilian war activities and tended to hinder the recruitment of volunteer workers" (p. 10) and that "films about women on the production line (*Swing-Shift Maisie, Beautiful but Broke*, etc.) . . . contributed little because of their general flippant approach" (p. 9). Her obsession with categorization can be seen in her attempt to classify films according to the six topics on which President Roosevelt, in his 1942 State of the Union address, believed the public should be informed: the issues, the enemy, the United Nations, the production front, the home front, and the fighting forces. In trying to classify films according to these categories (Annual Communications Bibliography, *Hollywood Quarterly*, 1946), she ends up putting *The Desert Song* under "Issues," *Janie* under "Fighting Forces," and *They Raid by Night* under "United Nations (Great Britain)." The irony is that Hollywood would have made movies that would have fit those categories anyway. Mrs. Jones only proved a given—and tediously at that.

Her later work, however, is more substantial. Her penchant for statistics is shown to much better advantage in "Communism and the Movies: A Study of Film Content," in John Cogley, *Report on Blacklisting*, vol. 1, *The Movies* (The Fund for the Republic, 1956; New York: Arno Press, 1972).

Except for a brief introduction, Ken D. Jones and Arthur F. McClure, *Hollywood at War: The American Motion Picture and World War II* (New York: Castle Books, 1973) is merely a listing of casts, directors, studios, and release dates of most of the American films that opened between 1938 and 1945 and that in some way reflected the war. Although the credits are incomplete (the most comprehensive credits are in *Variety* reviews), the stills, especially those from "B" movies, justify purchasing the book. On the same order as *Hollywood at War*, but more selective, is Joe Morella, Edward Z. Epstein, and John Griggs, *The Films of World War II: A Pictorial*

Treasury of Hollywood's War Years (Secaucus, N.J.: Citadel Press, 1980); the films range from *The Last Train from Madrid* (1937) to *The Best Years of Our Lives* (1946), from the war's prelude to its aftermath. Its distinguishing feature is excerpts from newspaper and magazine reviews.

The portrayal of war on the screen is the subject of five important studies, two of which focus entirely on the Second World War: Roger Manvell, *Films and the Second World War* (New York: Dell, 1976) and Colin Shindler, *Hollywood Goes to War: Films and American Society 1939–1952* (Boston: Routledge & Kegan Paul, 1979). The former is international in scope, comprising British, French, Russian, Polish, German, Italian, and American films. It does not attempt an exhaustive analysis, but its breadth and the author's ability to move easily from documentary to fiction film (as well as from country to country) make it a major work of scholarship. *Hollywood Goes to War* is well researched (but with incomplete footnotes) and written in a breezy style, but suffers from a forced wittiness in the captions that emerges as glibness. The worst are the captions for two stills from *The Best Years of Our Lives*. The first, showing Dana Andrews at the airplane graveyard, feeling as useless as the wrecks along which he stands, is captioned "Dana Andrews in successful pursuit of a job." Beneath it is a photograph of the famous deep focus shot of the wedding of Homer, the double amputee (Harold Russell, a double amputee in real life) and Wilma (Cathy O'Donnell); the caption: "Harold Russell in successful pursuit of Cathy O'Donnell." One should ignore the captions and read the text.

Three general studies of the war film devote considerable attention to World War II. The most elaborate is Clyde Jeavons, *A Pictorial History of War Films* (Secaucus, N.J.: Citadel Press, 1974), whose "coffee table" look belies the intelligence informing it. Like Manvell, Jeavons adopts an international point of view; although he is British, he does not sympathize with "hysterical British claims" that *Objective, Burma!* gives a "risibly biased account of American deeds in Burma" (p. 135).

Lawrence H. Suid, *Guts and Glory: Great American War Movies* (Reading, Mass.: Addison-Wesley, 1978), a study of the war film from the standpoint of military history, is primarily concerned with production details, historical accuracy, and military cooperation with the movie industry. It is not film criticism, but it can be appreciated for the valuable information it does contain such as Stanley Kramer's attempt to get Navy cooperation for *The Caine Mutiny* (1954) by stressing Queeg's instability, and James Jones's initial coolness to, and gradual endorsement of, the film version of *From Here to Eternity* (1953).Similar in concept is Steven Jay Rubin, *Combat Films: American Realism, 1945–1970* (Jefferson, N.C.: McFarland, 1981), which documents the making of *A Walk in the Sun, Battleground, Twelve O'Clock High, The Bridge on the River Kwai, Hell Is for Heroes, The Longest Day, The Great Escape,* and *Patton*. Again, this is not a critical study but a recreation of each film's production, gleaned from a variety of sources including personal interviews. Its only drawback is an absence of notes.

Dissertations

Doctoral students are prone (or prodded) to be objective, to enumerate and classify, to be scholars before they are critics. Thus the information in dissertations is often invaluable; the bibliographies are scrupulously up to date, and every source, no matter how irrelevant, is footnoted. Examples are Robert James Fyne, *Hollywood Fights a War: A Comparison of the Fighting Man of World War II Combattants in Selected Hollywood Films Produced between September 1, 1939 and December 7, 1941 with Those Produced between December 8, 1941 and August 15, 1945* (Ann Arbor, Mich.: Xerox University Microfilms, 1976) and Kathryn Kane, *Visions of War: Hollywood Combat Films of World War II* (Ann Arbor, Mich.: UMI Research Press, 1982). Occasionally, a dissertation appears in which, amid lists and catalogs, a judgment is expressed, revealing a critic in the making—see Russell Earl Shain, *An Analysis of Motion Pictures about War Released by the American Film Industry, 1939–1970* (New York: Arno Press, 1976) and Marjorie Valleau, *The Spanish Civil War in American and European Films* (Ann Arbor, Mich.: UMI Research Press, 1982).

The scope of Shain's dissertation is awesome; in addition to the forty-year span, there are seventy-one tables, chapter summaries, and appendices (and an occasional error, such as Robert Taylor for Robert Young in *Journey for Margaret*). Although Shain tends to rely too heavily on reviews, he has produced a major piece of research that deserves a place in every film scholar's library. Valleau compares radically different approaches to the same subject: the Spanish civil war as treated in six American and five European films. Her method is to discuss the production and content of each film. She concludes that European films are more political, but also shows how some American films are surreptitiously political.

Another Arno Press dissertation that merits consideration, although it is only indirectly concerned with the World War II film, is Charles J. Maland, *American Visions: The Films of Chaplin, Ford, Capra, and Welles, 1936–1941* (New York: Arno Press, 1977). Maland's study of the interrelationship between American culture and American films recalls Bergman's *We're in the Money* and is in the same tradition as Robert Sklar's *Movie-Made America: A Cultural History of American Movies* (New York: Random House, 1975), Michael Wood's *America in the Movies* (New York: Basic Books, 1975), and David Thompson's *America in the Dark: The Impact of Hollywood Films on American Culture* (New York: William Morrow, 1977). By concentrating on the work of four filmmakers during a crucial period in American history, Maland is able to counterbalance the agrarian, nineteenth-century vision of Capra and Ford with the industrial, twentieth-century vision of Chaplin and Welles, who were far more critical of the dominant culture—Welles even illustrating in *Citizen Kane* the failure of affluence and fame to insure happiness.

Hollywood Histories

A knowledge of the film industry during the time of the screenwriters' wars and the popular front is necessary to an understanding of the mentality behind the antifascist film. The industry's regression from comparative progressivism in the 1930s to self-righteousness in the 1950s has been superbly documented in Larry Ceplair and Steven Englund, *The Inquisition in Hollywood: Politics in the Film Community, 1930–1960* (New York: Doubleday, 1980), the best study of Hollywood politics ever written and by writers who were not even born when many of the events they describe so vividly were taking place. No other book has made the necessary connections between the founding of the Screen Writers Guild, the loneliness of the transplanted East Coast writers, their politics, the contempt with which studio heads often treated them, the Sunday salons, the background in radical theatre that characterized writers like John Howard Lawson and Albert Maltz, and the basic distinction between play writing where the author's contribution is acknowledged and screenwriting where it is often anonymous or ignored. Given their treatment, screenwriters would inevitably unionize. The book not only covers the founding of the Screen Writers Guild but connects the guild's attempt to become the screenwriters' sole bargaining agent with the prewar popular front and the postwar blacklist. While the authors' position on the blacklist is clear (a list of informers and the number of names named appears in an appendix), *The Inquisition in Hollywood* is not a liberal's vindication or a whitewash of Hollywood Communism. That Ceplair and Englund can write without hysteria is a tribute to their equanimity—a trait singularly lacking in many of their elders.

Nancy Lynn Schwartz's death of a brain tumor at twenty-six prevented her finishing *The Hollywood Writers' Wars* (New York: Knopf, 1982), completed by her mother, Sheila Schwartz. Although the book is not without errors, its essence is intact. Shocked by the injustices and betrayals of the McCarthy era, Nancy Schwartz sought to uncover their origins, finding them in the 1930s when anyone who talked union was a Red and screenwriters who favored unionization were potential blacklistees. Schwartz has successfully demonstrated how the greylist of the 1930s blackened after World War II, and also discusses the Hollywood left and its paradoxical infatuation with Communism, which allowed screenwriters to live like capitalists and champion the proletariat. She is not hard on them, believing that their "leftward leanings . . . seemed predicated less on dogma than on a desire to help humanity, a kind of sentimentality felt for the underdog" (p. 83).

Although Hollywood autobiographies are often suspect, Donald Ogden Stewart, *By a Stroke of Luck* (New York: Paddington Press, 1975) and Lester Cole, *Hollywood Red* (Palo Alto, Calif.: Ramparts Press, 1981) are a blend of eyewitness testimony and cultural history. More like a memoir but still pertinent is Jack L. Warner, with Dean Jennings, *My First Hundred Years in*

Hollywood (New York: Random House, 1964). Harry M. Warner was not as well known as his brother, but he enunciated the studio's policy far better in *United We Survive Divided We Fall! An Address Made June 5, 1940 by Harry M. Warner before 6000 Warner Bros. Studio Employees and Their Wives* (n.p.), available in the Margaret Herrick Library.

Film Criticism

Critical works, articles, and essays containing analyses of the films discussed include *Agee on Film: Reviews and Comments by James Agee*, vol. 1 (New York: Universal Library, 1969): *Hail the Conquering Hero*; Michael A. Anderegg, *William Wyler* (Boston: Twayne, 1979): *Mrs. Miniver, The Best Years of Our Lives*; John Baxter, *The Cinema of John Ford* (New York: A.S. Barnes, 1971): *They Were Expendable*; Rudy Behlmer, *America's Favorite Movies: Behind the Scenes* (New York: Ungar, 1982): *Casablanca*; John Belton, "Frank Borzage," in *The Hollywood Professionals*, vol. 3 (New York: A.S. Barnes, 1974): *The Mortal Storm, Till We Meet Again*; Leo Braudy, *The World in a Frame: What We See in Films* (New York: Anchor, 1976): *To Be or Not To Be*; Kingsley Canham, "Michael Curtiz," "Raoul Walsh," in *The Hollywood Professionals*, vol. 1 (New York: A.S. Barnes, 1973): *Casablanca, Northern Pursuit, Objective, Burma!*; Larry S. Ceplair, "The Politics of Compromise in Hollywood: A Case Study," *Cineaste* 8, no. 4 (1977): 2–7: *Blockade*; David Culbert, Introduction to *Mission to Moscow*, ed. Culbert, Wisconsin/Warner Bros. Screenplay Series (Madison, Wis.: University of Wisconsin Press, 1980); Bernard F. Dick, *Billy Wilder* (Boston: Twayne, 1980): *Five Graves to Cairo*; Idem, *Hellman in Hollywood* (Cranbury, N.J.: Fairleigh Dickinson University Press, 1982): *The North Star, Watch on the Rhine, The Searching Wind*; Raymond Durgnat, *The Strange Case of Alfred Hitchcock, or the Plain Man's Hitchcock* (Cambridge, Mass.: MIT Press, 1974): *Foreign Correspondent, Saboteur, Lifeboat*; Lawrence J. Epstein, *Samuel Goldwyn* (Boston: Twayne, 1983): *The North Star*; Lester D. Friedman, *Hollywood's Image of the Jew* (New York: Ungar, 1982): *The Mortal Storm, Address Unknown, The Purple Heart, Sealed Verdict*; Annette Insdorf, *Indelible Shadows: Film and the Holocaust* (New York: Random House, 1983): *The Pawnbroker, Seven Beauties*; Joseph McBride and Michael Wilmington, *John Ford* (London: Secker and Warburg, 1974): *They Were Expendable*; Axel Madsen, *William Wyler: The Authorized Biography* (New York: Crowell, 1973): *Mrs. Miniver, The Best Years of Our Lives*; Joseph R. Millichap, *Lewis Milestone* (Boston: Twayne, 1983): *Edge of Darkness, The North Star, Halls of Montezuma*; William Paul, *Ernst Lubitsch's American Comedy* (New York: Columbia University Press, 1983): *To Be or Not To Be*; Leland A. Poague, "Leo McCarey," in *The Hollywood Professionals*, vol. 7 (San Diego: A.S. Barnes, 1980): *Once upon a Honeymoon*; Dana B. Polan, "Blind Insights and Dark Passages: The Problem of Placement in Forties Film," *The Velvet Light Trap* 20 (Summer 1983): 27–33: *Pride of the Marines*; Joel E. Siegel,

Val Lewton: The Reality of Terror (New York: Viking, 1973): *Mademoiselle Fifi*; Donald A. Spoto, *The Art of Alfred Hitchcock: Fifty Years of His Motion Pictures* (New York: Hopkinson and Blake, 1976): *Foreign Correspondent, Saboteur, Lifeboat*; Michael Stern, *Douglas Sirk* (Boston: Twayne, 1979): *Hitler's Madman*; Lawrence Howard Suid, Introduction to *Air Force*, ed. Suid, Wisconsin/Warner Bros. Screenplay Series (Madison, Wis.: University of Wisconsin Press, 1983); Frank T. Thompson, *William Wellman* (Metuchen, N.J.: Scarecrow Press, 1983): *The Story of G.I. Joe, Battleground*.

The play may be the thing, but a film is much more; how much more this essay can only suggest.

Film Index

Subject Index